When Crisis Strikes on Campus

Edited by Wendy Ann Larson

Published in Cooperation with

American Association of Collegiate Registrars and Admissions Officers
American Association of Community Colleges
American Council on Education
Association of American Universities
Association of Catholic Colleges and Universities
Association of Governing Boards of Universities and Colleges
Association of Higher Education Facilities Officers
College and University Personnel Association
Council of Independent Colleges
International Association of Campus Law Enforcement Administrators
National Association of College and University Attorneys
National Association of College and University Business Officers
National Association of Independent Colleges and Universities
National Association of Independent Schools
National Association of State Universities and Land-Grant Colleges
National Association of Student Personnel Administrators

ISBN 0-89964-297-7

Printed in the United States of America.

In 1974, the American Alumni Council (founded in 1913) and the American College Public Relations Association (founded in 1917) merged to become the Council for Advancement and Support of Education (CASE).

Today, more than 2,800 colleges, universities, and independent elementary and secondary schools in the U.S., Canada, Mexico, and 25 countries belong to CASE. This makes CASE the largest nonprofit 501(c)(3) education association in terms of institutional membership. Representing the member institutions in CASE are more than 14,400 individual professionals in institutional advancement.

Nonprofit education-related organizations such as hospitals, museums, libraries, cultural or performing arts groups, public radio and television stations, or foundations established for pubic elementary and secondary schools may affiliate with CASE as Educational Associates. Commercial firms that serve the education field may affiliate as Suppliers.

CASE's mission is to develop and foster sound relationships between member educational institutions and their constituencies; to provide training programs, products, and services in the areas of alumni relations, communications, and philanthropy; and to provide a strong force for the advancement and support of education worldwide.

CASE offers books, videotapes, and focus issues of the award-winning monthly magazine, CURRENTS, to professionals in institutional advancement. The books cover topics in alumni relations, communications and marketing, fund raising, management, and student recruitment. For a copy of the catalog, write to CASE RESOURCES, Suite 400, 11 Dupont Circle, Washington, DC 20036-1261. For more information about CASE programs and services, call (202) 328-5900.

Cover design by Ann M. Williams.
Editing by Wendy Ann Larson.

Council for Advancement and Support of Education
Suite 400, 11 Dupont Circle, Washington, DC 20036-1261

Contents

Section 1: Troubled Times at the University of Florida

Section 2: Behind the Headlines: Case Studies in Crisis Communications

Section 3: CURRENTS on Crises

21

Why Crisis Plans Fail: Some situations—and people—resist good crisis management strategy   157
Bob Roseth

Section 4: CASE Issues Papers: Communicating Controversies on Campus

22

Racial Incidents on Campus   161

23

Animal Rights Break-ins and Demonstrations   163

24

Crime Incidents on Campus   165

25

Closing Academic Units   169

26

Student Alcohol and Drug Abuse   173

27

Sexual Harassment Incidents   177

28

The Abrupt Departure of a Chief Executive Officer   181

29

HIV/AIDS on Campus   186

30

Acquaintance Rape on Campus   193

31

Handling Issues of Sexual Misconduct at Independent Schools   199

Section 5: Crisis Resources

Acknowledgments

The Council for Advancement and Support of Education received invaluable assistance from the many authors and interview subjects referenced herein. Special thanks must go to President John Lombardi, staff, faculty, and students of the University of Florida for sharing their story in hopes of helping others cope with campus crises.

CASE is also grateful to the following cooperating educational associations for their guidance. From conception through completion, their support and suggestions have helped make possible this important publication.

- American Association of Collegiate Registrars and Admissions Officers
- American Association of Community Colleges
- American Council on Education
- Association of American Universities
- Association of Catholic Colleges and Universities
- Association of Governing Boards of Universities and Colleges
- Association of Higher Education Facilities Officers
- College and University Personnel Association
- Council of Independent Colleges
- International Association of Campus Law Enforcement Administrators
- National Association of College and University Attorneys
- National Association of College and University Business Officers
- National Association of Independent Colleges and Universities
- National Association of Independent Schools
- National Association of State Universities and Land Grant Colleges
- National Association of Student Personnel Administrators

On behalf of all campus administrators who will—sooner or later—face a crisis on their campus, we thank you all for your efforts.

Especially valuable support and insights were provided by the following individuals: Robert Atwell, David Merkowitz, Marlene Ross and Jim Murray of ACE; David Pierce, Margaret Rivera and Bill Reinhard of AACC; Cornelius Pings and Peter Smith of AAU; Richard Rosser and Gail Raiman of NAICU; and Peter Magrath and Roselyn Hiebert of NASULGC.

Ten associations also provided help early on in the process of compiling this book. CASE is indebted to: Tom Ingram and Rick Legon of Association of Governing Boards of Universities and Colleges; Elizabeth Nuss and Bob Ward of National Association of Student Personnel Administrators; Wayne Becraft and Laurie Robinson of American Association of Collegiate Registrars and Admissions Officers; Walter Schaw and Wayne Leroy of APPA: Association of Higher Education Facilities Officers; Benito Lopez of Association of Catholic Colleges and Universities; Richard Creal, Lourie Reichenberg, and Stephanie Jones of College and University Personnel Association; Buck Tilson of International Association of Campus Law Enforcement Administrators; Mike Grier and Linda Henderson of National Association of College and University Attorneys; Caspa Harris and Carla Balakgie of National Association of College and University Business Officers; and Margaret Goldsborough of the National Association of Independent Schools.

We should recognize the contributions of CASE's Commission on Publications and Periodicals and its Commission on Institutional Relations, as well as its own staff members, specifically Julie Landes, Ruth Stadius, Sarah Hardesty-Bray, Nancy Raley, Wendy Ann Larson, and Keith Moore. Finally, we wish to express particular appreciation to President John Lombardi; Assistant Vice President Linda Gray; and Vice President Art Sandeen of the University of Florida, without whose patience and support this effort could never have succeeded.

Foreword

Most campus communicators agree that sustaining a strong public relations program during times of calm will reap rewards during times of crisis. Perhaps then the primary prerequisite to surviving a crisis is maintaining effective communications at all times.

A crisis, though, will place unusual strains on even the strongest communications programs. These strains require cooperation across the academic institution. While communications pros must maintain strong relations with constituencies on and off campus, they must also rely on other administrators to make important management decisions during times of crisis.

The president, chancellor, or headmaster plays the most important role in managing the crisis and, often, in communicating with the public. The institution's trustees are also valuable allies in the process. On one campus, the CEO's cabinet may provide a ready-made crisis team—complete with one member to speak directly to the TV cameras. On another campus, the athletics director or the director of financial aid may speak for the institution in a crisis in their departments. A large campus may even employ a director of emergency response who is always on call and directs the crisis team. The varieties are endless.

In fact, depending on the crisis, the subject matter, the people involved, and the media's questions, almost *everyone* on campus should know how to deal effectively with a crisis. The institution's reputation depends upon everyone knowing his or her individual role (even if it is to be silent) and playing it.

Before you begin reading *When Crisis Strikes on Campus*, let me remind you that a crisis does not always wreak havoc or destroy and defeat. At least, not unless we let it. Often the unexpected event actually improves an institution in ways we cannot predict before or during the chaos.

Of course, no one believes the tragedy in August 1990 that befell the families of five students of the University of Florida has made them or the institution better. As our companion video illustrates all too well, the university community and the families of the slain students suffer losses beyond redemption.

Speaking before an audience nearly three years after the crisis began, Linda Gray, UF's assistant vice president for public information, related her memories of the first days after the tragedy. Students escorted professors to their homes for safety. Classmates randomly checked on each other in their residence halls. And staff members shared dinner after work to keep an eye on each other. This was caring and cooperation in action.

But today the news is not all bad. Gray can now list upgraded campus lighting and a larger security force as tangible improvements to the University of Florida environment. She proudly describes how a student initiative sparked a volunteer safety inspection program of off-campus apartments in Gainesville. Working in cooperation with the city and county law enforcement agents, UF officials now rate the personal security conditions of all off-campus apartments. Housing officers recommend only those with approved ratings. Yes, small gains in comparison, but important steps that may eventually thwart a serious crime or even save a life.

CASE extends special thanks for the contributions of President John Lombardi, Assistant Vice President Linda Gray, Vice President Art Sandeen, and the faculty, staff, and students of the University of Florida. The Council for Advancement and Support of Education hopes this important new book will help you and your institution communicate clearly and effectively before, during, and after a crisis.

Peter McE. Buchanan
President
CASE
October 1994

Preface

If people ever thought higher education was a place to hide from the problems of society, the events on our campuses over the last several years would set them straight. Our institutions have become front-page news—in stories ranging from crime, racism, and sexual harassment to what the curriculum should look like. Crisis management has come to consume more of our time than any of us ever thought possible.

Here at the University of Iowa, we faced our worst crisis in 1991 when a former graduate student fatally shot five people and critically wounded a sixth before turning the gun on himself. For a trauma of this magnitude, no campus can turn to a pre-set crisis plan in response.

But for the most part, crises follow a broadly predictable course, and presidents must take the lead. Whether your next crisis involves a budget cut or a natural disaster, the administration's response will say everything about your institution's integrity. What role does a president play in a crisis? What are his or her concerns? At the University of Iowa, I've found that these concerns lie in two areas: what leaders expect of themselves and what they expect of their administrators and staff.

It is critical that presidents first of all come to grips with their own responsibilities during a crisis. A leader does not run for cover when things get uncomfortable. Taking responsibility may seem alarming in the short run, but doing so will surely pay off in the long run with the respect of one's colleagues and the public.

Given today's media-driven communications, taking responsibility also means accepting the need to provide public information. It's easy to complain about being "on the media's schedule," especially during a crisis. But we do our institutions immeasurable harm if we withhold information, appear slow to respond, stonewall the press, or offer "no comment."

Having the president front and center during a crisis provides important benefits. It helps calm public concern and sets an example for the entire campus. My philosophy is clear: Denial or minimization of a problem will only delay solutions and lead to negative public perceptions. Candor and forthrightness are the essence of crisis management.

Staff members across campus know that I expect phone calls to be returned—whether the caller is a parent or a reporter. What's more, I expect each staff member to be open, willing to take the heat, and prepared to deal with the public aspects of any problem. In my opinion, any CEO should be able to ask for a high level of professionalism and commitment from the institution's staff.

My university relations staff also offers good advice on how a crisis will play in the public arena. Campus CEOs have to be careful, however, about trying to adapt to every public whim. Public relations advisers are at their best when they counsel CEOs to "do the right thing." A CEO's response to a crisis must be carefully considered, in line with the institution's mission, and consistent with its core values. That does not always win immediate praise from the public, but it will gain the institution respect over time. And, as hard as it may be to remember during the heat of the crisis, it is the long view that matters.

Whatever the crisis, my university relations staff and I rely on two essential steps in crisis management: bringing together a crisis team and designating an appropriate spokesperson. Of course, your crisis team will vary given the situation at hand. But as a rule, you should plan to include institutional relations staff members, key administrators, legal counsel, and perhaps experts in the subject at issue. When a meningitis outbreak hit our campus, for example, our team included an expert in epidemiology and the head of the student health service. When we discovered lead-based paint in our daycare centers, a pediatrician, a toxicologist, and staff members from our facilities management department all served on the crisis team. During the floods of 1993, a physical plant administrator and a structural engineer lent their expertise to the team.

Establishing a policy on spokespersons helps impose order upon chaos. Our policy simply states that the president or the vice president for university relations will designate our official spokesperson. Often this responsibility falls to a university relations staff member. But many times another administrator—someone experienced and well-versed in a particular issue—may be the most appropriate choice.

Despite the fact that we, like most of our colleagues, seem to have a crisis about every 15 minutes on our campus, it is clearly our responsibility to be at the center of the action. Our institutions are microcosms of our world, and from them will come many of the solutions to the challenges our society faces today. We just have to remember to review our crisis plan every few days.

Hunter R. Rawlings III
President
University of Iowa

Introduction

In *When Crisis Strikes on Campus*, we don't pretend to answer every question you may have on this hot topic. What we do attempt is to offer a basic handbook—complete with a companion video—to help you begin the complicated process of planning for crises at your institution.

We open the book with a behind the scenes look at a particular crisis—the 1990 murders at the University of Florida. **Section 1: Troubled Times at the University of Florida** offers tested advice from UF's veteran campus communicator, a first-hand account of the Gainesville crisis and the institution's reaction, and samples of the communication vehicles that helped keep campus and community constituents calm and collected. After learning from the experiences of your UF colleagues, you'll even have the chance to size up your own institution's crisis readiness. Our companion video, "The Worst of Times," captures on video the immediacy and uncertainty of the tragedy—and the regularity and consistency of the University of Florida's clearheaded response.

Knowing that your institutions' crises may come in many shapes and sizes, we turn our attention to a variety of other crises at different institutions. **Section 2: Behind the Headlines: Case Studies in Crisis Communications** features concise accounts of eight distinctly different campus crises. You'll learn how an independent school handled the arrest of a teacher involved in child pornography, how a community college overcame a broken reputation, and how a large university weathered Hurricane Andrew. And that's just for starters. As you read about what worked—and what didn't—for your colleagues at these institutions, you will be able put their advice to work for your institution.

Section 3: CURRENTS on Crises highlights the award-winning magazine's best and brightest articles on crisis communications in recent years. You'll find example-filled articles on everything from preparing for crisis before it strikes to learning the legalities of campus crises.

Section 4: CASE Issues Papers: Communicating Controversies on Campus showcases CASE Issues Papers on crisis communications. Each information-packed paper centers on such prickly issues as crime on campus, animal rights break-ins, and sexual harassment incidents. The papers not only describe the issue at hand but also offer successful communication strategies and campus contacts for follow-up research.

Section 5: Crisis Resources provides additional materials to help you prepare for the inevitable before it strikes. Legal advice from a college attorney, excerpts from campus crisis plans, and a bibliography of additional crisis resources offer practical examples. One caveat: Although we include sample crisis plans for your review, experts recommend that you begin with a blank sheet of paper when creating your own campus crisis plan. After all, no two institutions would respond in exactly the same way—even to identical crises. Every campus is different in history, culture, and goals. So every institution must draft its own crisis plan.

But we at CASE know how difficult this task can be. We hope *When Crisis Strikes on Campus* will make your own crisis planning a little less daunting.

Nancy Raley
Vice President, Marketing Operations
CASE

Troubled Times
At the
University of Florida

CHAPTER 1

Video Preview

"The Worst of Times: The University of Florida Story"

As University of Florida students arrived for the fall semester on Sunday, August 26, 1990, the police discovered two murdered female students in their off-campus apartment. Three other murders followed almost immediately. Each was similar to the first, suggesting a serial killer was on the loose. By Thursday, August 30, about half of UF students had left Gainesville. Media attention spread word of the University of Florida crisis around the world. Calls, more than 200 per day, came rapidly.

The Council for Advancement and Support of Education in cooperation with the students, faculty, and staff of the University of Florida has produced "The Worst of Times: The University of Florida Story." Developed from notes taken during the crisis, the video recalls the ensuing events through actual news footage. Commercial TV station news materials come courtesy of WUFT-TV, WCJB-TV, WTLV-TV, WFLA-TV, NBC News, and the *Independent Florida Alligator* and *Gainesville Sun* newspapers.

Newscaster Ray Moore narrates this story. A veteran communications professional, Moore served as news director for 10 years at WSB-TV in Atlanta and spent 13 seasons at the Georgia Institute of Technology as director of research communications. His 30 years in television news includes five years filing stories for the "Huntley/Brinkley Report" and investigative pieces for numerous award-winning documentaries.

The following people (in order of appearance in the video) help capture the concerns surrounding the University of Florida crisis.

- Ray Moore, Narrator
- Mike Browne, UF Student Government President, 1990
- Karelisa Hartigan, UF Professor of Classics
- Linda Gray, UF Assistant Vice President for University Relations
- John V. Lombardi, UF President
- Art Sandeen, UF Vice President for Student Affairs and Crisis Team Chair
- Larry Tyree, President, Santa Fe Community College
- Jim Scott, UF Dean of Student Services
- Rob North, Reporter, WFLA-TV

CHAPTER 2

The Gainesville Crisis

Behind the scenes at the University of Florida

Art Sandeen

At 6 p.m. on Sunday, August 26, 1990, the chief of campus police called to tell me that the bodies of two white females had been found in their off-campus apartment—the obvious victims of murder. Fall classes were scheduled to begin the next day. Dean of Students James Scott and I immediately went to the scene, an apartment complex about a mile south of campus that houses several hundred students from the University of Florida. We quickly learned that the two women were indeed UF students.

News of the murders spread quickly. By 7 p.m., we had called on several members of our student affairs staff from housing, student services, the counseling center, and the student union. About 18 of us were on site talking with student residents until after midnight.

The next day, we formed a 25-person crisis response team. The group included staff members from public relations, student affairs, academic affairs, the crisis center, business affairs, and legal affairs, as well as student leaders, campus ministers, and members of the campus, city, and county police forces. The response team came together—at least twice a day for the first several days of the crisis—to make all decisions and coordinate all communications. In fact, we continue to meet even now.

In the next 36 hours, the bodies of three more students were discovered in nearby apartments. Needless to say, students, faculty, staff, and the community felt grave concern. After consultation with the deans and our response team, President Lombardi announced at a press conference that the university would not penalize students for missed classes or late fee payments if they chose to go home. With Labor Day weekend approaching, the administration essentially set back all deadlines about 10 days to take the pressure off students. By Thursday, nearly 50 percent of our students had left Gainesville, and most had gone home.

Art Sandeen is vice president for student affairs at the University of Florida.

Reaching out

Our early responses focused on supporting students, getting out accurate information, and offering on-site assistance. Among the services provided during this unprecedented time were:

- free phone calls home;
- special phone lines set up to accommodate the large number of incoming calls;
- extension of academic and fee deadlines;
- 24-hour escort service on and off campus;
- meetings with student organizations;
- a grief counselor on campus;
- free housing on campus for students afraid to stay off campus;
- on-site counseling in student residences, day and night;
- cancellation of social events and parties;
- two letters from President Lombardi to the parents of all students;
- timely publication and distribution of crisis information;
- a rumor-control phone line;
- greatly increased security services everywhere;
- efforts to accommodate—not antagonize—more than 400 members of the press who were on campus for seven days; and
- staff working almost around the clock.

Spreading the word

The supplementary materials described below exemplify the various communication vehicles we used throughout the Gainesville crisis. Together, they summarize and embellish the University of Florida's actions before, during, and after the tragedy of August 1990. You will also find responses from neighboring Santa Fe Community College. The original communications appear at the end of this chapter for your reference.

- *Presidential correspondence.* University of Florida President John V. Lombardi kept parents and students informed throughout the crisis. In two letters to the parents of thousands of UF students (dated August 28 and September 4, 1990), Lombardi expressed his commitment to personal safety and described the university's response to the tragedies.

On December 28, 1990, Lombardi wrote to students pledging to "recognize the university's loss, to reaffirm his concern for personal safety, and to continue his commitment to the quality of life at the University of Florida." A fourth letter anticipated the media's coverage of the first anniversary of the tragedy and assured students of the administration's continuing concerns for personal safety.

- *Campus communication on student safety and personal security.* Throughout the crisis, UF's communications office sent several helpful pieces of correspondence on safety and administrative matters to the campus community.

- *Memorial Service guidelines.* Linda Gray, UF's assistant vice president for university relations, distributed this memo to media representatives attending the memorial service for the five students.

• *Santa Fe Community College responses.* During the tragedy, no one could predict where the killer would strike. As a result, neighboring Santa Fe Community College in Gainesville took swift action to coordinate its own safety measures with SFCC students and faculty. An August 28th memo from President Larry Tyree and SFCC's director of the women's programs and special projects illustrates the college's quick response to safety concerns. Two news releases from Information Director Larry Keen summarize vital actions for the media.

Taking time to grieve

One week after the tragedy began, the university held a memorial service on campus for the victims and their families. Today, a memorial scholarship and a special place on the campus also recognize our tragic loss. The university continues to maintain contact with each of the families.

Since the Gainesville crisis, law enforcement officials have captured a suspect and charged the individual with committing the slayings.

This tragedy could happen anywhere. Yes, written plans of action are useful but certainly are not sufficient in themselves. In our experience here at the University of Florida, we discovered that effective crisis communications will depend mostly on the good relationships among staff, faculty, police, and community leaders, established over a period of time. Involvement of student leaders in all actions and decisions from the start was also crucial for us. Of course, having a humane, energetic president sensitive to both students and the public helped us get through the crisis as well.

Although no one can offer a prescription to follow in tragedies such as this, we at the University of Florida do feel encouraged to have witnessed the wonderful and caring actions so many people were willing to perform for others.

Editor's Note: In early 1994, a jury convicted 39-year-old serial killer, Danny Rolling, and unanimously recommended the death sentence, which was also the recommendation of Judge Stan Morris. Rolling, who had initially plead innocent to the killings, finally confessed to the crimes, providing evidence of his guilt.

CHAPTER • 3

Coping with Campus Crisis

A campus communicator's guide to dealing with the demands of the job before, during, and after the crisis

Linda S. Gray

Pre-crisis preventive measures

Don't wait for crisis to call before you prepare for the inevitable. Take these proactive steps during calmer times so you and your staff will be ready to make your best moves when crisis strikes.

1. *Make campus connections.* Maintain a close working relationship with key university staff people—your president, vice presidents, deans, campus police, and student leaders. Ideally, the chief media relations person should report directly to the president. A crisis period is no time to get to know people.

2. *Get off campus, too.* Build similar working relationships with community leaders and key public relations professionals in your area.

3. *Keep an electronic Rolodex.* Maintain an up-to-date media list on computer. If possible, include both office and home numbers of key media representatives.

4. *Put your plan on paper.* Draft a written crisis plan that details:
- who decides what information is released;
- who speaks for the institution and releases material to media;
- who—on and off campus—must be notified in a crisis;
- what role the media relations staff will play;
- the composition of the crisis teams, depending on the nature of the crisis; and
- phone numbers and addresses of key people, including top administrators, crisis teams, and media relations staff.

5. *Put a lid on logistics.* Your crisis plan should also cover the following logistical details:
- potential news conference/media availability sites (specify sizes of rooms, whom to call to reserve the site, and the like);
- additional phone lines in your office (make sure you have designated phones for media representatives);

Linda S. Gray is assistant vice president for university relations at the University of Florida.

• an inventory of available equipment and space (where cameras can plug in, where laptops can be hooked up to phones, where computers can be used, etc.);

• details on the closest, best, and cheapest hotels and motels in the area;

• parking for the media (don't forget to designate spots for satellite trucks); and

• available staff support, including clerical and technical back-up people as well as communications staff to deal directly with media.

Crisis communications

The basic principles of effective communication all apply during times of crisis. But when an emergency situation turns up the heat on your campus, these additional guidelines should help you and your staff keep your cool.

• *Always return media calls.* A "bunker mentality" won't make a problem or the media go away. So make it a point to get back to reporters—even if they call more than once and even if they're hostile. The more cooperative you appear, the better.

• *Really communicate.* When you're talking with media representatives, that means both talking and listening. During crisis time, try to be informative, friendly, and patient. And take time to listen, too. Reporters can provide you with useful information.

• *Don't antagonize the media.* A sharp tone at a press conference, during a phone call, or elsewhere can affect your future relationship with a media representative and any other reporters who may have overheard the conversation.

• *Hold the phones.* Consider establishing a dedicated call-in telephone line for the media and other interested parties. Particularly useful when incoming calls tie up your regular phones, a dedicated call-in line allows you to record on tape and easily update important news such as times and dates of upcoming media events, rumor control information, and other newly acquired details.

• *Think about others.* Consider how the information you release to the media may affect other sources. If what you say will result in reporters calling other agencies or individuals, you need to call ahead to warn them of impending calls.

• *Share the spotlight.* When talking to media, be sure to give credit to other agencies, groups, or individuals working on the crisis, including your own staff. But don't do so just because it's courteous; do so because it will enhance your relationships and reflect well on you and your institution.

• *Take a proactive approach.* If you acquire new information about the crisis, reach out to media—even if things are frantic. Everybody's looking for a "twist" on the story that no one else has. If you can provide reporters with a special angle, it can pay off later.

Reporter relations

You're not the only one feeling the crunch of crisis communications. When a crisis hits your campus, reporters also face daunting deadlines and personal pressures. As a campus communications professional, it's your job—now more than ever—to practice good press relations.

• *Choose your words carefully.* When you notify the media of news conferences or availabilities, be sure to specify the kind of event you are actually having. Usually, if you announce a news conference, reporters expect you to provide them with information or to announce something. A press availability can simply mean you are making individual(s) available to answer questions from the media.

• *Never underestimate your audience.* Gauge the size of your crowd carefully when reserving a room. As a rule, it's better to have too much, than too little space. Make sure microphones, chairs, lighting, and water are in place at least 30 minutes before an event.

• *Plan ahead.* Choose an appropriate format in advance. Decide who will introduce speakers, who will decide when the question-answer period ends, and the like.

• *Hand out helpful background.* Decide whether you'll need handouts. If your speaker has prepared a written speech, you may want to distribute the text *after* the presentation to make sure reporters will stay and listen. But do tell them that you'll distribute a copy later, so they aren't irritated by having to take unnecessary notes.

• *Check the calendar.* Before you schedule your news conference or press availability, make sure you know what else is happening on campus and in the community. Don't lose effectiveness through time conflicts with other events.

• *Spread the word.* Consider whether you need to let other organizations and agencies know about your news conference. You may even wish to invite others to attend or participate in your event.

• *Know where the buck stops.* Decide who will maintain control at your media event. Someone may need to be the arbiter as to where reporters set up camera tripods, who sits where, and other details.

• *Stay on schedule.* Try to plan the length of your news conference/availability, but be flexible. Don't end it when there are still a dozen hands raised for questions.

• *Watch the clock.* Consider the time of the news conference/availability. If you want to make the noon, 6 p.m., or 11 p.m. TV and radio news, you need to allow time for crews to travel and edit tape. Remember, the time scheduled for your media event can send a signal—right or wrong—to the media.

• *Say cheese.* You may want to pre-plan still photo opportunities.

• *Keep the media informed.* If you have a satellite uplink or other equipment, be sure to let the media know in advance. And if you're going to set restrictions on a media event, put them in writing and let media representatives know at least 24 hours in advance.

Personal considerations

Coping with a crisis takes its toll on the most experienced campus communicators. The following suggestions will help you and your staff maintain your personal—and professional—demeanor during times of crisis.

• *Gather the facts.* In any crisis, try to find out as much information as you can. Even if you are not going to communicate that information, it's probably better to know as much as possible. In this way, you avoid inadvertently saying the wrong thing or sending unintended messages.

• *Don't misbehave.* Consider the parameters of your crisis and conduct yourself accordingly when dealing with the media and others. Although maintaining a sense of humor is important, inappropriate humor can work against you. Professional dignity is important particularly in unpleasant times.

• *Keep notes.* As the crisis progresses, take time to document the crisis and your institution's responses. These notes will not only help you remember things during the crisis, they will most likely prove useful for later review.

• *Dress for success.* If you're going to be on camera, always dress professionally. This may seem like "form over substance," but casual or mussed clothing can send signals to viewers that the situation is out of control.

• *Take care of yourself.* During the crisis, don't forget to give yourself some down time to sleep, relax, and reflect. Overwork and sleep deprivation can lead to misstatements, irritability, and loss of friends.

• *Say thanks.* When the worst of the crisis is over, send notes of appreciation to those who have been of service—on and off campus. And don't forget to acknowledge your own staff for a job well done.

• *Play catch up.* Apologize to the folks whose correspondence, projects, and other work you may have had to put off because of the crisis. Then catch up on that work. The consolation: You'll most likely find that much of the work will have taken care of itself.

UNIVERSITY OF
FLORIDA

Office of the President

226 Tigert Hall
Gainesville, FL 32611-2073
(904) 392-1311

August 28, 1990

Dear Parent:

No doubt by now you have seen or heard in the media of the recent tragic deaths of several young people in the Gainesville area. I know you join with us in mourning the senseless loss of these young people. I write to let you know that we at the University of Florida are doing all we can to protect our students and other members of the university community. Their safety is our primary concern.

We offer a variety of security, psychological, housing and food services to students and others. Many of those services have been expanded, with increased hours of operation and numerous additional personnel. As just one example of the expanded array of services we are offering, we are providing food and housing on our campus for those of our students who do not wish to remain in off-campus residences. We are encouraging everyone to take advantage of these services.

We have publicly encouraged all UF students who have not called home since the tragic deaths occurred to do so immediately. To make that easier for the students, we have established a phone bank at our Office of Development and Alumni Affairs where students can call home for free and let their parents know they are safe.

Our University Police Department is working closely with the Gainesville Police Department, the Alachua County Sheriff's Office, and the Florida Department of Law Enforcement to do all we can to mobilize our law enforcement services in the area and provide the best protection and safety possible.

Our Office for Student Services is available to help students at any time. Students who have questions or concerns are encouraged to call the Office for Student Services at 392-1261, and they may call the University Police Department at 392-1111 24 hours a day.

We hope you will encourage your child to do everything he or she can to preserve personal safety and to use the services we are providing. We appreciate your thoughtful concern, and assure you that we are mustering the considerable resources available to us to sustain a safe and supportive environment.

Sincerely,

John V. Lombardi
President

Equal Opportunity/Affirmative Action Institution

11

UNIVERSITY OF FLORIDA

Office of the President

226 Tigert Hall
Gainesville, FL 32611-2073
(904) 392-1311

September 4, 1990

Dear Parent:

The past week has been a difficult time for all of us associated with the University of Florida, including you and your son or daughter. We know that you will be making decisions this week about the future academic progress of you student, and I want you to know that we stand ready to do everything we can to work with you and with all of our students and their families to cope with this situation. I have had the opportunity to talk with many of you and want to thank you for the words of encouragement and tell you that we will extend our full support to our students as we move forward in our University activities, both academic and extracurricular.

Classes resumed today with our students present and determined to devote their attention to the usual activities of the fall semester. We are reminding our students that the deadlines to drop and add courses for this semester and to withdraw from the University without financial penalty are this Friday, Sept. 7. The deadline to pay fall term fees is Monday, Sept. 10. As you know, we extended these deadlines to the dates mentioned to accommodate our students and their families. We are determined that the terrible circumstances of the past week not cause permanent disruption to our University.

Provost Andrew Sorensen and I have talked with the deans who, in turn, are talking with faculty members, and we will work carefully to see that no student need suffer academically or financially from this situation. Our faculty will work with students to see they are brought up to speed in their class work. No one will be penalized for lack of class attendance before Sept. 7. We are, of course, encouraging students to work with faculty to ensure they are fulfilling course requirements.

Should your son or daughter experience any difficulties regarding their academic status or their personal reactions to this crisis, we encourage you to have them consult the Office for Student Services, 392-1261, the Office of the Provost, 392-2404, or the University Counseling Center, 392-1575. We will hold a memorial service for the five young people who died last week on Wednesday, Sept. 5, at 4:30 p.m. in the Stephen C. O'Connell Center, although that service will likely have taken place by the time you receive this letter. At that service we will remember those students and reflect on the meaning of their lives.

In the days that come we will carry on with the work of your university in the positive, meaningful and sensitive way that is our tradition. We ask that you and your student continue to sustain our pride in the accomplishments of the people at this fine university.

All of us at the University of Florida value your support and confidence.

Sincerely yours,

Equal Opportunity/Affirmative Action Institution

UNIVERSITY OF FLORIDA

Office of the President

226 Tigert Hall
Gainesville, FL 32611-2073
(904) 392-1311

December 28, 1990

Dear Student:

As the fall semester comes to a close, all of us recognize that this has been an unusual time. No one of us in this community will forget the pain, fear, and anger caused by the murders of five students, yet in that tragedy we found in ourselves and in our community the strength, compassion, cooperation, and caring needed to maintain the integrity of our lives and the continuity of our university. The University of Florida and its many communities here and through out the state combined our resources, our energy, and our belief in the fundamental values of a university community to carry us all through a most painful and difficult time. As the New Year begins, we must pledge ourselves to continue in this spirit to recognize the loss we have all suffered, to reaffirm our personal concern for all our safety, and to continue our personal commitment to the quality of life and achievement that is our purpose at the University of Florida.

When I came to join you here at the University of Florida, I expected to find a quality faculty and staff working with exceptional students, and you have exceeded all my expectations. I found a collection of students whose stellar academic achievements as measured by standardized tests, National Merit or Achievement Scholarships, and performance in our classrooms and laboratories included a passion for student-led activities and programs. Student campus life, whether in formal Student Government or an infinity of superbly organized and effectively run service organizations, all carried the same spirit of determined optimism, creative energy, and unquenchable enterprise. You, the students of the University of Florida, are a great resource for this state and this nation, and I am very proud to be a part of your university.

During this past semester, while we have lived with tragedy and confronted the challenge of confrontation in the Middle East and budget difficulties in the State of Florida, the university has extended its continuing tradition of accomplishment. Our extraordinary homecoming extravaganza, the student and faculty involvement in the filming of the movie Doc Hollywood, an effective expansion of the university's People Awareness Week, an exciting and successful football season with a new coach, and the achievement of a University of Florida-FSU-Los Alamos coalition of scientists in bringing the National Magnetic Lab to the state of Florida, each of these accomplishments represents but a sample of the quality work that is the hallmark of this university and that places us among the best of America's universities.

As we begin a New Year, the Lombardi family thanks you for the warm and enthusiastic welcome to your university. We could not have imagined the kindness and support you have given us. This is a university with an extraordinary spirit of achievement and an enthusiasm for life. We wish for all of you the warmth and kindness that you have given us. May your driving spirit enrich us all.

Sincerely yours,

[signature]

To: Faculty and Staff of the University of Florida

Safety and security of the entire university community is of utmost concern. In light of recent off-campus violent crimes, the University Police Department is stepping up on-campus crime prevention and safety services and recommending that faculty and staff take extra precautions to insure personal safety.

UF faculty and staff are encouraged to be familiar with on-campus safety services and preventive steps that may be taken to be more alert.

Safety Measures

- Do not work alone.

- Call University Police if you need escort services.

- Secure offices at all times.

- Do not travel alone -- travel only in groups.

- Avoid strangers.

- Be alert for suspicious individuals and situations.

- Use the "buddy system" to let your friends know where you are going, what route you plan to use and estimated time of arrival and return. For safety and crime prevention assistance, call UPD at 392-1111.

- UPD provides 24-hour police service seven days a week to the UF campus.

Personal Vulnerabilities

- Avoid dark and secluded places and do not bike, jog, or walk alone at night.

- Stay alert and tuned in to your surroundings.

- Have your key in hand before you reach the building or your car.

Summary Information for U.F. Students
September 2, 1990

1. **Classes:** Classes will resume on Tuesday, September 4, 1990. The drop-add deadline has been extended to Friday, September 7, and students needing to withdraw can do so until Sept. 7 without academic or financial penalty. If academic work has been missed, contact should be made with individual professors. The deadline to pay fees for fall term is 2:30 p.m. Monday, Sept. 10. Call 392-1374 (Registrar's office) or your College Dean's office in order to have additional questions answered.

2. **On Campus Housing:** There continues to be 24 hour front desk coverage in the residence halls, and radio dispatched security patrolling residence areas. Temporary spaces for students who need them will continue to be provided. Students choosing to withdraw from school who live on campus this semester can apply for on campus housing in January 1991 and will receive priority for such space. Call 392-2161 for information or go to the Housing Office.

3. **Financial Aid:** Financial aid packages are being dispersed according to the regular University schedule. Students who are Aid recipients and choose to withdraw from classes will not lose their financial aid for next semester. Contact the Student Financial Affairs Office, 392-1275, for further information, or go to that office in 101 Anderson Hall.

4. **SNAP Escort Service:** The SNAP Escort Service has extended its hours from 6:00 p.m. to as late as students need it at night. Students can receive escort service to campus locations and from the campus to their off-campus apartments. Call 392-SNAP for assistance.

5. **Counseling Support:** The University Counseling Center staff and the Alachua County Crisis Center staff are available to provide assistance to individuals and to student groups both during the day and evening. Call 392-1575 or 376-4444.

6. **Memorial Service on Campus:** The University will conduct a Memorial Service on Wednesday, September 5, 1990, at 4:30 p.m. in the O'Connell Center. All students, faculty, staff, and friends of the University are invited to attend.

7. **For Further Information:** The Housing Office will be open on Labor Day, Monday, Sept. 3 from 12:00 noon to 4:00 p.m. Call 392-2161. The Student Services Office will also be available for calls during the same time. Call 392-1261. To contact the University Police, call 392-1111.

Memorial Service Guidelines

To: Media Representatives

From: Information and Publications Services

During today's memorial service, we ask that you adhere to a few simple guidelines to help insure the dignity of the service.

* Do not use any artificial light source, including flash photography.

* Do not shoot stand-ups during the ceremony, or do live pick-ups with reporters in the O'Connell Center.

* Remain in place or on the photo platform until the conclusion of the service, which is expected to run 30-40 minutes.

(Please note that no one will be allowed to set up after 4:20 p.m.)

Thank you for your understanding and professionalism during what has been a difficult time for us all.

SANTA FE COMMUNITY COLLEGE

POST OFFICE BOX 1530
3000 N.W. 83 STREET
GAINESVILLE, FLORIDA 32602

OFFICE OF THE PRESIDENT

August 28, 1990

M E M O R A N D U M

TO: Faculty and Staff

FROM: Larry W. Tyree
          President

          Ann Bromley
          Director, Women's Programs and Special Projects

SUBJECT: "Security Measures for Students"

Santa Fe Community College has taken action in response to the tragic and brutal deaths of four female students and a male student, one of whom was SFCC student Christa Leigh Hoyt. Everyone's help is needed to prevent a reoccurrence of these crimes.

Please use some class time to explain precautionary measures and the safeguards already in place at Santa Fe. The students look up to you as instructors. Your wise and measured counsel in this time of justified concern would help greatly.

Please let your students know that night security has been increased with more officers and more patrols. For more information on security, call 395-5519 or visit Building T. Please tell your students that SFCC staff will provide night escort service. These staff will be wearing SFCC hats and college T-shirts with "security" imprinted on them.

There are free phones for local calls on campus. These phones are located in the concourses of Building R - financial aid, Building B - across from the bookstore, Building A - southwest entrance, Building K - concourse, Building H - southwest corner, Building W - lobby. Please give these locations to your students. A hotline so parents and friends can check on the status of SFCC students has been set up at 395-5502.

If students are deeply troubled and want personal counseling, have them call 395-5503. Attached is a brochure which lists numbers of outside agencies which also give personal counseling.

from **SANTA FE COMMUNITY COLLEGE**

**Office of
Information
and
Publications**
3000 N.W. 83rd St.
Gainesville, FL 32606
(904) 395-5235

Larry Keen
(904) 395-5235

ADVISORY ON SFCC SECURITY MEASURES

Almost 7,000 of Santa Fe Community College's 11,800 students live in apartments and other dwellings in the Gainesville area. SFCC President Larry W. Tyree thanks the Gainesville area media for helping to get word of Santa Fe's security measures out to the college's students.

The following is a summary of precautionary steps taken by SFCC as of Thursday (Aug. 30):

* Students can make free phone calls home from campus Building R or any of the five First National Union banks in Gainesville.

* Parents can reach students by calling (904) 395-5502 or visiting Building R. The college will send a runner to contact the student in class.

* Crisis counseling for students is available in Building R or by calling (904) 395-5503.

* Students can drop classes with full refunds until at least Sept. 10. Students will not be given grade penalties for missing classes until at least Sept. 10. The college will evaluate its policy on a daily basis after that date.

- MORE -

SFCC STUDENT SECURITY
Page 2

* Ten or more SFCC staff or faculty members will augment the regular security patrol of seven officers from 6:30-10:30 p.m. every class night. The auxiliary patrol will wear SFCC hats and clothing and will escort students to and from their cars.

* A safe house for SFCC students is at the Alachua County Girls Club, 2101 NW 39th Ave., 373-4475. SFCC does not have on-campus housing to use as a refuge.

* Free training in basic self defense for SFCC students, UF students and the public will be offered at 1 p.m., 2:20 p.m. and 4 p.m. Saturday (Sept. 1) in the SFCC Gym. Certified law enforcement officers will conduct the training.

- 30 -

news _____

from **SANTA FE COMMUNITY COLLEGE**

**Office of
Information
and
Publications**
3000 N.W. 83rd St.
Gainesville, FL 32606
(904) 395-5235

Larry Keen
(904) 395-5235

THE PUBLIC HELPS SFCC WITH EXTRA STUDENT SECURITY

A safe house, self-defense training and additional free phone calls home are new safety measures implemented Wednesday (Aug. 29) by Santa Fe Community College in response to five murders in Gainesville.

On Tuesday the college itself set up crisis counseling, added security patrols, free phone calls home, a hotline for parents to contact students and a suspension of financial or grading penalties for students who miss classes.

The college accepted outside help Wednesday. SFCC students have a safe house at the Alachua County Girls Club, 2101 NW 39th Ave., 373-4475. Santa Fe does not have resident housing to provide a refuge for students.

Free training in basic self defense will be offered at 1 p.m., 2:30 p.m. and 4 p.m. Saturday (Sept. 1) in the SFCC Gym, Building V. The Gainesville Aikido Association and certified law enforcement instructors from SFCC's Institute of Public Safety will conduct the training.

Any SFCC student can make a free phone call home from one of Gainesville's five First National Union banks.

- 30 -

Faculty and Staff
August 28, 1990
Page 2

Lastly, please give your students some precautionary tips. They are young, perhaps naive and most certainly afraid. You can help. Warn them to:

Use the buddy system leaving class and going to parking lots.

Know their friends and stay with them if possible.

Once they get home, students shouldn't answer the door unless they know who the person is. If the person at the door appears to be a security officer, maintenance man or medical worker, call the applicable organization to find out if someone has indeed been sent to their residence.

Your concern and help are deeply appreciated.

Attachment

Larry Tyree

Ann Bromley

CHAPTER • 4

Crisis Readiness Test

When crisis strikes on your campus, will you be ready?

Now that you've viewed "The Worst of Times" video and read the University of Florida background materials, take time to complete this Crisis Readiness Test. Your answers to the following questions will help you size up the strengths—and weaknesses—of your institution's crisis preparedness. "Prepared" can mean that you have existing relationships, lines of communications, and mutual trust among those with whom you must collaborate during a crisis—both on and off campus. It also means you are armed with backgrounders on things that could go wrong.

But remember, be honest in your responses. There's no time like the present to prepare for crisis. So get out your pencil and get ready.

1. For which types of institutional crises are you prepared?
- Community-related?
- Accident?
- Natural disaster?
- Disease?
- Crime?
- Scandal?
- Administrative or governance problem?

2. Have you drafted a crisis plan for your institution?
- Is everyone prepared to use it when needed?
- Who heads the crisis response team?
- Have you distributed your crisis plan to the appropriate campus colleagues?

3. How fast can you assemble a crisis team?
- Does your crisis plan specify the team's composition for a variety of crises?
- Do you have a crisis communications chain in place?
- Have you identified alternate team members in case any first draft picks are out of town or otherwise unable to serve?
- How will you communicate with area and campus residents when power and phone lines are down?

4. Who are the members of your crisis team?

- Campus CEO?
- Other top administrators?
- Key academic officers?
- Student affairs administrators?
- Faculty?
- Students?
- Campus security?
- Trustees?
- Legal counsel?

5. Who will speak for your institution?

- Your campus CEO?
- Vice president for student affairs?
- Director of public relations?
- Others?

6. Do you have a phone notification list that includes the following key audiences?

- Members of the crisis team?
- Local agencies and outside officials?
- Updated information for all media representatives?

7. Have you worked out the following logistical details in advance?

- Potential news conference sites?
- Availability of phones, fax machines, and computers at campus sites?
- Inventory of video and uplink equipment on or near campus?
- List of area hotels and motels?
- Parking for media representatives?
- Staff availability?

8. Are your media relations sound?

- Did you work to build—and maintain—good working relationships with the media before the crisis hit?
- During times of crisis, can your staff handle media requests calmly and truthfully in a relationship of mutual trust?
- Does your PR director have direct, immediate access to your CEO?

9. How swiftly can you meet the following communication needs?

- Get word to everyone on campus?
- Develop a complicated news release?
- Send a sensitive letter from your campus CEO to parents?
- Provide a news briefing?
- Hold a campus informational forum?
- Set up a rumor-control hotline?

10. Are your ties to the local community strong?

- Neighborhood groups?
- Police, fire, safety, health departments?
- Mayor and town, county, or state officials?

Behind the Headlines: Case Studies in Crisis Communications

CHAPTER • 5

Surviving the NCAA's Death Penalty
Southern Methodist University

Patricia Ann LaSalle

The crisis at a glance

In 1986, a former Southern Methodist University football player revealed on live Dallas television that several athletics boosters had made improper payments to team members. Because the SMU football program was already on probation for recruiting violations, the NCAA issued its so-called "death penalty," suspending the football program for a year. Within days, the director of athletics and the football coach resigned. The president, who had earlier been on medical leave, also resigned.

Elevating and prolonging the local and national newsworthiness of the story, the governor of the state, who had been chair of SMU's Board of Governors, revealed his involvement. Not only did he admit to knowing about the improper payments, but he had approved of their continuation because of agreements made with the players.

Deeds before words

The most important element of responding to a crisis is to begin steps to fix what's wrong. Action must accompany communication. In addition to changes in athletics department personnel, SMU disbanded its powerful Board of Governors, which was intended to serve as the executive committee of the Board of Trustees but had, in fact, become somewhat isolated from the full Board. An ad hoc committee revamped SMU's governance system, achieving a larger, more diverse, and more representative Board of Trustees with fewer opportunities for power to become concentrated in one small group. Another ad hoc committee reformed the athletics program, now governed by stringent controls and strict accountability to the University's administration and faculty. SMU's interim president abolished the football program for a second year to allow sufficient time for reforms to be established. Within a few months, SMU had recruited a distinguished, nationally known, no-

Patricia Ann LaSalle is associate vice president for public affairs and university editor at Southern Methodist University. At the time of the football scandal she edited the university magazine and other publications.

nonsense educator as president: A. Kenneth Pye, former chancellor of Duke University. Through these actions, the atmosphere of crisis was turning into the foundation of credibility.

The crisis team

As soon as the news broke, we called together a crisis team including our director of news and information, the editor of our university magazine, vice president for development and alumni relations, alumni relations director, faculty senate president, and other PR officers of SMU's individual schools. To coordinate our efforts, the University's various PR officers formed a Communications Council, which still exists.

The audiences

Throughout the crisis, we worked to deliver timely and accurate information to a variety of constituencies, including the media, alumni, students, parents, donors, high school counselors, prospective students, church officials, and community leaders.

The communication mix

As soon as the NCAA levied its sanctions, the director of news and information and the university's magazine editor collaborated to create a special *SMU Update* newsletter. Three, four-page issues provided alumni, donors, and parents up-to-the-minute details on the complex controversy. This action was necessary because our quarterly university magazine could not be produced quickly enough to meet our communication needs. Instead, we used two issues of the magazine for more comprehensive coverage: not only articles summarizing our crisis, but opinion pieces from a student, a professor, a football player, and an alumnus offering different views on the proper role of athletics at SMU. The magazine included a chronology of the crisis and the reforms, but also elevated the discussion to a national context—athletics and education in general. Thus, the newsletter and the magazine complemented each other.

SMU also sent personal letters to certain groups, such as alumni, donors, parents, and prospective parents. For example, the associate provost recruiting top academic scholarship students wrote to their parents assuring them that the teaching and research they expected to benefit their students continued as usual and explaining the reforms that would address SMU's problems before their students enrolled.

To assist campus communication, the Faculty Senate and the Student Senate sponsored a "town hall" meeting to air the issues and concerns of the University community. Attended by more than 300 people (some had to be turned away), the meeting was open to faculty, students, staff, alumni, and other friends. In addition, students held a "teach-in" on the steps of the main campus building with invited speakers that included the sports reporter who broke the story and members of the SMU Board of Trustees. Anyone who wanted to express a view was able to do so.

Above all, as local and national news representatives virtually camped out at the university, the office of news and information responded promptly and completely to all questions. Because of this cooperation, media professionals promised to return to give full coverage to our reforms and the university's turnaround. In fact, the arrival of our new president and the return of football gained positive national coverage on the networks and in such publications as *The New York Times Magazine*.

Words to the wise

1. *Pick a leader.* Although teamwork is essential in any crisis situation, ideally one person should manage all communications. Before SMU's NCAA crisis broke, our public relations vice president had left to take another position, and the interim president had left the position vacant. This meant we had no overall "PR leader." Fortunately, staff members from various campus units were able to work together as a team to handle crisis communications.

2. *Make a plan.* If you didn't have one before, prepare and follow a written crisis communication plan. If you did have one, follow it and look for ways to improve it based on your recent experience.

3. *Go right to the top.* Make sure your staff has access to key campus officials to gather the full facts of the crisis. Contact these officials regularly to be certain you stay abreast of ongoing developments. The chief public relations officer should be a part of the decision-making process to advise on the perceptual ramifications of actions considered.

4. *Provide training.* A crisis can cast into the limelight campus individuals who may not have experience dealing with the media. Provide training on how to answer questions succinctly to get a specific message across and rehearse questions and answers with campus officials.

5. *Tell it like it is.* Report as candidly as possible to your constituents and the news media. Honesty and cooperation with the media pay long-lasting dividends when it's time to communicate the university's turnaround and ongoing success stories.

6. *Prescribe—and dispense—effective remedies.* Be sure to communicate the actions your institution has taken to solve the problems revealed and prevent their repetition. In our case, this included governance reform, athletics reform, hiring a new president, and developing a monitoring board for athletics.

7. *Make the most of bad news.* Accept the fact that the crisis will generate bad publicity. But use this time productively to establish good working relationships with the media. When the crisis passes, those relationships will remain.

8. *Deliver the good news, too.* Maintain your efforts to communicate other newsworthy events at the university. Don't let the crisis paralyze ongoing efforts to market your institution's strengths.

9. *Get in touch with their feelings.* Continuously gather information about what your constituents are thinking during the crisis. This will help you to address their concerns and clarify areas of confusion.

10. *Spread the word.* Meet regularly with other campus communicators to coordinate

the flow of information to all constituencies.

11. *Focus on the big picture.* Help constituents view the larger aspects of the situation. Here at SMU, we put our crisis in the context of skewed values about the importance of big-time athletics nationwide.

12. *Consider the setting.* If the campus is engaged in heated debate, help constituents understand that such discussion is a healthy and productive part of the academic enterprise.

13. *Keep your mission in mind.* Emphasize that, although the institution is busy responding to the immediate situation, education continues. Let your constituents know that the crisis has not compromised the educational process. Our provost did this through an op-ed published in the major daily newspaper and reprinted in the university magazine.

14. *Keep it in perspective.* Don't lose your sense of humor. No matter how daunting a crisis seems, remember that this too shall pass.

15. *Look for the opportunity in crisis.* Recognize that sometimes a crisis can be the shake-up an institution needs to re-examine its fundamental values and correct its course. Try to see the positive aspects of a negative situation. SMU was able to institute reforms that otherwise might have taken years to implement.

16. *Come together.* Rather than be divisive, a crisis, if properly managed, can enhance a sense of community as faculty and staff work toward a common goal. The way these individuals conduct themselves can serve as valuable lessons to students who will face complex difficulties in their own lives. Remember, others will judge us not only by the circumstances of our crisis or scandal, but also by our own conduct during the hard times and their aftermath.

December 1986

SMUUPDATE

SPECIAL TO ALUMNI AND FRIENDS

Interim president named

L. Donald Shields   *William Stallcup, Jr.*

Acting Provost William B. Stallcup, Jr., has been named President *ad interim* of SMU, following the early retirement of President L. Donald Shields November 21.

Shields' retirement, effective immediately, came as the result of serious health problems. A victim of adult-onset diabetes, he has experienced a worsening of the condition over the past several months despite a four-week medical leave in October. Increasing tension caused by recent allegations of misconduct in SMU's football program further aggravated his condition. It became imperative that he retire, his physician said.

The appointment of Stallcup to the interim post was announced November 25 by the Board of Governors. An SMU alumnus, Stallcup is a longtime member of the Biology Department in Dedman College and has served in a number of administrative positions at the University.

Shields said his decision to leave the University after six years as chief executive officer was extremely difficult. "It pains me to leave the University in this critical time in its life, and I very much regret that my health does not permit me to contribute to the solution of the University's current challenges."

He added, however, "I am confident in the ability of the University community to confront and overcome even the most serious challenges and to have the strength and spirit to continue striving to achieve our high aspirations for excellence."

In a November 25 resolution, the Board of Governors said: "Dr. Shields has led the University with extraordinary vigor and creativity, winning the affection and loyalty of all segments of the University and the respect of the community." It declared that "SMU has benefitted enormously from Dr. Shields' leadership."

Dr. Shields, 50, who came to SMU in 1980, was formerly president of California State University at Fullerton.

William Stallcup ('41) has twice served the University as acting provost, first in 1980-81 and most recently since April 1986, following the resignation of Provost Hans Hillerbrand. *(Continued on page 4.)*

Governors act on athletics

SMU's Board of Governors has established a blue-ribbon commission to re-examine the role of intercollegiate athletics at the University. The Board also adopted a resolution abolishing special admissions for student football players and initiated an investigation into new allegations of wrongdoing in the football program.

The action came in the wake of alleged football improprieties made public in early November, which aroused renewed concern among SMU constituencies about the football program.

"The Board of Governors has one objective only in this matter," said Board Chairman William P. Clements, Jr., at a November 25 news conference. "We feel strongly that the University must bring into focus that our primary, fundamental objective is academics. . . .Anything that detracts from that goal must be corrected."

In further addressing SMU's football problems, the Board will consider all options,

Clements said, including the possibility of eliminating the program, if necessary.

Details on the implementation of the special admissions termination are being worked out now by University officials. SMU has specially admitted about 28 athletes a year, about half of them in football. Under the Board's action, SMU football recruits will be considered for admission using the same standards as those applied to other students.

By tightening admissions requirements and "putting the emphasis where it belongs," Clements said the Board understood that SMU's football program "may approach a less than fully competitive position. But that remains to be seen."

At its specially called meeting November 25, the Board also announced that SMU's investigation into alleged football improprieties will be conducted, in cooperation with the National Collegiate Athletic Association, by Dr. Lonnie Kliever, professor of religious *(Continued on page 3.)*

To alumni and friends

Dear Friends:
The events of the past few weeks have been distressing for all members of SMU's family—faculty and students on campus, alumni in Dallas and across the nation and the world, as well as many other friends and supporters of the University. As President *ad interim* of the University, I have had the opportunity to discuss these events with numerous individuals and groups who are close to the University, who cherish it, and who have given freely of themselves in support of it.

Among SMU people, there is concern about the integrity and reputation of the University and its programs. There is sadness at the departure of Don Shields, under whose leadership the University has progressed greatly in the past six years.

There also is the recognition that this is a time of opportunity—opportunity for redirection, clarifying the central purposes of our University, and for reaffirming our commitment to SMU's mission. In emphasizing SMU's academic priorities, the Board of Governors on November 25 initiated actions that provide an important starting point for redirection and rededication. During the next several months, in the special University commission on athletics, in the search for a ninth President of the University, and in many other undertakings, we shall have further important opportunities to strengthen SMU.

As we concern ourselves with the events of recent weeks, however, it is important to remember that the heart of the University's functioning remains intact—education continues. The outstanding teaching, research, and service that have brought distinction to SMU continue to do so. In this we can all take pride.

When I enrolled as a freshman at SMU not quite 50 years ago, I came here as a scholarship student, truly grateful for the privilege of attending this fine University. Since then, whether as a student, a professor of biology, or in my administrative assignments in the Office of the Provost and now in the Office of the President, I have labored under a strong sense of indebtedness to SMU, as well as a sense of loyalty to it. I know that you and others who share this sense of indebtedness and loyalty will join with me and the University's leadership now to ensure a continued strong future for our University.

William B. Stallcup, Jr.
President *ad interim*

31

Faculty seeks active role in athletics reform

Members of the Faculty Senate and other professors at the University are calling for a re-examination of the proper role of athletics at an academic institution, are seeking to play an active part in those deliberations, and have sponsored a series of discussions to open up dialogue on the issues.

"The participation of the faculty should be central to the whole process of educating ourselves" and others on the issues at hand, Anthropology Professor David Freidel, a member of the Faculty Senate, told the group at a recent meeting.

According to Faculty Senator and Economics Professor Carter Murphy, "What is called for is a continuing dialogue in this body and with the faculty at large, in the Board of Governors, and among the alumni and students with an interaction of ideas throughout the year."

John Deschner, holder of the Lehman Chair in Christian Doctrine, Perkins School of Theology, brought the issue of the balance between academics and athletics beyond the SMU campus when he told the Senate: "I have an impression that what SMU is going through is a local version of a profound problem in this country at many universities."

Beginning November 19 and continuing November 24 and December 3, the Senate took up the question of athletics in open sessions and passed a number of resolutions reflecting the thinking of that body.

It adopted the language of a petition from some 200 professors to urge "the immediate, unconditional and permanent abolition of quasi-professional athletics at this institution." It called for establishment of a committee to evaluate the role of athletics "in a University dedicated to academic excellence and moral integrity" and to recommend specific athletic reforms.

Further, the Senate expressed opposition to "privileged academic treatment" for athletes and to the maintenance of a staff to recruit and manage "quasi-professional athletic teams." Specifically, it said, "We are categorically opposed to subsidies of any kind to athletes as athletes, to special admission criteria for athletes and to any other form of privileged academic treatment for athletes."

In other action to halt what Senate President Leroy Howe called "a crisis in confidence" in athletics at SMU, the Senate called for a prompt investigation of the allegations against the football program.

Faculty concern surfaced immediately after new allegations against the football program were made public. At a meeting of the faculty of Meadows School of the Arts, that body endorsed unanimously a statement expressing its "absolute and unwavering commitment to maintaining and strengthening the academic quality of our school and the University." The statement continued, "We abhor the excesses and ethical compromises which are fostered by the present system of big-time intercollegiate athletics and, in particular, the continuing abuses associated with the SMU football program."

A letter from Dedman College Dean R.

Hal Williams declared, "The (Dedman) faculty . . . feels that there is something very wrong with the way athletics are currently conducted on this campus . . . .We believe that action must be taken to end this situation." The letter, later adopted as a statement from Dedman College, supported "traditional honorable amateur athletics for students who have an interest in such endeavors, and intercollegiate competition with only those institutions unambiguously committed to honorable amateur athletics.

At a November 21 meeting of the faculty of the Edwin L. Cox School of Business, resolutions were approved expressing "deepest concern about the impact of the

SMU football program on the moral and academic integrity of the University," and calling for the formation of a University-wide committee to evaluate the role of athletics at SMU. The findings of such a committee, the business school faculty said, should be made public to the university community before the end of the school year and be acted on by the president and the Board of Governors.

Among the resolutions passed by the Senate was a statement of support for President *ad interim* William Stallcup. It pledged "to work with him to reassert the traditional educational values espoused by SMU and to resolve promptly and responsibly the basic issues now confronting the University."

Alumni board solicits opinions

Calling for enhancement of "the basic moral fiber and the values upon which this University was founded," the SMU Alumni Association Board of Directors has issued a statement urging "immediate, decisive action to strengthen the integrity of the University, which has been put in question by recent accusations involving the intercollegiate football program."

The statement to the SMU Board of Governors was drafted by 20 members of the alumni board's Executive Committee. The statement further recommends that an Alumni Association representative take part in SMU's football program investigation as well as the special commission appointed examining the role of athletics at the University. The Executive Committee nominated William W. Aston ('61), Alumni Association president-elect, to serve on the athletic commission.

"The alumni board felt a statement was important because alumni are so strongly af-

fected by SMU's actions and how they are perceived in their home communities," said Alumni Association Executive Director Gary A. Ransdell. "The Board felt it could not make specific recommendations because of the diversity of alumni opinion being expressed. It would be wrong at this point to assume there is a consensus. We hope alumni will continue to express their views in writing to the University on the issues involved."

To assist the communication process, the Alumni Association will sponsor forums for discussion in conjunction with regional chapter events throughout the United States, Ransdell said.

In other action, the Association asked the SMU Board of Governors for official alumni representation on the search committee to select SMU's next president. The alumni board nominated Association President Lindalyn Bennett Adams ('52) as its representative.

Students call for accountability

The SMU Student Senate has passed a resolution reaffirming its commitment to a program of honorable amateur athletics, condemning "any individual or body that jeopardizes the integrity" of the University, and calling for an external investigation of alleged football misconduct.

Passed 26-6 at a special meeting called by Student Body President Trevor Pearlman, the resolution says, in part, that the Student Senate "would support efforts to hold responsible boosters accountable for their actions, which could include their disassociation from the University and being subject to due process of law. . . . "

The resolution also sounded a note of optimism : ". . . we, the Student Body, commit ourselves to a belief in the pursuit of excellence of our University and its potential for its athletic as well as academic integrity."

Mixed feelings of the student senators echo those of the student body at large, according to Pearlman. He says many students are concerned that their SMU degrees are devalued as the school's integrity is ques-

tioned. On the other hand, many students support the idea of retaining a football team to encourage school spirit.

"They want a football team that enables them to get together as a whole, but I think they recognize that SMU doesn't need to become national champions. A mediocre team is okay," Pearlman added.

The student body president also said students feel "encouraged" by recent actions of the SMU Board of Governors. During a November 25 press conference following a specially called meeting of the Board, Chairman William P. Clements, Jr., said he hoped members of the student body would nominate students to serve on the newly formed special commission to examine the role of athletics at the University. He also said that student representatives would be involved in the search committee to select a new president.

Pearlman said that students on the presidential search committee and athletic commission will "represent a significant perspective of the school."

Hitch, Collins submit resignations

Athletic Director Bob Hitch and Head Football Coach Bobby Collins resigned their positions December 5, amid controversy over allegations of wrongdoing in the football program. Their resignations were effective immediately.

In a statement issued following the actions, President *ad interim* William Stallcup said, "During their years of service, SMU sports teams have enjoyed marked success. Under the prevailing circumstances, however, it is my judgement that Mr. Hitch's and Mr. Collins' resignations are in the best interest of the University." Stallcup continued, "I offer Bob and Bobby our gratitude for their many efforts on behalf of SMU, and our best wishes for them and their families for the future."

Stallcup appointed Dudley Parker, associate director of athletics, to manage the department temporarily. He said an acting director will be appointed shortly, and a search

for successors to Hitch and Collins will be initiated "in due course."

At a news conference both Hitch and Collins cited "the best interests of the University" as their reasons for leaving. Hitch said, "SMU is a fine institution and it deserves better than it's getting at this point. It's time for someone else to take (the program) another step or two without this embarrassment."

Bob Hitch was in his sixth season as athletic director at SMU. Under his administration, the Mustangs have earned three NCAA championships and 11 Southwest Conference titles. They have earned 32 national Top-Ten finishes in all sports. For the past five years, SMU has ranked number one nationally among privately supported intercollegiate sports programs. Hitch came to SMU in 1981 from the University of Wyoming.

Collins, who previously was head football coach at Southern Mississippi University, has

Bob Hitch   *Bobby Collins*

produced a 43-14-1 record since he came to SMU in 1982. He was named Southwest Conference Coach of the Year in 1982, after leading the Mustangs to a Cotton Bowl and conference championship.

Governors (cont.)

studies and University representative to the NCAA. Dallas attorney Robert Hyer Thomas ('53), a member of the Alumni Association Board of Directors, has been appointed the legal counsel assisting Kliever. Findings will be reported to the NCAA.

The new special commission on athletics will have a broader focus, to include such issues as the relationship of intercollegiate athletics to academic goals and priorities; liabilities as well as benefits of the intercollegiate athletics program; the question of continued participation in the Southwest Conference; the funding and organization of the Athletics Department, as well as its relationship to the central administration; and special admissions and special academic assistance policies and practices for student athletes.

William L. Hutchison ('55) has been selected by the Board of Governors to head the special commission. A Dallas business leader, Hutchison is a member of the Board of Governors and a longtime supporter of the University. Membership on the commission will include faculty, students, trustees, alumni and possibly participants from outside the University community, Clements said.

The current allegations against SMU's football program came to light November 12, when WFAA-TV aired an interview with David Stanley, a former Mustang football player. Stanley said he received $25,000 in 1983 from a former Athletic Department staff member for signing with SMU, and was then paid $750 a month until December 1985, four months after the football program was placed on probation. On November 14 *The Dallas Morning News* reported that senior Mustang Albert Reese allegedly is living in a rent-free apartment provided by an SMU booster.

Under the NCAA's new "death penalty" rule, SMU could lose its football program for two years if the institution is found guilty of further violations within five years of receiving sanctions. In August 1985, the football program was placed on three-year probation after an NCAA investigation revealed 35 instances of recruiting violations.

Mustang Club urges support of athletics

The Mustang Club has issued a statement to the SMU Board of Governors supporting "the continuation of all men's and women's intercollegiate athletic programs at the competitive level that students, alumni and friends of the University have come to appreciate."

Approved unanimously by the club's Board of Directors, the statement further says that "we expect to see these programs conducted with integrity."

The Mustang Club is a non-profit organization which serves as the fund-raising arm of the Department of Athletics.

The statement said the club shares the "frustration" over recent allegations of foot-

ball misconduct and urges the University to cooperate fully with the NCAA "in a joint effort to restore the integrity of our athletic program."

The statement continued: "We recognize the proud tradition of intercollegiate athletics at SMU during the past 75 years and the tremendous positive impact the men's and women's athletic programs, including football, have had on the University, the greater Dallas community and the Southwest Conference." The Mustang Club also expressed its disagreement with recent resolutions passed by the Faculty Senate regarding athletics at SMU.

Morgan named interim provost

Ruth Morgan

After serving eight years in the Provost's Office, Political Science Professor Ruth Morgan was granted a sabbatical leave for 1986-87. She was completing a book on Dallas politics and looking forward to returning to full-time teaching next fall. But last month she received a call asking her to return to the administration as provost *ad interim*. (She replaces William Stallcup, who was named president *ad interim* upon the retirement of L. Donald Shields.)

"When called to return to administrative service at this particular time, I felt that I could do no less," Morgan said. "The character of the University is measured by the way it responds to challenges. I have confidence that this faculty and this staff and these students will rise to the occasion. My first goal is to ensure stability and continuity and

to maintain the momentum on the course we have charted toward excellence and integrity in everything we do."

Ruth Morgan has been a member of the faculty since 1966 and has served the University in a number of administrative roles. She joined the staff of the Provost's Office in 1978 as assistant provost, and chaired the Steering Committee on Self-Study and Program Review. She became associate provost in 1981 and continued in that position until last spring, when she asked to be relieved of her administrative duties so she could devote full time to teaching, research and writing.

Morgan has also served as director of the Master of Liberal Arts Program and as academic director of SMU-in-Paris. Previously she served as president of the Faculty Senate (1972-73).

Morgan was named "Outstanding Professor" in 1969 and 1974. In 1972 she received the "M" Award for outstanding service to the University. An expert on the American presidency, Morgan is the author of *The President and Civil Rights*, and has three other books in progress.

Highlights of the Shields presidency

Progress toward *The Decade Ahead*

L. Donald Shields became SMU's eighth president in December 1980. He came to SMU from California State University at Fullerton, where at age 34 he had been the nation's youngest president of a state university.

When he arrived in Dallas, Shields announced ambitious goals for SMU—to make it one of the premier private universities in the South and Southwest.

After six years in office Shields has taken an early retirement because of his health. During his tenure the University made significant strides toward the goals he established. Some of the highlights of his presidency follow:

• Early in his tenure Shields defined his goals in a planning document, "The Decade Ahead," which outlined priorities for SMU's six schools, student life, athletic programs and other areas of the University. The document called for emphasis on undergraduate education of high quality and "selective excellence in graduate and professional programs."

• The financial resources of the University grew dramatically during the Shields administration, with endowment increasing from $92 million in 1980-81 to $282 million in 1985-86. Total gifts during the same years rose from $12.3 million to $29.9 million, an increase of 144.7 percent.

• Endowed professorships; one measure of a university's academic stature, increased from a total of 29 when Shields came in 1981 to 50 currently.

• Students have shown increasing academic strength in the first half of the 1980s. SAT scores for entering freshmen rose from 1020 in 1980-81 to 1100 this fall, against a current national average of 906.

• Contributing to the rising SAT averages at SMU are two academic scholarship programs instituted during the Shields administration—President's Scholars, who get full tuition, and University Scholars, who get partial assistance. SMU competes with some of the nation's top universities for its President's Scholars. Those who entered the program

this fall have an average SAT of 1394; freshman University Scholars average scores of 1258. There are a total of 104 President's Scholars and 623 University Scholars currently on the SMU campus.

• New facilities recently completed or nearing completion on the campus include: expansion of the Edwin L. Cox School of Business with two new buildings made possible by major gifts from Cary M. Maguire and Trammell Crow; construction of the Hughes-Trigg Student Center, provided by Charles and Katharine Trigg, which is scheduled for completion in September 1987; and a five-level, 822-space parking garage near Moody Coliseum.

• Externally funded research increased from $3.2 million in 1981-82 to more than $6 million already in 1986-87, as of November.

Interim president named (cont.)

A member of the biology faculty since 1945 and a former department chair, he has also served as associate dean of the faculty in the School of Humanities and Sciences, now Dedman College (1971-73), associate provost (1973-80 and 1981-83) and special assistant to the president (1982-83). A native of Dallas, Stallcup earned a bachelor's degree in biology from SMU in 1941 and his doctorate in zoology in 1954 from the University of Kansas.

Regarding Stallcup's appointment as president *ad interim*, the Board of Governors issued a statement November 25 expressing "enormous gratitude to him for his willing-

ness to serve the University in this demanding role." At a news conference the same day, William P. Clements, Jr., chairman of the Board, said, "Bill Stallcup is a distinguished professor, he was a student here, and he has long been in the service of the University. We are blessed to have him to pass the baton to."

The Board of Governors shortly will name a search committee for the ninth president of SMU. The committee will be representative, the Board said, of all segments of the University community, including faculty, students, administrators, alumni, trustees, and representatives of the United Methodist Church.

This special newsletter is being sent to alumni and friends in an effort to summarize the events that have taken place at Southern Methodist University in the last few weeks. A joint project of the Office of University Relations and the Office of Alumni Relations, the newsletter also represents an invitation for members of the University family to express their views on the various issues under consideration. University President William B. Stallcup, Jr., welcomes your letters. (Please address them to the Office of the President, SMU, Dallas, Texas 75275.) If you wish to share your views with other alumni, the *SMU Mustang* magazine will be pleased to publish signed letters. (They should be sent to the Office of Alumni Relations, 3000 Daniel Avenue, Dallas, Texas 75205.) SMU will continue to keep alumni informed about this issue and other important aspects of University life.

SMUUPDATE

Southern Methodist University
Dallas, Texas 75275

Important Information About Recent Events at the University.

CHAPTER 6

Weathering Andrew's Aftermath

University of Miami

Susan Bonnett

The crisis at a glance

On August 22, when a hurricane warning was issued for South Florida, the University of Miami president convened our hurricane planning group. We'd had a comprehensive hurricane plan in place for many years, so we were confident that our thorough planning would help the university successfully weather the storm. But we would soon discover that no amount of planning could have prepared us for what has been called the worst natural disaster in U.S. history.

Hurricane Andrew hit the University of Miami on what was to be the first day of freshman orientation just before the start of the fall 1993 semester. Most freshmen were already on campus (some with their parents) and chose to ride out the storm along with the housing staff and faculty in the residential colleges. Other students en route to Miami with their families decided to stay in motels further north. And local students braced for the storm at their homes across South Florida. Not yet knowing the severity of the storm, we issued a media advisory on August 23 announcing that the university would be closed on August 24 and freshman orientation would be canceled.

Our annually updated hurricane plan—complete with the university's disaster policies, emergency preparations, and communications strategies—prepared us to be without power and water for two or three days. But when the storm had passed, sources predicted several *weeks* without power. Decisions on when to reopen were made and remade as damage reports came in. Two days after the hurricane, the president decided to close most residence halls for repairs and to postpone the start of classes until September 14.

Managing the crisis

The hurricane plan includes a Disaster Advisory Committee headed by the president. The committee includes communications but is strongly oriented toward maintaining facilities and providing food, shelter, and medical care for resident students. While this group pre-

---

Susan Bonnett is associate vice president for university relations at the University of Miami.

pared for the hurricane, after the storm the needs changed and an ad-hoc crisis team emerged that included the university's senior administrators.

Obviously the primary focus after the storm was on safety, assessing damage, and beginning repairs and clean-up. However, communication with employees, students, parents, and key constituencies emerged as the next highest priority. University relations staff played a crucial role working nonstop with the president as the chief media spokesperson.

The audiences

During the hurricane and its aftermath, our three primary constituencies were students already on campus and those on their way, parents, and university employees. The downtown medical campus focused its communication efforts on patients as well as employees.

The communication mix

The lack of power and impassability of roads made initial communication efforts difficult. But next to the safety of students and employees, communication became our highest priority. Our primary communication objectives were (1) to provide a means for families of students who stayed on campus to obtain information immediately after the storm; (2) to determine the safety and housing status of all employees and provide assistance when needed; (3) to inform students, parents, faculty, and staff of the scheduled changes; (4) to keep students from returning to the residence halls during the clean-up; and (5) to dispel rumors and misinformation about the condition of campus and to encourage out-of-town students to return.

Once we had delivered these immediate safety messages, we were able to turn our attention to the following post-hurricane communication objectives: (1) to gain recognition and support for the volunteer efforts of students, faculty, and staff working on hurricane-relief projects; (2) to build credibility of faculty members as experts on a variety of hurricane-related topics; (3) to forge stronger ties with the news media by making key faculty members available as resources; and (4) to demonstrate the university's concern for the community.

Two days after the storm, the *Miami Herald* and every local radio and TV station had interviewed UM President Tad Foote or another UM spokesperson about closings and schedule changes. Stories in *USA Today* and the *New York Times* helped us communicate with out-of-state students. After identifying key recruiting markets, we worked quickly to broadcast information about closings on radio stations in New York, Chicago, Boston, and Baltimore.

Once the storm had passed, we were able to send source sheets, news releases, and media advisories—complete with campus experts and faculty and student volunteer efforts—to local and national media. As a result, news coverage began to shift from simple status reports to positive coverage about UM faculty experts and their role in understanding Hurricane Andrew's wrath. In the month after the hurricane, the communications staff initiated daily placements in the *Miami Herald*, seven placements in the *New York Times*, and comparable coverage in the *Washington Post, USA Today*, and national network news shows.

On campus, a comprehensive telephone campaign helped the university contact directly some 4,840 of our 8,600 undergraduates to keep them informed and answer any questions they had. In a similar effort, staff members and volunteers reached some 4,600 university faculty and staff in three days. The successful phone campaign helped the university identify and find temporary housing for 419 homeless families.

Several times a week, we published our own *Hurricane Update*, which student volunteers delivered to employees and key offices and sent across campus via e-mail. A special edition of our internal tabloid covered the hurricane and its aftermath for faculty and staff, while our university magazine delivered a feature on Andrew's impact to all alumni. We also sent letters outlining schedule changes to all undergraduate students. A presidential appeal letter updated all alumni outside the affected ZIP code areas and raised nearly $200,000 for the UM Hurricane Relief Fund.

An 800 telephone line helped make sure families could stay in touch with students even if regular phone lines were overloaded or out of service. University employees could seek assistance through a variety of special seminars on everything from dealing with insurance claims to coping with post-disaster stress.

Words to the wise

1. *Allow enough time for recuperation.* Having a crisis *recovery* plan is just as important as having the crisis plan itself. Because our plan dealt primarily with the crisis and immediate aftermath, we soon realized that we had underestimated the recovery period and work required. Depending on the nature of the disaster, the recovery period may extend over weeks—or even longer.

2. *Prepare for power outages.* After Hurricane Andrew, UM's office of university relations was without power for two weeks. Staff members were forced to use equipment and space at several locations, at times making communication less than effective and coordination difficult. Make sure your administration understands the importance of post-crisis communication and is willing to make the institutional commitment to provide the necessary resources, such as emergency generators, cellular phones, and the like.

3. *Offer support to staff.* Develop strategies that allow for alternative staffing and shifts. A natural disaster may affect certain geographic areas more than others, so some employees will face more difficult situations depending on where they live. Also remember that crisis and post-crisis work is extremely stressful. Be prepared to relieve staff to handle personal concerns when necessary.

Office of Media Relations
P.O. Box 248105
Coral Gables, Florida 33124-4020
305-284-5500

August 31, 1992

H U R R I C A N E   U P D A T E

The University of Miami has delayed opening as a result of Hurricane Andrew. This "Hurricane Update" will be issued each morning until routine operations are underway.

MEDICAL SCHOOL CAMPUS

- The medical center received minimal hurricane damage, and the School of Medicine re-opens Monday, August 31. Faculty, staff and students resume regular schedules on August 31.

- Although the health needs of the community are being met, Jackson Memorial Hospital is beginning to show signs of strain. All non-trauma cases among faculty, staff, and students should be directed to the University Health Center. (See additional information on the Health Center that follows).

- All clinical faculty should contact their chiefs of service as soon as possible.

- All freshman and sophomore medical students should report to their classrooms at 8:30 a.m. Monday, August 31. All junior and senior medical students should report to their teams at that time.

- Classes for non-medical graduate students begin Monday, September 14.

- Classes for the Cuban Exile Physician Program begin Monday evening, August 31.

- The Sylvester Comprehensive Cancer Center is fully operational and ready to assist physicians and their patients obtain cancer care interrupted by the hurricane. Medical care, radiation therapy, and chemotherapy are available. Emergency staff privileges are being extended to physicians who need a facility to treat their cancer patients. Patients or their physicians should call 545-1000 to make necessary arrangements.

CORAL GABLES AND ROSENSTIEL MARINE CAMPUSES

- The Coral Gables campus re-opens on Monday, August 31. All employees should return to work if they are able. Cafeterias will be open, and drinking water will be available for employees.

- The Rosenstiel campus on Virginia Key re-opens on Monday, August 31. Graduate classes begin on Monday, August 31. An information desk has been established at 361-4000.

- UM employees are being paid even if they were unable to work due to the emergency situation. Regular payroll for monthly employees takes place on August 31, as scheduled (including Direct Deposit). Payroll for bi-weekly employees will take place Thursday, September 3, as scheduled (including Direct Deposit). Follow established procedures for check pick-up and distribution.

HEALTH CENTER

- The Coral Gables campus Health Center is fully operational and is open Monday-Sunday, 9 a.m. to 5 p.m. After 5 p.m. (emergencies only), call 284-5927/5921.

- The University Pharmacy is open Monday-Friday, 9 a.m. to 5 p.m., and Saturday and Sunday, 12 p.m. to 5 p.m. For more information, call 284-5922.

- Psychological/psychiatric services are available for all University employees covered under health plans and HMOs:

  * United States Behavioral Health: 1-800-333-8724
  * Dade (Jay Wolfstead): 621-2217
  * Dr. Alisa Lamnin: 372-3550

- The Health Center is conducting a series of "Rap Sessions" for faculty and staff to discuss their experiences with the hurricane. The one-hour sessions will be held Monday and Wednesday from 3 to 4 p.m. and 4 to 5 p.m. in Whitten University Center, Rooms 237 and 245. Sessions will also be held Tuesday from 3 to 4 p.m. and 4 to 5 p.m. in Room 245. For more information, call 284-5927.

- Drinking water is available outside Eaton Residential College. Please bring a clean container. Water in water fountains may not be safe to drink. Do not drink this water until notified that it is safe.

-2-

CHILD CARE

- UM/Canterbury Preschool will provide emergency child care for University of Miami faculty, staff, and students, Monday, August 31-Friday, September 4. Child care is available in sessions from 8 a.m. to noon or from 1 to 5 p.m. Each session includes lunch, games, stories, videos, and art. The location is Pearson Residential College, 5185 Ponce De Leon. Bring your child's blanket, pillow, and favorite toy. For more information, call Susan Rosendahl at 666-2031 or 666-0635.

RELIEF AND ASSISTANCE

- An operations center has been established to locate and provide relief for faculty, staff, and alumni who are suffering from the effects the hurricane. The program -- UM Cares About Neighbors (UM CAN) -- is fully staffed and will work daily to identify and assist members of the University community in need. If you need assistance, or if you have information about individuals who need assistance, please call 284-2872.

- A collection center has been established at the University. It is located at the Ibis Cafeteria. Faculty, staff, and students are asked to donate non-perishable food, drinking water in sealed containers, disposable diapers, baby food and formula, and wearable clothing. The drop-off point is the loading dock at the back of the cafeteria (across from the entrance to Gusman Hall). Hours are 9 a.m. to 5 p.m., until further notice. Please note that this is a collection center only and not a distribution center. The items will be distributed by local agencies.

- Carrie Edmundson, 284-2318, is coordinating a volunteer and job program for students, both on campus and in the community.

- Human Resources has organized an employee volunteer housing program. Human Resources is also identifying apartments and homes that are available for rent. Please call 284-6709 for more information.

- Facilities Management and the Purchasing Department have developed a list of contractors that can be used by members of the University community for repair of their homes. For more information, call Jim Balter at 284-5751 or 284-2291.

- Employees who have had major housing damage and need assistance in dealing with insurance claims can call Bill Coombs in Risk Management, 284-3163. The Purchasing Department, 284-5751 or 284-2291, has guidelines for dealing with your insurance claims.

-3-

- A residence halls project has been set up to assist FPL workers. Approximately 200 FPL workers from the Carolinas, Georgia, and Virginia, are being housed in the Lane Recreation Center.

SAFETY AND SECURITY

- The Department of Public Safety has worked diligently to maintain safety and security during and after the hurricane. All staff members have been working long shifts, and ten additional officers are on loan from Virginia Tech.

- If you see or are a part of a situation that requires the attention of the Department of Public Safety, call 284-6666. Please limit these calls to important issues of safety and security.

- In order to keep the campuses secure, it is imperative that each member of the faculty and staff do his or her part. Please take extra care to lock doors and close windows, and do not prop doors open.

- All employees are asked to carry their 'Cane Cards with them at all times. If your card has a clip, please wear the 'Cane Card at all times.

- Anyone who has contractors who need access to campus buildings should call the Purchasing Department (284-2291). A temporary ID card will be issued.

BUSINESS AND FINANCIAL AFFAIRS

- Authorized staff should spend funds prudently, but do what is necessary to get the University operational. Vice presidential approval is required for amounts over $15,000. All major expenditures affiliated with the clean-up should be carefully documented.

- Check-cashing is available for students at the Cashiers Office, Ashe Lobby. Emergency loans are available through Student Account Services, Ashe 158.

- The normal check requisition process resumes on Monday, August 31, in the Orovitz Building (2nd Floor). Petty cash is available for emergency purchases.

- The University Credit Union (Coral Gables Office) is open 10 a.m. to 2 p.m. The medical campus office will open on a limited basis beginning Monday, August 31, at 10 a.m.

-4-

IMPORTANT STUDENT INFORMATION

A new academic schedule has been developed. The provost has written to undergraduate students regarding the following schedule:

- September 10, Thursday -- New student orientation begins, residential facilities will re-open. Orientation and registration begin for first-year law students.

- September 11, Friday -- Registration begins.

- September 14, Monday -- Undergraduate, graduate, and law classes begin.

- December 18, Friday -- First semester ends.

- There will be no separate final examination period. There will be no cumulative final examinations. Faculty are encouraged to use alternatives to final examinations such as take-home examinations and final papers where due dates can be staggered. The intent is to avoid overload on the final two days of the semester.

- Orientation, academic advising, and registration for the Spring 1993 semester will be extended, as necessary, through January 16-17, Saturday-Sunday.

- The University will be closed Monday, January 18, for Martin Luther King, Jr., holiday.

- Spring semester classes begin, as originally scheduled, Tuesday, January 19.

ON-CAMPUS RESIDENTIAL FACILITIES

- Students currently housed in campus housing are being encouraged to return to their homes. However, the University will provide housing and food for those students who choose to remain on campus.

- Students now on campus will be reimbursed for the trip home (within the contiguous U.S.) and back to campus. The reimbursement rate will be 15 cents per mile. Receipts should be saved to provide documentation.

- Delta Airlines is providing a discount airfare program for students. Delta's number is 1-800-241-6760. Ask for file number L0810.) For more information, call Jim Balter in the Department of Purchasing at 284-5751.

-5-

- International students will be reimbursed for travel (within the state of Florida) if they return home with a U.S. student.

- Residential facilities are being sealed off for repairs and maintenance; only one entrance will be open and identification will be required.

MISCELLANEOUS

- The local E-Mail system is not yet operational for most users. Bitnet, however, is operational.

- The Richter Library can assist in salvaging books damaged by the storm. Contact Frank Rodgers, 284-3551.

- The Lowe Art Museum can assist in the repair, storage, and safe-keeping of works of art. For more information, call Brian Dursum at 284-5414.

- Until further notice Dining Services is not offering catering for University meetings.

- The ATM machines in Whitten University Center are fully operational.

- As reported in the media, several hundred monkeys escaped from a University facility in south Dade County during the hurricane. None of the loose monkeys have infectious diseases, but they will bite if provoked. All but about 50 of the monkeys have been recovered, although monkeys also escaped from the Manheimer Foundation and Monkey Jungle. A hotline has been set up to aid in the recovery of any of the monkeys. If you have information, call 547-6804.

-6-

Edward T. Foote II
President

August 31, 1992
(dictated August 28)

Members of the University of Miami Family

Dear Colleagues:

First, I pray that you and yours are safe and that the damage to your homes and other properties is not severe. But I know that many of you are hurting a lot. Some loved ones may have been injured. Some lives may have been lost, though to my knowledge none yet have been reported. Many have lost their homes. We are doing everything possible to assist members of the University family in the aftermath of the hurricane. We are trying to reach all of you by telephone. Please call your supervisor if you have not already.

Please call 284-6709 if you need emergency assistance.

Here is a brief report on the status of the University following the hurricane, written five days after that terrible night.

Our medical and marine schools, the south campus and the Koubek and Knight centers sustained only moderate damage.

The Coral Gables campus took the worst hit, but no one was killed or seriously injured. Please recall that the hurricane struck the night of the first day of orientation (shortly after Bosey and I were to have welcomed parents of new students), so virtually the entire freshman class, hundreds of transfer students and hundreds of parents were stranded in our residential colleges and apartments, a total of 4,000-5,000. Thank god no one was killed or injured. We lost power, water, air conditioning, telephones, etc., but survived through the extraordinary work of our colleagues, many of whom worked more than 48 hours straight. There was a time three days ago when we were literally running out of food and potable water, but deliveries resumed just in time. Now, we have basic services restored to most of the campuses. Monumental cleanup work continues.

Many of our colleagues--particularly in the Residential Colleges, Physical Plant, and Public Safety--worked around the clock for days. Their effort has been heroic. I salute them for all of us, and thank them warmly for their dedication.

P.O. Box 248006
Coral Gables, Florida 33124
(305) 284-5155

University Community
August 31, 1992
Page Two

As always, School of Medicine personnel served the broader community splendidly by providing vital medical services at Jackson Memorial Hospital and other sites.

By this time you will have received news coverage of the extensive property damage in some parts of our community. It is difficult to comprehend the extent of the human suffering in the aftermath of such a savage storm.

Since immediately following the hurricane, I have met daily with the University's senior officers and academic deans. We have decided to delay the opening of the University.

- New student orientation and registration will begin on Thursday, September 10. Residential facilities also will re-open on September 10. The start of classes on the Coral Gables campus has been postponed until Monday, September 14.

- Students in campus residential facilities have been encouraged to return to their homes, and most have. The University will provide reimbursement for travel expenses within the continental United States computed on a mileage basis with documentation of the expense. The University will provide housing and food for those students who choose to remain on the campus.

- Since the medical and marine campuses sustained little damage, those programs re-opened on August 31.

Beginning today, news will be distributed University-wide daily until normal communications are restored.

Please recall that the opening of our University was delayed in 1926 because a disastrous hurricane struck South Florida. Now Hurricane Andrew has been labeled the worst natural disaster in the history of our nation. We prevailed then. We will again.

I look forward to greeting you soon again, healthy and safe, I pray.

Cordially,

Edward T. Foote II

ETF:db

Edward T. Foote II
President

September 2, 1992

Members of the University of Miami Family

Dear Colleagues:

As we near the end of the second week following Hurricane Andrew, I write with this brief report on the status of the University family and I pray that you and yours are not suffering. (This letter will be widely available on the several campuses of the University and delivered with paychecks.)

Last week there was widespread anguish and confusion--and courage. This week there is returning normalcy and the growing confidence that our community and our University will, indeed, prevail.

Virtually all offices of all campuses opened Monday morning. Even those that did not open in the usual way opened elsewhere while repairs were completed. The School of Medicine and Rosenstiel School of Marine and Atmospheric Science began classes Monday and are functioning well. The South campus and the Koubek and Knight Centers are functioning normally. Following the massive cleanup, the Coral Gables campus incredibly is nearly restored to such beauty as could be salvaged after the loss of many trees.

At the peak of the storm, approximately 3,000 students were in our residential colleges and apartments. They were joined there by another 2,000 stranded parents, friends, staff members, and others. As soon as the hurricane was over and we knew that they were safe, we asked students to move elsewhere if possible, and all but 350 did. Our plan remains to begin freshman orientation September 10 and classes for the rest of the University September 14.

Beginning just as soon as it was physically possible on the Monday following Hurricane Andrew, we began systematically finding our people. By the end of last week we had established a telephone bank in the Alumni House to try to reach every one of our 7,000 employees. With the help of scores of volunteers we were able to find out how they were, whether they needed help, or conversely whether they were able to help others. Simultaneously, deans and division heads fanned out across the county to find their own colleagues. The result was that by Wednesday afternoon

P.O. Box 248006
Coral Gables, Florida 33124
(305) 284-5155

University Family   -2-   September 2, 1992

we had located all but two of those 7,000 members of our University family. Thank God, none were seriously injured. We have sent special teams to find the last two.

Sadly, however, we also have confirmed that many of you suffered grievous damage to your homes and properties. More than 400 have experienced total loss or great devastation to your homes. Every one of you in that desperate condition has found at least temporary shelter, and many are moving to more permanent arrangements.

Please let us know if you need help. **Call 284-6709. We will help you**.

Communications during this ordeal have been difficult at best. Our resourceful colleagues have been publishing a hurricane bulletin throughout the week, which will continue as necessary until normal communications return sufficiently.

For nine days, traveling to every part of our University, including the front-line emergency medical center operated by our doctors, nurses, and students, I have met with many of you. I have a tremendous admiration for what you are doing. The services countless numbers of the University family have performed for others have been extraordinary. Even as we dig out of our own misery, we are mobilizing institutionally to help our community.

As you will have read, so is the broader community mobilizing to help itself. President Bush has been joined in recent days by various members of the Cabinet, with whom I have met. Many federal, state, and other officials are here to help us and our community.

Rebuilding will be a massive effort, but we will rebuild.

Take care of yourselves. Many thanks for everything. If one must suffer such a devastating hurricane, one should do so in the company of people like you.

Cordially,

Edward T. Foote II
President
(Dictated but unsigned)

ETF:LLS

WINDS *of* CHANGE

HURRICANE ANDREW LEAVES AN IMPRESSION ON THE UNIVERSITY

Floridians had been warned for years that "The Big One" was long overdue. But when a hurricane watch went into effect on Saturday, August 22, few took it seriously. It wasn't until Sunday, when meteorologists confirmed Andrew was heading straight for South Florida, that people began taking action. Grocery stores were filled with shoppers loading up on canned goods, building supply stores were fast running out of plywood, and bank machines were coughing out the last of their $20 bills. By midnight, when the storm was scheduled to unleash its fury, everyone from Palm Beach to Key West was sitting nervously behind boarded-up windows in anticipation of this unknown force that would soon be upon them.

BY SUSAN MAY

WHAT HAPPENED BETWEEN THE TIME THE HURRICANE HIT AND THE TIME UM OPENED ITS DOORS IS A STUDY IN HUMAN COMPASSION BORN OF THE TRAGEDY OF THE HURRICANE.

Above: Volunteer Eric Sapp sticks UM labels on donated canned goods in this makeshift grocery store set up on campus.

Right, above: The day after Hurricane Andrew, the Coral Gables campus looked like an eerie ghost town of leafless trees and deserted buildings.

Right, center: An intensive phone campaign was launched to locate every one of UM's 7,000 employees. All were found safe.

Above: Shortly after the hurricane, Secretary of Education Lamar Alexander (left) toured the Coral Gables campus with President Edward T. Foote II.

Left: Just two weeks after the destructive storm, downed trees had been removed or replanted, roofs had been repaired, and windows had been replaced.

Earlier that day, several thousand students and parents from all over the country had begun to arrive at the University of Miami. Unaware of the impending crisis, they were looking forward to a jam-packed week of orientation activities, beginning that evening with a welcome reception hosted by President Foote.

Instead, they found themselves hunkered down in mattress-lined hallways with ferocious winds howling outside. The residential college faculty and staff quickly took charge, improvising advice, support, and provisions throughout the night and into the next morning when they were faced with no power and little food or water.

"It was a terrifying experience," says Rebecca Hoffman (B.A. '92), program assistant at Hecht Residential College, who helped evacuate people from the top floors.

"The whole building was vibrating violently, the doors were rattling, and we could hear large objects slamming against the building."

Hoffman was one of thousands of people in South Florida who prayed for their lives that night. As she was quietly reciting a prayer of her Jewish faith, her best friend, a devout Catholic, sat next to her holding tightly to her rosary beads.

The first thing Hoffman noticed when she looked out a window the next day, was a lone mourning dove with no feathers hopping among the fallen trees and debris.

Watching television coverage of the hurricane's devastation to South Florida from his home in Baltimore, Maryland, Jeff Olrick (B.A. '92) knew he had to get here. He had been a resident assistant at Eaton Residential College and knew that the staff would need help.

"More than anything I wanted to offer moral support to the people in the University community," says Olrick. "My loyalties to UM really came through after the hurricane. It greatly affected me that so many people I knew and a place I considered home for four years were in trouble."

He jumped into his car and drove 17 hours straight, stopping only in South Carolina to load up his car with food and water.

Olrick was one of hundreds of alumni, students, and faculty and staff members who came to the aid of the University community in the aftermath of what would turn out to be the one of the worst natural disasters in the United States.

Hurricane Andrew swept through the Bahamas before hitting South Florida with winds of up to 175 miles per hour. Much of the southern end of Dade County was demolished, leaving 160,000 people with no place to live and countless others with severe damage to their homes. President Bush declared South Florida a national disaster area with $20 billion worth of property damage.

Fortunately, the University of Miami was spared the total devastation of its neighbors to the south. But there was still much work to be done.

The Coral Gables campus was hit the hardest of all, with 35 damaged roofs, 800 windows blown out, 3,000 trees downed, and power lines left hanging like licorice sticks. Worst hit was the Ponce Building. The roof blew off, the storefront windows shattered, and the interior flooded. The next morning, the copy machine was found in the middle of the street.

After the storm, the entrance to the Rosenstiel School of Marine and Atmospheric Science was marked with shattered remnants of its sign. The hurricane also destroyed fences, pumps, and other equipment, and knocked down the satellite dish used to receive meteorological data. Most of the experimental hatchery's brood stock of redfish and valuable biological cultures in various labs also perished when the power shut down.

The South campus, which is a research facility, sustained considerable damage, including that which led to the release of 300 monkeys being bred for research at other medical facilities. All were accounted for.

The medical campus suffered the least physical damage, but the economic toll was great because of delayed patient appointments.

Through telephone calls and newspaper ads, students from the Coral Gables campus were told that classes would begin on September 14, two weeks later than planned.

But what happened between the time the hurricane hit and the time UM opened its doors is a study in human compassion born of the tragedy of the hurricane.

THE BIG ONE
Hurricane of our nightmares is knocking at the front door

Just hours after the hurricane had left its path of destruction, President Edward T. Foote II was plucked from his damaged home by University police and brought to the institution he has guided for 11 years. In the aftermath of the crisis, he would provide the leadership that would get the University back on its feet again in record time.

Shedding his coat and tie, Foote spent the first few days after the hurricane checking out the situation on all four campuses and talking to employees and students about their experiences. What he found were hundreds of volunteers who had left their own private tragedies to help their colleagues.

"I made a decision early on that I was going to do what I could to keep the University in touch with itself," says Foote, who went through six mobile phones in the process. "I considered that to be a major part of my responsibility—communicating, sharing with others the sense of enormous accomplishment that their brothers and sisters were doing out there."

Although the University of Miami was spared a severe blow, the homes of many of its employees who lived further south were not. Through an intensive telephone campaign, in which all 7,000 employees were called, it was discovered that more than 400 members of the UM family had lost their homes.

Roy J. Nirschel, Jr., vice president for University Advancement, led this and all other community efforts, which were given the designation UM-CAN (UM Cares About Neighbors).

"Thirty-six hours after the storm hit, we had organized phone banks at the Alumni House to track down our employees to see where they were, how they were, and if they needed help," says Nirschel. "We had 100 members of our staff, along with faculty, staff, students, alumni, and community members making calls. That's when we discovered the full extent of the devastation."

Within a week, almost all of the 7,000 employees had been accounted for, and the University police were sent out to track down the missing. All were found safe.

Safe, but not necessarily sound.

Employees whose homes had been destroyed or badly damaged needed repairs to their homes, food and water for themselves and their families, and a place to live.

Once again, the University community rallied together to help co-workers, neighbors, and friends in their time of need. Many of those helping had gone through traumatic experiences themselves.

Liz Markowitz, administrative assistant for University Advancement, thought she and her husband, Gary, and their 11-month-old daughter, Meagan, were not going to make it to the next day. After a harrowing five hours seeing their trees crash down around them, their patio blow away, and their windows smash to the floor, Markowitz watched in horror as the powerful wind began to bend their sliding glass doors inward. At that point she did the only thing she could think of to do during the worst crisis of her life. She called her mother.

"I really thought it was the end, and I had to call my mother one last time," says Markowitz, her voice breaking as she recalls the moment. "I said 'I'm calling you to say good-bye.' My mother just cried. She felt so helpless."

Markowitz and many others consider themselves very fortunate to have survived the storm unscathed. The word "miracle" comes up often among those who experienced the hurricane's full force. "We were lucky Andrew was only after our possessions," says Markowitz. "He had mercy on people."

Within a few days after the storm, Markowitz was among the volunteers at the University who were calling others to see how they fared. "It was the least I could do," she says. "And it made me feel better hearing people say they were okay."

Efforts were also begun to find housing for faculty and staff who had lost their homes and students who needed a place to live.

An emergency child-care center was set up on the Coral Gables campus, bringing relief to many employees whose children's schools were destroyed or closed.

The Student Health Center was kept open 24 hours a day for anyone who needed it, but

Above: The Coral Gables campus was the hardest hit, with 35 damaged roofs, 800 blown-out windows, and 3,000 fallen trees.

Right, above: This campus sign took on new meaning after the devastation caused by Hurricane Andrew.

Right, below: Drex Dobson, third-year medical student, offers consolation and advice at a Salvation Army clinic.

Above: The Ponce Building was flooded after it lost its roof and windows. The next morning the copy machine was found in the street.

FOR MEDICAL STUDENTS, THE DISASTER PROVIDED A ONCE-IN-A-LIFETIME LEARNING EXPERIENCE THAT ALSO OPENED THEIR HEARTS TO SPECIAL NEEDS IN MEDICINE.

fortunately there were no serious emergencies.

The Ibis Cafeteria was turned into a grocery store of donated goods for UM employees from hard-hit areas. Shoppers could choose from canned goods, water, paper products, baby supplies, charcoal, and hundreds of other products.

"At first it was very difficult for people to accept our help because they're the kind of people that are usually helping others," says Mary Sapp, director of planning and institutional research, who organized the effort along with co-worker Kerry Foster. "They couldn't think of themselves as homeless."

But the "store" ended up helping more than 200 grateful families in its short existence.

At the medical campus, attention turned to the health concerns of the storm's victims. Medical teams from the Schools of Medicine and Nursing descended on the hardest-hit areas to the south in a matter of hours. They established their presence at numerous clinic sites, some already existing at migrant workers camps and others created by them in Andrew's wake. Doctors, nurses, residents, and students staffed the clinics daily, caring for thousands of victims.

For medical students, the disaster provided a once-in-a-lifetime learning experience that also opened their hearts to special needs in medicine.

"I want to go into emergency medicine," said third-year medical student Chris Parks as he examined a two-year-old girl who had cut her chin on broken glass. "Before I wasn't sure, but this has definitely made up my mind."

Throughout the two weeks following the hurricane, President Foote held daily "crisis management" meetings to exchange information about volunteer efforts and to make on-the-spot decisions about getting the campus back in shape.

On September 14, right on target, the Coral Gables campus proudly opened its doors to students. Roofs had been repaired. Windows had been replaced. Trees had been replanted.

The changes Hurricane Andrew imposed upon the University of Miami's buildings and grounds were temporary. But that cannot be said for the University family, many of whom were brought together through a traumatic experience and whose lives were changed permanently in the process. It was a lesson in heroism that was learned by many and will be forgotten by few.

"I am so proud of the people of this University," says President Foote. "They did a super job under the most difficult of conditions and with real bravery." Hemingway said 'courage is grace under pressure,' and it's difficult to imagine more pressure than this place has been under. There couldn't be more courage in so many wonderful people than I saw displayed at this University."

Susan May is associate editor of Miami magazine. Photography by Lenny Cohen, P. David Johnson, and Todd Simmons.

CHAPTER • 7

Mending a Broken Reputation
Pima County Community College District

Krista Neis

The crisis at a glance

In February 1989, a regional accrediting agency placed Pima Community College on probation because of governance problems. In March, Pima's board removed our president from office after discovering he had falsified his resume. And from February to July, four of five governing board members left office for reasons ranging from misuse of college property to illegal campaign practices.

The crisis team

Our acting president, headed up Pima's crisis team, which included the executive vice president for academic and student affairs and the vice president for college relations, our directors of media/community relations and marketing (both of whom were new to campus), the president's cabinet of provosts from our five campuses, and the campus police chief.

The audiences

Due to the complexity and duration of Pima's series of major and ensuing minor crises, we had to take care to keep a variety of constituents informed. These constituents included Pima faculty and staff members, current and prospective students, parents, media representatives, our board of governors, the accrediting agency and state board, as well as our supporters in business and education communities and the general public.

The communication mix

When the accrediting agency put Pima on probation, the college bought space in the next

Krista Neis is assistant to the chancellor for community relations at Pima County Community College District.

issue of the student newspaper to run a letter from the president. The letter explained the terms of the agency's decision but emphasized that the probation would affect neither academic credits nor financial aid. Students found a similar letter in their home mailboxes.

Faculty and staff received news of the probation in special editions of the college's weekly internal newsletter. Over the summer, the president's office also sent letters to faculty members' homes to deliver probation progress reports.

Within a week after the board removed the president from office, we broadcast a 10-minute videotape announcing the appointment of the acting president on the internal TV network to cafeterias and student centers on our three campuses. The tape also appeared on the cable channel designated for students taking courses off-campus via television. The acting president personally phoned key campus leaders shortly after her appointment.

Pima also worked hard to stay in touch with our off-campus constituents. We set up a telephone hotline for prospective students, alumni, and other concerned constituents. The acting president kept high schools, colleges, and universities informed. The college reached out to the general public with local newspaper ads. We also provided progress reports through media interviews and civic club speaking engagements. Finally, a variety of alerts, press conferences, background summary pieces, special interviews, and the constant availability of our acting president helped us keep the media informed.

Words to the wise

1. *Know your audiences.* Establish and maintain good relations before, during, and after the crisis. Despite the immediacy of the situation at hand, always take a long-term approach to constituent relations.

2. *Speak for yourself.* Designate a crisis spokesperson, structure your institution's messages, prepare background information, assign a devil's advocate, and rehearse your statements if possible.

3. *Get the story straight.* Although the accrediting agency was careful to specify that our "institutional" probation did not reflect on the college's academic status, the media repeatedly referred to Pima's "academic" probation. In retrospect, we should have sent a reminder with all releases that pointed out the error and reiterated the correct terminology.

4. *Consider the long—and short—of it.* Separate complex crises into more manageable issues and identify the short-term and long-term strategies to help you address each issue.

5. *Develop a nose for news.* Although local media coverage of Pima's crisis was unusually evenhanded, many internal constituents complained of too many negative stories during the crisis. Internal constituents may not understand the media, their priorities, and how they work. So be ready to explain why crisis news takes precedence over routine campus news and why regional or national media coverage may occur.

6. *Get back to basics.* Anticipate and be prepared to respond to requests for timely updates. Maintain a good file of basic resource materials and information sources to provide both staff and media representatives with the necessary context.

7. *Document your crisis.* Keep good records and notes for ongoing follow-up and analysis.

8. *Make lemonade.* No one looks forward to a crisis, especially one that develops into multiple mini-crises with long-term repercussions. But the duration of such crises do offer unique opportunities for new initiatives that don't surface during more normal times or in a short-term emergency.

After the announcement of Pima's institutional probation, for example, we set up a marketing council to develop a new student recruitment/retention plan designed to keep enrollment strong (it did), and demonstrate continued confidence in Pima's academic program. We also launched a year-long internal and external communications campaign. And midway through the crisis period, at just the right moment, our alumni association sponsored a recognition dinner honoring a well-respected local leader (alumna) that proved pivotal in reversing negative publicity and refocusing the media on Pima student and alumni achievements.

District Service Center
200 North Stone Avenue
P.O. Box 3010
Tucson, Arizona 85702-3010

Office of the President
(602) 884-6047

27 February 1989

Dear Pima Student,

It is my fervent desire that this letter reach you as soon as possible to address your fears and concerns about the meaning of institutional probation and how it might affect your educational program. For that reason I am unable to address you each personally, as I would prefer.

It is important that you know:
* Pima Community College accreditation is in tact and not at issue at this time;
* Your credits will continue to be accepted for transfer to other institutions;
* Those of you receiving financial aid are in no danger of having it discontinued, if you are meeting the guidelines.

Notice was received Wednesday, February 22, from the NCA Commission on Institutions of Higher Education, that the College might be placed on probation for two years. Probation would be directed at four specific items of concern. They are: 1) "Serious disputes among Board members;" 2) "Allegations of misconduct and misuse of public funds by Board members;" 3) Inability of the Board to "differentiate between policy-making and administration;" 4) "A large number of" interim positions where "little or no progress" has been made toward permanent appointments.

We must respond in writing by February 28 and the recommendation for probation will be considered by the Commission at its regularly-scheduled meeting, March 2 and 3. Action at that time may be to accept the recommendation as is, alter it in some manner or postpone action until a future meeting.

Meanwhile, the administration of this College is committed to keeping you, the students, informed of all developments through direct communication. Watch for letters such as this, ads placed in campus and local newspapers, campus visits, television and radio talk shows and other efforts to inform students. We will initiate and maintain direct dialogue with the state's three universities to assure the integrity of our academic programs. And, we will direct diligent attention to ameliorating the items of concern raised by the NCA Commission.

As your President, and on behalf of all dedicated and concerned faculty, staff and administrators at this College, I guarantee every effort will be made to handle your concerns collectively and individually. Information hotlines will be forthcoming. Meanwhile, please direct any personal concerns not answered here to 884-6060.

Respectfully yours,

Diego A. Navarrette, Jr.
President

BulletinBulletinBulletin
❋ PimaCommunityCollege

March 20, 1989

SPECIAL EDITION
From Brenda Marshall Beckman, Acting President

As most of you already know, the Board of Governors of Pima Community College acted at their March 15 meeting to suspend President Diego Navarrette with pay effective 8 a.m. Thursday, March 16.

The Executive Deans were directed to advise the Board regarding the appointment of an Acting President and prepared a memo for their consideration at a special Board meeting for March 22, 1989. At the moment of the President's suspension, the Acting Vice President for Academic and Student Affairs, Carol Gorsuch, assumed responsibility for routine matters as has been standard practice in the absence of the President. But her job description does not include the assumption of the full powers of the President.

The Board therefore scheduled an emergency meeting for 4 p.m. Friday, March 17, for the purpose of appointing an Acting President.

Acting Executive Vice President Gorsuch formally requested that she not be considered due to her faculty status, the acting nature of her current appointment, and a possible conflict of interest.

At the special meeting last Friday the following was presented to the Board on behalf of all the Executive Deans by Executive Dean Miguel Palacios:

The Executive Deans believe it is imperative that the following matters be addressed immediately to stabilize the College and assure its future.

I.   A chief executive officer must be selected by the Board.
    Recommendations:
    ● Filling of the chief executive officer position on a regular basis should be delayed until the College's probationary status has been removed.
    ● The Board should immediately appoint an Acting President from among the Executive Deans to serve as chief executive officer of the College until the position is filled on an interim basis.
    ● While some temporary administrative reassignments may be necessary to carry out day-to-day administrative responsibilities, no organizational restructuring should be made without prior consultation with NCA and the State Board.
    ● Procedures to fill interim positions should be expedited.
    ● Persons currently under investigation should not be appointed to any permanent position until final legal determination has been made.
II. The Acting President should establish a timetable for removal of probationary status.
    Recommendation: <u>Optimum Timetable for Removal of Probationary Status</u>
    ● March 1989...The Acting President appoints a self-study coordinator and team to complete a self-study by March, 1990.
    ● April 1989...The self-study process commences.
    ● March 1990...The College's President contacts NCA requesting a comprehensive evaluation visit.
    ● Sept 1990....Comprehensive evaluation visit by the NCA team occurs.
    ● Nov 1990.....Formal action by the NCA Commission.

Community Campus ▪ Community Services ▪ District Service Center ▪ District Service Center Annex
Downtown Campus ▪ East Campus ▪ Education Center South ▪ Skill Center ▪ West Campus

Published weekly on Monday. Contributions to Department of Marketing by noon the week prior. EOE/AA

III. Serious attention must be focused on maintaining a positive information exchange and working relationship with the State Board of Directors of Community Colleges.

Following receipt of the above recommendations **the Board appointed me Acting President to serve until an Interim President can be selected.**

At this point I would like to make a personal comment. The circumstances which led to the suspension of President Navarrette are a personal and a professional tragedy for him and they are clearly of great consequence to the institution.

Diego Navarrette has been and will remain a dear friend and a person I value greatly for his many special qualities. It is my hope as events move forward that his decades of dedication and service to this institution will not be forgotten and that his unfailing commitment to Pima Community College students and their achievements will be acknowledged. There are countless successful citizens in this community who would not be where they are today without Diego Navarrette's help and support in the past.

Now, to provide some additional clarification:

● I agreed to serve as Acting President because the full range of sanctions which could have been applied to our institution would have caused our students to pay the price. The Executive Deans could not in all conscience allow such a thing to happen.

● I do not know how long I will be in this role. I hope that the time will be very brief. The Board will consider on Wednesday night (March 22) how they wish to proceed on filling the presidency with an Interim President.

● <u>Under no circumstances</u> will I consider serving in either the interim or permanent presidency. **That is absolute.**

This is a critical time for the College. Many urgent matters must be addressed immediately and cannot await the appointment of an Interim President. **I am setting as the highest of all priorities for the institution the restoration of our full accreditation status and the redemption of our good name.** Our immediate objectives must be to stabilize the College, to rebuild our reputation in the eyes of the community and the State Board of Directors of Community Colleges (which has oversight responsibility for the College), and to work with the NCA to remove probationary status. I am directing that the activities necessary to achieve these objectives be given maximum attention. After consultation with the College Executive Staff, some other matters may be set aside and attended to later.

As was stated in a recent editorial:
> "Pima College deserves respect. Respect is what it has always given those who came to it for a start. Or a second chance. Or the opportunity to take a life they didn't like and change it, enhance it, turn it around."

That is the challenge. To take the life of this College as it is currently playing out, to change it, enhance it, turn it around, restore its deserved respect. **And we are ALL, every one of us, involved. We all know that the substance of the College is sound. I call for every single employee of the College to play a part in restoring our image. Everything we do has an impact. How we work together, how we conduct ourselves, the words we choose, what we say to our neighbors, how we respond to questions in the community, all send messages about this College. Please help to send the message that the heart of this College is sound and its limbs are strong. And let people know as the storm clouds clear that the community can once again take great pride in Pima Community College and everything about it.**

**A Message
From Acting President
Brenda Marshall Beckman**

Events of the past months have caused a great deal of attention to be focused on Pima Community College. Since stepping into the role of Acting President on March 17, 1989, it has been necessary for me to analyze these events in order to report to the State Board of Directors for Community Colleges and the North Central Association of Colleges and Schools the key events or changes and their significance to the College.

The catalog of positive actions and favorable responses to them by the State Board and NCA is accumulating daily. The college community may find it encouraging that the list is so long, and I thought I would share some of the items with you:

- The Board of Governors has acted to realign the Board Office staff to report through the Office of the President. (This was a serious NCA concern.)

- Considerable progress has been made on meeting State Board requirements to assure release of fourth-quarter funds to the College.

- Relationships between board members have been consistently cordial during the past weeks.

- The decorous conduct of the most recent board meeting earned favorable press comment.

- Relationships between the Board of Governors and the administration, particularly the Office of the President, have improved.

- County Superintendent of Schools, Anita Lohr, has appointed Katharina Richter as the new board member in District 2.

- Filling of other vacancies is likely to proceed without undue delay.

- Work to begin the self-study process, which is necessary for reconsideration of the College's probationary status, is already under way.

Our positive record is growing and is likely to continue. I am convinced that, while much remains to be done, Pima Community College has already turned the corner. We are on track to a very positive future.

Aztec Press, April 13, 1989

**A Message
From Acting President
Brenda Marshall Beckman**

The past week has been an eventful one for the College. Many matters of considerable importance have been decided which will have very positive impact on the College. They include the following:

• The State Board of Directors for Community Colleges considered the progress made by Pima Community College in meeting the set of requirements established in February. In the unanimous judgment of the State Board, sufficient progress had been made to warrant the release of the fourth quarter payment of state funds in the amount of $3.3 million.

• The State Board, recognizing that the composition of the Pima Community College Board of Governors is already changing, voted down a resolution of no confidence in the board. The matters discussed which led to this vote included the following:
1. New board member Ms. Katharina Richter has been seated to replace resigned board member Ed Wagner.
2. Ms. Carole Miller has resigned from the board.
3. County Superintendent of Schools Anita Lohr has indicated she expects to appoint a replacement for Carole Miller by mid-May.
4. Ms. Janet Vasilius has indicated clearly her intention to resign, but has delayed taking this action only after discussion with Ms. Lohr, North Central Association Executive Director Dr. Patricia Thrash and me regarding the need to keep a functioning quorum of the board and assure a smooth transition as the board composition changes. This is particularly crucial at this phase of the budget process.
5. Court action relating to Ms. Karleen Kaltenmark's status is proceeding through the court system to final legal determination.

• The Executive Committee of the State Board of Directors for Community Colleges approved the appointment of James B. Tatum as Special Advisor to the Pima Community College Board of Governors. We are delighted that Mr. Tatum has agreed to serve in this capacity. Mr. Tatum is recognized as a trustee leader across the country and his assistance to us will be warmly welcomed.

• Work has begun on the process of the self-study we must undertake as a required step on our way to removing the College's probationary status. We are delighted that West Campus Writing Instructor Bob Longoni has agreed to serve as the chair for the self-study. This all-important task could not be in more capable hands.

In summary, Pima Community College is on track, we are moving forward without hesitation to the kind of tranquil future for which we all long. I hope our students will carry that message to the community.

Aztec Press, April 20, 1989

A Message
From Acting President
Brenda Marshall Beckman

While a great deal of media attention has been focused on Pima Community College in the recent past, very little has been noted of the quality of the College's programs, the excellence of the instruction provided or the achievements of our students.

Our record on these matters is strong and long-standing. For two decades, Pima Community College has offered small classes and committed personal attention on the part of its faculty. Through that same period, the range of supportive services for students has been developed, expanded and enhanced. The area of advising, which has been so key to student success, has been of particular importance.

Pima Community College is enormously proud of the many students and alumni who have been able to grow personally, succeed academically, and achieve so much in their fields of employment, as a result of their own efforts and their experiences at PCC.

Just to mention a few examples:

- PCC student Lee Sword was one of ten outstanding students selected nationwide to be honored by Phi Theta Kappa at the American Association of Community Colleges annual convention last month. I was immensely proud to be present at the ceremony when Lee was so honored.

- One of Pima Community College's nursing students, Terry Balley, passed her state nursing examination last July with a perfect score, a rare achievement indeed.

- Both our baseball and soccer teams have earned national prominence again this year, bringing honor to the College for their success.

These are but a few of the stories of achievement and success that tell the real story of Pima Community College.

Whatever some perceptions may be, the following remains absolutely true and has never faltered:

- Pima Community College is a place where students can receive excellent advising to help them make wise choices as they select their courses of study.

- Pima Community College is an institution that sets a high value on the quality of instruction available to its students.

- Pima Community College provides a broad range of supportive student and academic services to help students to be successful.

- Pima Community College has faculty and staff who are deeply committed to serving the needs of individual students.

In summary, Pima Community College is a caring, high-quality institution. It is also the very best place for many many students to receive the kind of education they so urgently need.

Stay with us. We will not let you down.

This space purchased by the Office of the President

Aztec Press, April 27, 1989

A Message
From Acting President
Brenda Marshall Beckman

President's Column

The present and the future of Pima Community College are looking brighter. It is particularly encouraging to have this news shared publicly by independent voices. James B. Tatum, Advisor to the Board of Governors, who spent several days at the College last week, issued the following press release a few days ago:

"My visit to Pima Community College on April 23, 24 and 25, allowed me to meet a large number of people associated with or interested in the College. I came away with a strong sense of quality in many areas of the institution. This is demonstrably so in the academic offerings at the College as well as other areas of operation. I believe there is a bonding together among various groups occurring which bodes well for the future. It can be said with surety that no student or prospective student should have any question whatsoever as to the quality of instruction and earned credit hours being transferable to other educational institutions.

"The commitment on the part of many active citizens and Anita Lohr, the County Superintendent of Schools, leads me to believe that Pima will have outstanding individuals named to the board where vacancies exist. This means that work can begin in the very near future to ensure that Pima not only has a governing board that the North Central (accrediting) Association and the Arizona State Board will find to be functioning at an acceptible level, but also one which will be outstanding.

"I look forward to my association with all of the people at Pima as we jointly explore ways to serve the needs of the citizens of the county."

In addition to Mr. Tatum's statement, we received the encouraging news that the Pima Community College Foundation has decided to reschedule the fundraising dinner which had been canceled earlier this year. Such recognition by others of the positive happenings at Pima Community College is heartwarming and much appreciated. We really do have good times ahead.

This space purchased by the Office of the President

Aztec Press, May 4, 1989

CHAPTER • 8

Taking Back University Hall

Brown University

Robert A. Reichley

The crisis at a glance

On April 22, 1992, at 8:30 a.m., when University Hall opened for the day, a group of 77 students filed in, sat down in the first-floor hallway, and announced their intention to stay in the building until their demands were met. Their demands:

• More than double the University's fund-raising campaign goal for undergraduate financial aid endowment.

• Arrange for the Brown Corporation (the University's ruling body) to hold an open meeting for the entire University community to discuss need-blind admissions.

• A later, additional demand requested amnesty for any arrested students and open hearings for any University disciplinary proceedings.

The students were addressed by deans, who reminded them of the University's policies about noise and disruption. The noise level—chanting, singing—continued to rise, as did the number of complaints from employees in the building.

Later that morning on the College Green, just outside University Hall, a larger group of students gathered for a rally in support of need-blind admissions. Shortly after noon, that rally got out of hand and several hundred students stormed University Hall, which is the University's main administration building. The building's estimated 65 employees were evacuated.

The leadership of the takeover group—Students for Aid and Minority Admissions (SAMA)—had evidently planned a communication strategy well in advance. Several video cameras entered the building with the rush of students. News releases were written and distributed to media in advance of the takeover, one of which described the student occupation of President Gregorian's office—an event that never happened. Highly propagandistic accounts of the events, including a selectively edited video, were distributed. Subsequent letters from parents reflected their belief that the students had been well-behaved, quiet, and principled. In fact, several deans and unarmed University police officers were pushed and shoved; secretaries were terrorized, harassed, and threatened; attempts

---

Robert A. Reichley is executive vice president of university relations at Brown University.

were made to secure doors with 2x4s; and some employees, fearing for their physical safety, locked themselves in their offices. The 238 students who were subsequently arrested ultimately and individually signed a letter of apology to the staff of University Hall in which they admitted to all of these activities that violated the University's rules.

Resolution

At 3:30 p.m., students in the building were read a short document informing them that arrests would begin at 5 p.m. and that anyone could leave the building with no questions asked until then. Many left.

At 5 p.m. students were still allowed to leave and avoid arrest, although they would face University disciplinary action. More left.

At 6 p.m. arrests began. All arrests were made individually by the University's own police, each officer accompanied by a dean. (At the University's request, neither Providence Police nor State Police were involved.) By 9:15 p.m. the building was emptied. A total of 291 students faced university disciplinary action. Two hundred and thirty-eight of them also faced five civil charges, although the University pressed only two and asked the judge for leniency. Ultimately, 291 students were placed on two semesters' probation. The 238 arrested students pled *nolo contendere*, paid total fines of $75 each, and offered written apologies. No students received permanent criminal records.

The crisis team

The University's president and provost were both out of town when the crisis hit. The crisis team included executive vice president-university relations, senior vice president-administration and finance, news bureau director, dean of the college, dean of students, chief of police and security, general counsel, and chairs of the faculty executive and campus minority committees.

The audiences

The takeover of University Hall touched many constituents, including the entire campus community, the parents of arrested students, local and state government officials, eventually the entire alumni and parent bodies, and potentially large segments of the general public through media.

The communication mix

Because the University anticipated the takeover, the president had issued a letter in advance to the entire 10,000-member campus community, setting the record straight about Brown's financial aid policy and record. Student life deans also distributed copies of University rules and described possible consequences if students tried to take and keep the building. The University spokesperson was available on site to speak with media and remained in the building after most employees had gone home.

The News Bureau generated most of the University's documents, including a chronology of the takeover, description of charges, and, ultimately, distributed the full text of statements by students facing civil charges and University discipline. At one point, the News Bureau sent more than 300 overnight packages—complete with all relevant documents—to the parents of arrested or charged students. The News Bureau also made these documents available to the local and student press and certain national press. As state legal cases developed along with internal discipline charges, the News Bureau followed up with more press releases to area media outlets.

Other crisis coverage included a special edition of the president's newsletter to all parents, a feature on the demonstration in the *Brown Alumni Monthly*, and communication to 5,000 alumni recruitment volunteers.

Words to the wise

1. *Think ahead.* Anticipation and good intelligence are critically important. At Brown, for example, the deans communicated in writing with students of interest before the takeover so there could be no doubt that the policy options were clear. Such early communication efforts, when possible, provide valuable context for whatever happens and an assurance that students knew in advance the consequences of their actions.

2. *Know who's in charge.* With the president and provost both off campus, the crisis team had to work together, but the takeover tested the university's organizational chart.

3. *Follow the rules.* It's essential for the crisis team and all involved constituents to understand University policies and procedures relating to the crisis at hand. In this case, the crisis team needed to become familiar not only with campus policies but also those of the police, the courts, and the mayor's office.

4. *Do a crisis communications audit.* Review all messages to secondary audiences. Determine whether other offices responsible for communications with special groups have done their job, whether the communications have been effective, and what sort of reactions were received (e.g., deans' communications to affected parents and students).

5. *Meet the press.* Evaluate the media coverage your crisis garnered and let the appropriate media representatives know what you liked and didn't like about their stories. Consider meeting with the editorial board of area newspaper(s) to discuss the institution's actions further.

6. *Take advantage of hindsight.* As soon as the crisis is over, call the crisis team together one last time and conduct a thorough postmortem. You may even want to ask other senior staff members to size up the crisis team's success. Now is the time to consider what worked —and what didn't—so you're even better prepared for the next crisis.

The following statement was read on Wednesday afternoon, April 22, to students who had taken over University Hall:

Your actions have disrupted normal business operations and have required us to close the building. You are requested to leave immediately.

If you have not left by 5 p.m., you will be asked to present your ID or otherwise identify yourself as a member of the Brown community.* You will be escorted from the building by a University official and your case will be handled through the University's normal disciplinary process.

University discipline may lead to a written reprimand, sanction, probation, suspension, dismissal or expulsion.

If you cannot or will not identify yourself as a member of the Brown community and if you refuse to leave, you will be arrested and removed from the building. Following your removal, you will be transported downtown to the Providence police station and booked for willful trespass. You will also be subject to University discipline.

* It is a specific offense of the University code to alter, forge or contribute to the fraudulent use of University identification cards or to refuse to identify oneself or to refuse to present University identification to an Officer of the University, including Police and Security personnel.

The Brown University News Bureau   Mark Nickel, Director

38 Brown Street / Box R
Providence, RI 02912
401 863-2476
FAX 401 751-9255

news

DISTRIBUTED APRIL 22, 1992   NEWS BUREAU CONTACT
FOR IMMEDIATE RELEASE   MARK NICKEL

Background on Undergraduate Financial Aid at Brown University

Issues involving the University's financial support of its undergraduate students have
been the subject of discussions, deliberations and action for many years. The following is
a chronology of recent developments.

A Chronology of Undergraduate Financial Aid

June 1982   The Corporation makes explicit a policy which the University had been
               following for several years: Brown should provide scholarship support to
               at least 30 percent of each entering class.

Sept. 1986   A Corporation study group, acting on a report prepared by the senior vice
               president for finance and administration, the dean of the College and the
               dean of the Graduate School, evaluates the long-range implications of that
               policy. The University is committing an ever-larger portion of unrestricted
               funds to undergraduate financial aid. This trend cannot be sustained. The
               report calls for higher level of permanent endowment for financial aid.

Spring 1989   The Advisory Committee on University Planning (ACUP) recommends
               that the fiscal 1990 budget provide financial aid for 31.5 percent of the
               Class of 1993

Summer 1989 President Gregorian commits an additional $1 million annually of Uni-
               versity reserves to the undergraduate financial aid base to cover the cost of
               an overexpenditure on the part of the Admission Office for the Class of
               1993.

Fall 1989   Preliminary models used by ACUP for fiscal 1991 include financial aid
               for 31 percent of the Class of 1994

Nov. 1989   The Committee on Admission and Financial Aid (CAFA) proposes that
               33.5 percent of the incoming class be on aid for fiscal year 1991. CAFA
               requests an additional $1.5 million to cover the cost of additional students
               on aid and cost increases for continuing students.

Dec. 1989   A majority of ACUP members endorses a financial aid budget which
               provides funding for 31.5 percent of the incoming class.

                                                              MORE ...

Jan. 1990   Three student members of ACUP propose that the committee recommend a tuition increase of 7 percent and an undergraduate financial aid budget with funding for 32 percent of the incoming class. ACUP rejects this proposal.

Feb. 1990   ACUP delivers its final report to President Gregorian and the Budget and Finance Committee. The report includes a recommendation for a financial aid budget with funding for 31.5 percent of the incoming class. The Coalition for Need-Blind Admission delivers a petition endorsing need-blind admissions at Brown.

March 1990   President Gregorian exempts the financial aid budget from the 1-percent cuts he had imposed on other areas of the University for fiscal 1991.

              The President announces that he will seek a change in the policy used to set the financial aid budget so that:

              • The financial aid budget base would be indexed to rise in direct proportion to increases in overall tuition and student charges.

              • Income from any new gifts to financial aid endowment would be added to the budget over and above the budget base.

              The President announces that he will ask the Corporation to include $40 million for undergraduate financial aid endowment among the goals for the upcoming fund-raising campaign.

April 1990   The Coalition for Need-Blind Admissions endorses the President's policy changes but calls for a campaign goal of $80 million for undergraduate financial aid. The President asks ACUP to evaluate both his plan and an alternative plan submitted by the Coalition.

May 1990   ACUP endorses the President's proposed policy changes and his recommendation of $40 million as the campaign goal.

              Four members of the Coalition for Need-Blind Admissions meet with the Budget and Finance Committee of the Corporation to discuss admission and financial aid.

              The Corporation approves the fiscal 1991 budget, including financial aid for 31.5 percent of the incoming class. Financial aid budget was set at $16.3 million.

Oct. 1990   The Brown Corporation approves the President's proposal to change the policy used to determine the undergraduate financial aid budget.

March 1991   The President exempts the financial aid budget from the $1.5-million in base budget cuts he imposed on other areas of the University for fiscal 1992.

MORE ...

BROWN UNIVERSITY

FINANCIAL AID CHRONOLOGY

PAGE 3

May 1991   The University adds another $125,000 to the undergraduate financial aid budget to meet the needs of the incoming Class of 1995. Thirty-four percent of that class receives University-funded scholarships.

Aug. 1991   The President establishes an emergency assistance fund for financial aid students, setting aside up to $700,000 to be used for this purpose. This fund provides one-time increases in scholarships for students whose families were adversely and markedly affected by the recession.

Nov. 1991   The President exempts financial aid from the budget cuts, ranging from 6 to 9 percent, which he had imposed on all other areas of the University for fiscal 1993 through fiscal 1996.

Jan. 1991   ACUP recommends 7% increase in student fees, including 7.5% tuition increase.

Feb. 1992   The Corporation approves the President's request that increases in student charges be held to 6.4 percent, less than ACUP's recommendation.

The Corporation sets the campaign goal at $450 million and includes Gregorian's goal of $40 million for endowment of undergraduate scholarships. Also included in the campaign is $35 million in endowment for graduate and medical student support, making a financial aid total of $75 million.

March 1992   Gregorian provides a reserve fund of $500,000 to the undergraduate financial aid budget (over and above the increase resulting from increases to overall student charges) for fiscal 1993 to continue providing relief to families affected by the recession. Between the base budget and this increase, Brown will spend $19.2 million on undergraduate scholarships in the 1992-93 academic year.

Representatives of Students for Aid and Minority Admissions (SAMA) and other student groups present the President with a petition signed by 1,700 members of the Brown community, asking that the new director of financial aid be a person of color.

The President sends all members of the Brown community a memo outlining the University's progress and policies on financial and minority admissions and outlining prospects for the comprehensive campaign.

April 1992   Brown launches its new comprehensive campaign and announces that it has already raised $163 million, more than one-third of the goal.

Itzhak Perlman donates his services and performs with the Brown Orchestra in a benefit concert at Lincoln Center in New York. All net proceeds of the concert are given to undergraduate financial aid endowment.

MORE ...

BROWN UNIVERSITY

FINANCIAL AID CHRONOLOGY

PAGE 4

How Brown's Endowment Supports the University[1]

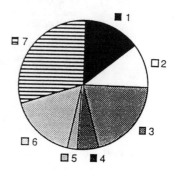

	(in $ millions)
1. Endowed chairs and faculty support	$67.3
2. Other instructional purposes	52.0
3. Scholarships (graduate and undergraduate)[2]	95.0
4. Libraries (including John Carter Brown)	25.2
5. Graduate fellowships and stipends	12.2
6. Miscellaneous restricted purposes[3]	78.1
7. General purpose unrestricted	140.2

Ivy League Comparisons for Fiscal 1990-91

	Class of 1995 % on Grant Aid[4]	Grant Aid from All Institutional Sources[5]	% of Tuition and Fees Devoted to Grant Aid[6]	Endowment Value 6/30/91
Brown	34%	$16.6	14.5%	$431.4
Columbia	51%	13.9	14.4%	1,525.9
Cornell	43%	24.5	15.1%	953.6
Dartmouth	39%	14.7	18.5%	594.6
Harvard	45%	24.3	9.0%	4,669.7
Penn	37%	28.4	19.5%	825.6
Princeton	41%	13.3	1.4%	2,624.1
Yale	42%	16.2	8.0%	2,566.7

(Source: Brown Budget Office)

---

[1] Based on an endowment valuation of $470 million (12/31/91). This excludes life-income trusts and other funds which the University manages on behalf of donors who continue to receive income.

[2] Undergraduate scholarship funds account for more than $86 million of this total.

[3] Various small endowments restricted to support of certain buildings, programs, athletic teams, centers, offices, prizes and premiums, etc.

[4] The Class of 1995 entered in the fall of 1991. Expenditures for those students are in fiscal 1991-92 and are not reflected in the financial data shown here.

[5] Institutional Sources include unrestricted revenue (including tuition and fees), endowment earnings and gifts.

[6] The percentage of tuition and fees devoted to grant aid can be a misleading statistic. Institutions that are more tuition-dependent and that devote a large share of tuition income to financial aid are committing a greater portion of the institution's own resources to financial aid. For example, Brown and Columbia devote about the same percentage of tuition and fees to grant aid. However, tuition accounts for 75 percent of Brown's unrestricted revenue, but only about 65 percent of Columbia's. As a result, Brown is committing almost 11 percent of its unrestricted funds to Financial Aid while Columbia is committing less than 6 percent.

MORE ...

BROWN UNIVERSITY

FINANCIAL AID CHRONOLOGY

PAGE 5

How Brown's Endowment Provides Undergraduate Scholarships

During the 1992-93 academic year, Brown will spend $19.2 million of its own money on undergraduate scholarships. That money will come from three sources:

$1.0 million from gifts and grants designated for current undergraduate financial aid
3.6 million generated by the financial aid endowment
14.6 million from the University's general, unrestricted income

Financial aid endowment is not the only source of endowment support for undergraduate scholarships. The $14.6 million of general funds to be provided by the University will be raised partly by income from the University's general-purpose endowment funds.

In calculating how much support will come from the endowment, Brown uses a 12-month moving average of the endowment's value. This protects the budget process from volatility in the market. Although the endowment for undergraduate financial aid had a market value of approximately $86 million in December of 1991, the 12-month moving average value was closer to $70 million.

Yearly Increases in Brown's Operating and Undergraduate Financial Aid Budgets

Fiscal Year	University	Financial Aid
1989	6.4	9.3
1990	8.6	16.9
1991	7.5	9.3
1992	4.6	8.9
1993	4.3	7.0

(Source: Brown Budget Office)

######

91/136

The Brown University News Bureau   Mark Nickel, Director

38 Brown Street / Box R
Providence, RI 02912
401 863-2476
FAX 401 751-9255

news

DISTRIBUTED APRIL 22, 1992   NEWS BUREAU CONTACT

FOR IMMEDIATE RELEASE   MARK NICKEL

Brown University Is Committed to Achieving Need-Blind Admissions
A Statement by Robert A. Reichley, Executive Vice President

No one in the Brown University community disagrees with the principle of achieving need-blind admissions. The issue now and in the future remains: Who will pay?

Next year, Brown will distribute more than $19.2 million of its own money in the form of scholarships to undergraduate students, based solely upon the individual student's financial need. That amount is comparable to most of the select few schools with which Brown competes for students. Each of those schools has greater endowment resources than we do. Therefore we are proud of the commitment we have made to make a Brown education accessible to many students.

Unfortunately, a disproportionate share of that $19.2 million will come from the University's unrestricted funds (derived mostly from tuition revenues and the Brown Annual Fund) rather than from endowment income. Brown's tuition is already one of the highest in the nation, and we must do our utmost to keep tuition increases as low as possible.

As for fundraising, only a week ago, the University announced the largest campaign in its history with a goal of $450 million. That goal includes $75 million for financial aid endowment: $40 million for undergraduates, $25 million for graduate students and $10 million for medical students.

Some students have suggested that the overall campaign goal should be raised to $500 million and the goal for undergraduate financial aid raised to $90 million. Other students have mistaken the amounts specified within the overall campaign goal for faculty, student aid, academic programs, facilities, etc., as allocations rather than as well-considered goals to be raised over the next few years.

MORE ...

BROWN UNIVERSITY
NEED-BLIND ADMISSIONS
PAGE 2

The University spent more than three years analyzing the fund-raising potential of its alumni and donor community, including reviews by outside consultants and lengthy discussions within the Brown community and the Brown Corporation, the University's governing body. Only then did the University set its campaign goals. No goal was more painstakingly reviewed, analyzed and discussed than the goal for undergraduate financial aid, as the attached chronology clearly illustrates. At one point, the President directed Brown's Advisory Committee for University Planning (ACUP) to consider and evaluate a student plan to set the undergraduate financial aid goal at $80 million. ACUP considered the student plan and ultimately endorsed the $40 million goal.

Working with the best information at hand, the Brown Corporation in February set a minimum goal of $450 million as the amount it feels the University can raise given the size of its alumni body and giving potential of its donors. The Corporation pledged that it would do its best to exceed that goal, as the University did during its last major campaign, which ended in 1983.

Brown values the diversity it has built into its educational community over the years and realizes the role scholarship endowment plays in preserving and strengthening that asset. We are committed to continue building a student body and a faculty which reflect the breadth and diversity of the nation's talent. But we will require resources to accomplish that goal, including greater participation of the federal government. It is, after all, in the nation's long-term interest that Brown and other institutions of higher education are working to provide an education for the broadest segment of our nation's youth.

######

91/137

BROWN UNIVERSITY
Providence, Rhode Island 02912

April 23, 1992

University Statement on the Demonstration and Building Takeover of April 22

Brown University is and always has been committed to an open exchange of ideas and expression of all views. At the same time, a Brown education is characterized by all members of the community taking active responsibility for what they do, whether that means developing a course of study or participating in civil disobedience.

Accountability is a hallmark in this regard. Yesterday, a significant number of students expressed their views, and many of them made an informed and conscious decision to violate University regulations. These individuals were informed of the University's planned response, the ramifications for the students, and they were repeatedly told their options throughout the afternoon.

The administration regrets that these actions occurred, particularly because it shares with the protestors the goal of increasing financial aid for all Brown students, undergraduates, graduates and medical students alike. The administration also respects the students' right to demonstrate and to participate in civil disobedience and expects that those engaging in such activities accept the consequences that ensue.

Questions and Answers About the University Hall Takeover

(A brief chronology of activities on Wednesday, April 22, is on the reverse side.)

1. What happened to the students arrested?

Yesterday evening between 5 and 9:15 pm, 253 students elected to be arrested and were charged with five Rhode Island violations: Disorderly conduct; willful interference with employment; disturbing the peace; and two willful trespass charges. The students were released on their own recognizance and are scheduled to appear in court in groups, beginning Monday, April 27.

The consequences of these charges, all of which are misdemeanors relating to disorderly conduct, range from a $50-$500 fine and/or up to one year in jail.

These 253 students <u>also</u> face University disciplinary charges, yet to be determined.

In addition to the 253 arrested, 42 students left the building before the arrests. These students also face University disciplinary charges.

2. Will the University drop the state charges?

No. The University believes that its students should be accountable and responsible for their actions. It intends to let the cases go to court for adjudication.

3. What will be the consequences of a second building takeover or disruption?

The court order under which the students were arrested is in effect for 10 days and for all campus buildings. If a second incident occurs involving the same students and they are re-arrested, <u>they would not be released again on their own recognizance.</u> It should be understood that being released on one's own recognizance implies that any illegal behavior would not be repeated.

4. Where was President Gregorian during the demonstration?

The President was in New York conducting fund-raising business for the campaign. He was in touch throughout the day with University administrators concerning events on campus.

A Brief Chronology of Events, Wednesday, April 22, 1992

8:30 About 70 students enter University Hall and representatives meet with some deans. The students state that there will be a noon rally at which demands will be presented and that they will not leave the building until their demands are met.

10:00 Students in University Hall are warned by Dean Bechtel about increasing level of noise and complaints received.

10:30 Dean Bechtel distributes to students passages from the Student Handbook (pp. 99-101) that outline possible violations.

11:30 Professors Billy Wooten and Lina Fruzetti, chairs of the Faculty Executive Commitee and Campus Minority Affairs Committee, respectively, speak to students in the University Hall rotunda. Prof. Fruzetti urges them to "return to our normal duties and responsibilities and set in motion the process of the dialogue." The student demands, presented later in the afternoon, are: to increase the campaign goal by $50 million and to allocate those funds for undergraduate financial aid; to have an open meeting of the Brown Corporation in May to discuss the issues of admission and financial aid in general.

12:15 Some 250-300 additional students forcibly enter University Hall. Several University Police and Security officers and deans are pushed and shoved in the process, but not seriously injured. Students demand that administrators and officers leave the building and declare a takeover. Student leaders calm students and security officers leave and station themselves outside.

Students congregate in Corporation Room where they are told that they must vacate by 5 pm and that the University was in the process of getting a Temporary Restraining Order from the Superior Court of RI. In the temporary restraining order, Judge Cresto orders students to vacate the building.

3:30 Students are read a short document stating, "Your actions have disrupted normal business operations and have required us to close the building. You are requested to leave immediately." The statement also described their options and the consequences of those options. Some 175 copies of that document are distributed. The options included: 1. Leaving the building by 5 pm and suffering no consequences; 2. leaving at 5 pm or later and suffering University disciplinary action; 3. not leaving and being arrested for criminal trespass and suffering University discipline.

3:30-5:00 Three times more the students are requested to leave the building immediately. Before 5 pm, a considerable number of students leave.

5:00 Some 42 students leave voluntarily before arrests begin. Deans take their names and ID's.

5:30 Students are read the temporary restraining order in full and given one final opportunity to leave the building.

5:45 Col. Boucher, chief of Brown Police and Security, explains arrest procedures.

6:00-9:15 The arrests are made and students are transported to the Providence Central Police Station. Arrests in University Hall are made by Brown police officers and, in the presence of a University staff member, students are escorted to transportation. Brown faculty members and deans are present at the Providence Police Station through much of the evening.

The Brown University News Bureau   Mark Nickel, Director

38 Brown Street / Box R
Providence, RI 02912
401 863-2476
FAX 401 751-9255

news

DISTRIBUTED APRIL 24, 1992   NEWS BUREAU CONTACT
FOR IMMEDIATE RELEASE   DON DEMAIO

Brown To Press Two of Five Possible Charges Against Arrested Students

Brown University officials have decided to press two of five possible charges against 253 students who were arrested Wednesday evening, April 22, following a day-long takeover and occupation of University Hall, Brown's main administration building.

According to administrators and faculty members who were present, the students clearly violated five state statutes. The decision to press only two charges was made in an effort to moderate the severity of penalties imposed on students while ensuring that they remained accountable for their actions.

"Since we made these decisions on Wednesday, my administration and I have been looking for accountability, not punishment for its own sake," said President Vartan Gregorian. "We believe strongly that students must take responsibility for their actions; at the same time, the University must take the appropriate steps to prevent further disruption of our educational activities."

The two charges being filed are Rhode Island statutes 11-11-4 "Prevention from carrying on employment," and 11-44-26.1 "Mandatory minimum fine for willful trespass within school buildings." Three other charges will not be filed. Those charges are: Rhode Island statutes 11-11.1 "Disturbing the peace," 11-44-26 "Willful trespass: remaining on land after warning," and 11-45-1 "Disorderly conduct."

The "disturbing the peace" and "disorderly conduct" charges will not be filed because the University may pursue those offenses through its own internal disciplinary process. The prosecution on the "willful trespass: remaining on land after warning" charge will also be dropped since the University is seeking to continue the restraining order, received on

MORE ...

BROWN UNIVERSITY
UNIVERSITY TO FILE CHARGES
PAGE 2

April 22, through the remainder of the academic year, thus barring by court order further building takeovers during that period.

"Prevention from carrying on employment" is a petty misdemeanor which carries a penalty up to a $100 fine and up to 90 days in jail. This charge is being filed because the takeover of University Hall not only disrupted the conducting of University business, but also because staff in the building were threatened and some had to lock themselves in their offices to ensure their own safety.

"Mandatory minimum fine for willful trespass within school buildings" is a violation that does not carry any criminal record for first offenses, but can be punished by a minimum fine of $50 up to a maximum fine of $500. This charge is being filed because it is the most applicable statute covering the refusal of the 253 students to vacate University Hall until they were arrested.

During the incident, approximately 250 students forcibly entered University Hall. Several University Police and Security officers and deans were pushed and shoved in the process. Students demanded that administrators and officers leave the building and declared a takeover. Throughout the day, the students were repeatedly requested to leave the building and told that if they did not do so by 5 pm, they would face arrest for trespass. They were also warned that a temporary restraining order had been acquired ordering them to vacate the building and not obstruct Brown in the use of its property. By 5 pm, many students had left the building voluntarily. Brown Police Lieutenant Zaccardi read the summons, the complaint which included the charges, and the restraining order to those who remained. Students were again given the opportunity to leave the building without arrest. The 253 students elected to be arrested by refusing to leave.

Information on what charges the University may file within its own disciplinary system will be made known next week.

######

91/140

Brown University

Robert A. Reichley

Executive Vice President
Alumni, Public Affairs
and External Relations

April 28, 1992

Dear Parents:

President Gregorian has asked me to provide you with information about the takeover of University Hall on Wednesday, April 22. I have assembled the enclosed copies of statements, news releases and newspaper clippings for your information. The packet includes:

• President Gregorian's March 31 memo to the community discussing issues of financial aid and minority admissions.

• **My statement and the accompanying chronology of undergraduate financial aid, issued by the University April 22.** Copies were provided to all students, faculty and staff as well as to media.

• The statement read Wednesday afternoon to students who were occupying University Hall, informing them of their options with respect to the court order and their eventual arrest.

• The University's description of events of April 22, dated April 23 and placed in all student, faculty and staff mailboxes by Friday morning April 24.

• A news release announcing the University's decision to press two of five possible charges against the 253 arrested students. This was placed in all mailboxes by 5 p.m. on Friday April 24.

• A selection of newspaper accounts, from both student newspapers and the *Providence Journal.*

• A news release from SAMA (Students for Aid and Minority Admissions) distributed in advance of the takeover. It is important to note that the occupation of President Gregorian's office mentioned in the release did not occur.

• President Gregorian's response to a letter from Bruce Ratner, parent of an arrested student. Mr. Ratner sent the President a copy of a letter he and his wife, Julie, had sent to parents of arrested students.

Finally, President Gregorian's latest newsletter for parents is currently on the press and will be mailed later this week. Because the President used a portion of that letter to discuss the events of April 22, I have enclosed a photocopied press proof to round out this information packet.

Sincerely,

Box 1920
Providence, RI 02912
401 863-2453
FAX 401 863-7070

The Brown University News Bureau   Mark Nickel, Director

38 Brown Street / Box R
Providence, RI 02912
401 863-2476
FAX 401 751-9255

news

DISTRIBUTED APRIL 29, 1992   NEWS BUREAU CONTACT

FOR IMMEDIATE RELEASE   MARK NICKEL

Brown Asks Leniency for Students Who Plead Guilty or Nolo Contendere To Charges Stemming from April 22 Takeover of University Hall

In a letter to Judge Albert DeRobbio this afternoon (Wednesday, April 29), Brown University President Vartan Gregorian asked DeRobbio to consider a filing without conditions for students who plead guilty or nolo contendere to charges stemming from the April 22 takeover of University Hall, Brown's main administration building. Such a filing would allow all records of the students' arrest to be expunged after one year.

The letter was read to the court by Beverly Ledbetter, vice president and general counsel at Brown.

Students are able to change their pleas prior to their preliminary hearings in two weeks.

"While it wants students to be accountable for their actions, the University has no interest in punishment for its own sake or in unnecessarily compromising the ability of its students to become the nation's next generation of leaders," said Robert A. Reichley, executive vice president (alumni, public affairs and external relations).

The University, together with lawyers for the arrested students, prevailed upon the court to allow students one week to meet bail requirements. Gregorian also announced that he will, upon request, provide financial assistance from discretionary funds to any student who is unable to meet bail which was set by the court this afternoon.

(The full text of Gregorian's letter follows.)

MORE ...

75

The text of Gregorian's letter

April 29, 1992

The Honorable Albert DeRobbio and Associate Judges
District Courthouse
Garrahy Judicial Complex
One Dorrance Street
Providence, Rhode Island 02903

Dear Judge DeRobbio:

I have very high regard for students of Brown University. We are proud of our school and attending students who will be our future leaders. As a national university, it is part of our mission to recruit the best talent regardless of their ethnic, racial and economic status. Toward that end, we have set aside $19.2 million of scholarship to meet the financial needs of our students.

I welcome dissent, freedom of speech and assembly; they are fundamental to the fabric of our society. However, I cannot condone extralegal and disruptive means employed by anyone, including our students. Though I understand their motivation and appreciate their aims, I cannot condone their tactics.

Our University cannot fulfill its educational mission when any group of its members attempts to impose its will upon another.

Yet we have high hopes and expectations for these students, and when a student demonstrates a willingness to assume responsibility for his or her action, I believe we should arrive at a judgment that will not constitute a long-term mark on the student's record.

I am therefore requesting that for those students who plead nolo contendere or guilty that you consider a filing without conditions. It is my understanding that a filing would allow a complete expungement of all records of the arrest after one year, that there would be no record of the arrest and that fine or other sanction would not be imposed so long as the student does not break the law.

We do not want, because of one apparent mistake, to jeopardize the careers and achievements that remain ahead for our students. We need our entire community's support to insure access to higher education for all of our nation's talent.

I am most grateful for your kind consideration of this plea.

Sincerely,

Vartan Gregorian

######

91/143

Brown University

Robert A. Reichley

Executive Vice President
Alumni, Public Affairs
and External Relations

April 30, 1992

Dear Parent:

Two significant developments occurred yesterday in the aftermath of the April 22 takeover of University Hall. Approximately 250 students were arraigned in Rhode Island District Court on two charges, and all students involved in the takeover received a formal notice of internal University disciplinary proceedings. I am writing to provide you with information about both developments. A packet of information about the April 22 events was mailed to you earlier this week.

At 2 p.m. yesterday (Wednesday, April 29), Judge Albert DeRobbio assembled the students who had been arrested, read them their rights, explained the charges against them and described the pleas they could enter. Judge DeRobbio explained that each individual who had been charged could enter one of three pleas: guilty, not guilty, or *nolo contendere* (no contest). He stated that if any individual entered a plea of guilty or *nolo,* he or she would pay the minimum mandatory fine of $50 on the charge of "willful trespass within a school building." That charge is defined as a "violation," and a *nolo* or guilty plea would not result in a criminal conviction. There would be no criminal record in the student's name. On a second charge, of "prevention from carrying on employment," a petty misdemeanor, Judge DeRobbio stated that no fine would be imposed and the complaint would be "filed." He also stated that any individual who pled guilty or *nolo* would be assessed statutory court costs of $3.50 on the violation and $83 on the petty misdemeanor.

According to Julius C. Michaelson, a former Rhode Island attorney general now acting as an attorney for the University, when a complaint is placed on "file," it is held for a period of one year. If the individual charged with the offense is not involved in any illegal activity for that one-year period, the complaint is quashed and destroyed. Under those circumstances, any and all records as to the complaint, charge or plea will be expunged.

A letter from President Vartan Gregorian to Judge DeRobbio was read in open court by Brown's general counsel. In the letter, President Gregorian asked that those students who pled guilty or *nolo* not receive a judgment which would constitute a long-term mark on their record. Judge DeRobbio acknowledged that he had been advised of President Gregorian's request and that he had taken the University's views into consideration. A copy of the President's letter is enclosed.

According to Mr. Michaelson, individuals who entered pleas of not guilty may change their pleas at any time before a final determination of their guilt or innocence. (The first trial date is May 29.) This opportunity normally arises at a scheduled court proceeding. However, where an individual indicates to the court that he or she desires to change a plea of not guilty, the court may at its discretion schedule a proceeding for that purpose.

As you know, the University has established rules and regulations governing student behavior. All students receive copies of these regulations. The University has charged all students involved in the takeover of University Hall with two offenses against the

Box 1920
Providence, RI 02912
401 863-2453
FAX 401 863-7070

4/30/92

Page 2

University code. Your student has received a "charge letter" describing the allegations, citing relevant portions of the *Student Handbook,* listing witnesses and evidence, and outlining administrative procedures, including group information sessions to be conducted by Dean Thomas Bechtel.

I wish to assure you that the University has no interest in punishment for its own sake and has attempted to remain as flexible as possible while preserving the principle that students are accountable for their own actions. Thus during the building takeover, students were notified of their impending arrest and were given four hours to leave the premises without consequences. By charging students with violations of its internal code, the University reduced from five to two the charges it pressed in district court. In addition to asking the Court to consider a filing without condition, President Gregorian has offered financial assistance to any students who are unable to meet bail requirements set by the court. The University, together with lawyers for the charged students, asked the Court to grant students up to a week to meet bail requirements.

If you have questions or would like more information about the University's disciplinary processes, you may write to Dean Thomas Bechtel / Brown University / Box P / Providence, RI 02912. The Office of the Dean of Student Life has also set up a voice mail service for charged students and parents. You may telephone 401/863-2087 and leave a message. The line is monitored by members of the dean's staff, and your call will be returned as soon as possible during normal business hours, 8:30 a.m. until 5 p.m. Monday through Friday.

Sincerely,

Robert A. Reichley

Enclosure: A copy of President Gregorian's letter to Judge Albert DeRobbio

The Brown University News Bureau   Mark Nickel, Director

38 Brown Street / Box R
Providence, RI 02912
401 863-2476
FAX 401 751-9255

news

DISTRIBUTED MAY 5, 1992   NEWS BUREAU CONTACT
FOR IMMEDIATE RELEASE   MARK NICKEL

University Settles Internal Discipline Cases in April 22 Building Takeover
Students Request Probation, Seniors To Do 20 Hours of Community Service

Brown University announced today that it has accepted a statement of accountability from students involved in the April 22 takeover of University Hall. The statement will allow resolution of internal disciplinary charges brought against 291 students by the University.

Under terms requested by the students, freshmen, sophomores and juniors will be placed on probation for two semesters; graduating seniors will be placed on probation for the remainder of the academic year and will perform 20 hours of University community service prior to Commencement.

Editors: Full text of the student's document is attached.

Counsel for the students and others acting on the students' behalf approached the University several days ago with a proposal which led to the final statement of accountability. The statement was received by Robin Rose, dean of student life, who recommended that the University approve the proposal. As of midafternoon Tuesday, more than 280 of the 291 students had signed the statement, as advised by their attorney.

"I am gratified that we have been able to take this step toward community reconciliation," said Brown President Vartan Gregorian. "This resolution of internal discipline brings us closer to the point where we will be able to move forward with the crucial work of building support for all University priorities, including financial aid."

The statement of accountability and the University's imposition of probation apply only to the University's internal disciplinary proceedings. Although some students arrested in University Hall on April 22 have pled *nolo contendere,* most still face a misdemeanor and a violation charge in Rhode Island district court.

MORE ...

79

BROWN UNIVERSITY
DISCIPLINARY SETTLEMENT
PAGE 2

Text of the Agreement

We, the undersigned, having been noticed of the charges pending against us before the University Disciplinary Committee, wish to make the following statement in support of our request that the University place us on probation for two semesters. This request on our part should be viewed as our intentional, voluntary act to acknowledge our actions and be accountable for the adverse impact of the same on the University.

On April 22, 1992, we were individually and/or collectively involved in a series of actions which were contrary to the University *Tenets of Community Behavior* and specifically failed to show respect for the rights and concerns of others. We understand why the University feels that this behavior disrupted or materially interfered with the exercise by others of basic rights to which they are entitled by the University on University property and accept full responsibility for these actions and the inconvenience or apprehension caused by our behavior. No one in the Brown community should ever be put in fear, intimidated or harassed by another. We sincerely apologize.

This statement is being freely given, is a voluntary and uncoerced statement prepared with the advice of our legal counsel. It is an honest representation and is intended to demonstrate our remorse. We respectfully ask that the University accept these statements in lieu of continuance of the proposed University Disciplinary Council proceedings and that the same, including the presentation of witnesses and evidence against us and our right to present witnesses and evidence in our behalf be waived by both parties in consideration of the imposition of a penalty of probation for two semesters for each and every one of us. We hereby waive any right to appeal the penalty of probation and any other relief to which we might be entitled arising out of or connected with the internal disciplinary process.

Graduating seniors further request that in addition to being placed on probation for the remainder of the school year, they be permitted to acknowledge their actions and be accountable for them by performing twenty hours of University community service prior to Commencement.

######

91/145

The Brown University News Bureau   Mark Nickel, Director

38 Brown Street / Box R
Providence, RI 02912
401 863-2476
FAX 401 751-9255

news

DISTRIBUTED MAY 12, 1992   NEWS BUREAU CONTACT

FOR IMMEDIATE RELEASE   MARK NICKEL

University Hall Staff Receives Student Apology for April 22 Disruption
Misdemeanor Charge Is Dismissed for Students Who Sign Apology

Brown University President Vartan Gregorian assembled approximately 75 University Hall employees at 3:45 p.m. today and read them a statement of apology and acknowledgement of actions signed by students who participated in the April 22 takeover of University Hall. The statement acknowledges events which took place during the takeover, including occupation of the building, excessive noise, attempts to barricade doors, occupation of the registrar's office and interference with its operations, and communications to employees "which might be perceived as harassing, threatening or intimidating."

Seventy-six of the 238 students who still faced charges in the University Hall takeover had preliminary hearings this morning. All chose to sign the statement and plead *nolo contendere* to a violation charge of "willful trespass within a school building." The violation carries no criminal record. Preliminary hearings for the remaining students will continue tomorrow; the total number of students who have signed the statement will be available later this week. *Editors: Full text of the student statement is attached.*

The University supported a dismissal of the petty misdemeanor charge of "prevention from carrying on employment" for those students who signed the statement. (The misdemeanor was the only charge for which a conviction would have resulted in a criminal record.) As a condition of dismissal of the petty misdemeanor charge, Chief Judge Albert DeRobbio required court costs in the amount of $16.80 and a reimbursement to the City of Providence of $6.30. The violation charge carries a mandatory minimum fine of $50 and court costs of $3.50. The total charge to each student who signed this morning was $76.60.

MORE ...

81

BROWN UNIVERSITY
APOLOGY TO STAFF
PAGE 2

The statement acknowledges that although each act was not engaged in by all students, all of the arrested students, by their collective presence, blocked passageways and stair cases, prevented egress and ingress and interrupted the conduct of business in University Hall.

The student statement comes exactly one week after the University announced a resolution of internal disciplinary charges against 291 students. In that case, students voluntarily signed a statement of accountability for their actions on April 22, admitted involvement in actions which were contrary to the University's rules of conduct, and apologized. Freshmen, sophomores and juniors received two semesters of probation; seniors received probation for the remainder of the academic year and pledged to complete 20 hours of University community service. After Gregorian reported that resolution at last Tuesday's faculty meeting, the faculty voted without dissent to thank the administration for its efforts, to support Gregorian in his actions and to commend the arrested students for their willingness to accept responsibility for their actions.

After reading the student statement of apology to University Hall employees this afternoon, Gregorian also read it to Brown faculty who had assembled for a continuation of the previous week's faculty meeting.

Text of the Student Statement

To the Staff of University Hall:

This statement is to acknowledge the actions of those of us who took part in the sit-in and takeover of University Hall on April 22, 1992, for the events which took place on that date.

When the first group of approximately 70 students entered University Hall at around 8:30 in the morning, Dean of Student Life Robin Rose advised the students that they were being admitted to the building for purposes of a peaceful demonstration and would be constrained by a number of parameters. These included keeping the number of students in the building within the requirements of the fire code, keeping noise to a level which would permit the employees of University Hall to continue their work without interruption, containing the sit-in to the first floor of the building and not bringing food and drink into the building. Students were also advised that they would have to leave the building by 5 p.m.

These parameters were not adhered to. Food and beverages were brought into the building and students sang and chanted and did not desist despite repeated requests to do so by

MORE ...

the Deans. Notwithstanding the distribution of materials stating that such conduct was in violation of the University rules, the activity continued. Although this activity was initially fairly orderly, it became less orderly and the noise level more intrusive as the rally on the Green began to become more active.

When an additional 300 or more students entered the building at midday, University personnel who were in the doorway through which the students from outside rushed were pushed and shoved out of the way. There was a period of confusion during which the pushing and shoving occurred when the additional large numbers of students suddenly entered the building. The students spread to the hallways and stair cases of the building and announced that they would not leave the building. The noise level and sheer numbers of students, of which I was one, made it difficult or impossible for the employees of University Hall to continue their work. During this period there were also isolated incidents and random acts of students confronting staff members. These acts, engaged in by some students, included (1) communications inside and outside the building informing persons that the building was closed and under the control of the students occupying the building; (2) rapping and banging on doors coupled with verbal demands to employees to leave the building; (3) attempts to barricade doors; (4) communications to senior administrators demanding the expulsion of security personnel from the building; (5) attempts to isolate office personnel; (6) communications to employees which might be perceived as harassing, threatening or intimidating; and (7) physical occupation of the Registrar's Office by students who prohibited or significantly interfered with office operations and/or telephone communications. Although it was our commitment to the underlying issue which led us to enter University Hall for the purpose of protest, the above described actions inappropriately interfered with employment. Although each act was not engaged in by all students, all of us who were arrested did, by a collective presence, block passageways and stair cases, prevent egress and ingress and interrupt the conduct of business in University Hall.

I sincerely apologize to the employees working in University Hall for the disruption of employment and any acts by members of our group which intimidated, threatened or placed employees in fear. I apologize to those members of the student body and others who were unable to complete registration or conduct other University business due to our actions. Although I make this statement in support of my request that the University support the withdrawal from prosecution of the pending charge against me relating to "prevention from carrying on employment (11-11-4)", it is nevertheless a voluntary statement which sets forth honestly our actions and their impact on others.

Prior to signing this statement, I was fully advised by counsel of my rights and options including the right to contest this charge and have the matter heard on the merits before the Sixth Division District Court and chose this manner of resolution instead.

######

91/155

BROWN UNIVERSITY
PROVIDENCE, R. I. 02912

THE PRESIDENT

May 15, 1992

Dear Brown parents, alumni and friends of Brown:

Since the unfortunate events of April 22, I have received many phone calls and letters from parents, as well as a number of letters and calls from concerned alumni and alumnae, regarding the takeover of University Hall and subsequent events. I believe that all who have written deserve a timely reply now that developments of the past few days have changed the sequel to the occupation of University Hall. I am sorry that I cannot answer each letter individually, but you can certainly understand that the number of letters and inquiries do not permit me to do so. I hope, however, that this letter will respond to most of the questions and concerns you raised in your letters regarding the incident and its consequences.

Your letters varied from those who simply wanted more information, to those who denounced the administration, to others who expressed support or support mixed with concern. Some wrote to say that the takeover was a "peaceful demonstration" and the University reacted inappropriately in its response, while others—some in the legal profession—questioned their children's understanding of civil disobedience. As a parent, I can appreciate your love and solidarity with your children. I also understand why some of you empathize with their lofty aims. I'm sure that as a parent in a similar situation I would be inclined to do the same. It's neither desirable nor necessary to impugn the character or veracity of one's offspring.

At the same time, I ask your understanding why I cannot impugn the integrity and veracity of some 100 individuals working in University Hall on the day of the incident, including the provost, the chair of the Faculty Executive Committee, the chair of the Campus Minority Affairs Committee, deans, faculty, other senior administrators, secretaries and clerks by repudiating their accounts of the occupation of University Hall. Several days ago, I met with more than 100 staff members who were working in the building at the time of the takeover and was astonished at their description of the incident and the amount of anger and frustration they expressed, believing that my concern for the students' welfare should extend as well to them as employees. Their reports made it clear that the action of April 22 was not a peaceful sit-in, but a well-planned takeover of the building that represents the nerve center of the University.

On May 5, the University responded positively to a letter from the involved students who faced our disciplinary sanctions. In the letter they unanimously accepted responsibility for their actions, expressed remorse and requested that the University put them on probation. On May 12, in response to a letter from these students to employees of University Hall, acknowledging their actions and extending apologies, we agreed to support the dismissal of one count in District Court that could have resulted in a criminal record. (See enclosures.) As a result of these actions, I consider this unfortunate episode closed. I am delighted that our students will have no permanent disciplinary or criminal record. I'm gratified that our faculty on May 5, after hearing a full report of the incident, supported me and my administration's actions without dissent. I'm equally delighted that they thanked the students involved for their willingness to be accountable for their actions.

On that occasion, I told our faculty that I am proud that Brown has a spectrum of political views ranging from the extreme left to the extreme right, including moderates. Freedom of thought, speech and assembly are all part of the fabric of this University. We all share common aspirations for Brown. We should not allow tactics or diverging ideologies to divert us from our common goals. I also reaffirmed my position that the cause of diversity will not be held hostage by any faction or factions.

Access to higher education is a national issue. In addition to doing our best at Brown, we should not forget that Brown is only one of more than 3,000 public and private colleges and universities that share a responsibility for increasing access to higher eduction for all members of our society. Leadership at all levels—including federal and state government—must help by providing not only answers but also resources to ensure that this national responsibility is fulfilled.

I am sure that the two enclosed documents from the students involved will move our discussion, as well as your understanding of these complex events, to a new plane— one which is compatible with dialogue and reasoned discourse.

I'm relieved that this episode is over. We have all learned valuable lessons about our community and the fragility of our universities, as well as the burden of our responsibilities.

With best regards,

Vartan Gregorian

P.S. In view of the urgency of this matter, and with the financial support of a sympathetic grandparent, I am sending this letter by priority mail in order to respond to your questions and concerns, and end your anxiety, as quickly as possible.

Encl. 2

CHAPTER • 9

Dealing with Sexual Misconduct

Phillips Exeter Academy

David W. Johnson

The crisis at a glance

On Thursday, July 16, 1992, without prior warning, police arrested Exeter faculty member L. Lane Bateman on charges of possessing and shipping child pornography. The next day, after hearing further information from police and consulting with legal counsel, the Academy's principal fired Bateman.

The arrest marked the beginning of a seven-month crisis management challenge for Exeter. Local, regional, and national media all arrived on campus to investigate. After the initial flurry, a *New York Times* article in August reporting—incorrectly—widespread student involvement provoked a second round of intense coverage. The story was picked up by *Time, Newsweek*, and CNN. *Vanity Fair* published a lengthy feature in its December 1992 issue.

In a frequently shifting and confusing scenario, a number of actions took place that made it difficult for the Academy to be proactive. For instance, New Hampshire charges were dismissed to make way for consolidated federal charges against Bateman. Under the jurisdiction of the United States attorney for New Hampshire, the secrecy surrounding the case gave the Academy little or no access to information. As with the *New York Times* story about widespread student involvement, the media were liable to report something first—leaving us in a reactive position throughout.

As time went on, we became better able to predict times of heightened media attention: the opening of school, the beginning of the trial in October 1992, the day of the verdict in December, and the sentencing in January. Still we were caught by surprise when we had to react to new information introduced in the U.S. attorney's 58-page sentencing memorandum, filed just a few days before Christmas 1992.

During the trial, videotapes offered as evidence showed that Bateman had involved a former Exeter student in one of his videos and had secretly videotaped other students near a dormitory bathroom. Though less extensive than early reports, Bateman's activities were damaging to the school's reputation. On January 11, 1993, the former drama department chair was convicted of two counts each of possessing and shipping child pornography. He was sentenced to five years in federal prison with an additional three years' probation.

David W. Johnson is director of communications at Phillips Exeter Academy.

The crisis team

The crisis team consisted of the principal, vice principal, dean of faculty, dean of students, and director of communications. The four-person Academy communications office dealt with the 80-100 media involved while maintaining its normal schedule of publications and projects. Though not specifically on the crisis team, the director of studies emerged as a major resource, assisting the principal in answering the most difficult letters received from alumni and alumnae. We received approximately 300 letters, and we wrote a personal reply to each. We also relied on the letters as a good source of feedback from our stakeholder constituencies. The letters were generally sympathetic to the school and favorable regarding the principal's decision to fire Bateman. A number of letters were critical of both.

Important members of the crisis team were the Academy's legal counsel and a public relations firm. The team met almost daily during the early days of the crisis, and during times when it intensified, such as in August and before the trial in October. Their advice helped us with our decision that although newspapers and television wanted interviews with the principal, almost all media requests were handled by the communications office. The principal allowed herself to be interviewed only twice—once by the *New York Times* and later a follow-up interview with the *Boston Globe*. She was not comfortable with the results of these interviews and, in hindsight, would not do them again. Two thoroughly briefed senior administrators took part in interviews with these two newspapers at the conclusion of the crisis to help bring about closure. Part of the responsibility of the communications office was to enlist the support of such administrators in dealing with the media, who wanted to hear from the academic side, not just the "PR" side.

The trustees were not directly involved during much of the crisis, though several of them extended their support to the principal and—in the fall—drafted a resolution commending her handling of the situation. She and the trustee president were in more frequent communication. The trustee president appeared in person before the faculty to read the statement—an important gesture of support.

For more than seven months, the office of alumni/ae affairs and development also had to deal with the impact of the arrest and charges as did the admissions office. In both cases, the communications skills of administrators were brought to bear in response to questions from alumni and alumnae and parents of prospective students. The dean of students' office handled queries from parents of current students. Neither fund raising nor admissions interests suffered in the wake of the crisis.

The audiences

The school's primary concern was the welfare of its current and former students. Thus the audiences given the most attention were students and their parents, alumni and alumnae, prospective students and their families, faculty and staff, and the surrounding New Hampshire communities. The school attempted to meet the information needs of the media while recognizing that it should communicate directly with its internal audience (students) to provide accurate information in the face of exaggerated or conflicting media reports.

In keeping with our primary concern about student welfare, we arranged for additional campus security personnel at the opening of school and issued guidelines to the media requesting, among other things, that media representatives not visit the campus without checking in first with the communications office, and that they not enter Academy classroom buildings or residence halls. With the exception of one television reporter whose progress across campus was measured by complaints from different departments that we received in the communications office, these measures were generally effective.

The communications mix

The Academy maintained straightforward and open communications with its most closely related audiences throughout the crisis. Communication with the campus community began only four days after the arrest with a letter from the principal to Exeter parents and friends. The principal outlined the charges, described the school's actions, and offered support to students and parents alike, including the establishment of a confidential help-line to the school's counselors. She also met twice with faculty who were on hand during the summer. As we had done in the past, we used my editor's column in our winter 1992 alumni/ae magazine as another means of informing our 25,000 constituents about the school's position and our assessment of the media coverage we had received.

After the sentencing, the principal wrote a second letter to the full internal audience, summarizing the circumstances leading up to Bateman's conviction, emphasizing the school's commitment to moving ahead, and thanking members of the Exeter family for their support during a difficult time. Finally, with the crisis behind us, we devoted another magazine column to the subject in an effort, similar to the principal's letter, to bring about some closure on this painful episode.

Throughout the crisis, Exeter's posture toward the media was as open and cooperative as possible, while attempting at the same time to protect the privacy interests of our students, faculty, and staff, including the defendant. In taking this position, Exeter wanted to show that it had nothing to hide. Our policy was to let reporters speak with students, faculty, and staff as long as they checked in first with the communications office and did not interfere with the educational process. We issued three statements during the crisis: one immediately following the arrest and firing; a second after the *New York Times* story in August; and a third at the time of the jury's verdict. All were brief, stressing the school's concern for its students and—ultimately—its relief that the lengthy ordeal was over. We faxed these statements to selected media so that the school's reaction would be included in the initial story.

Since Phillips Exeter Academy is a high-profile institution in the secondary school field, our tally of print media clips numbered more than 1,000. In addition, of course, was television and radio coverage, which is harder to quantify. We maintained a sampling of television coverage for reference both during and after the crisis.

Words to the wise

Crises are bound to happen. In a community with a large number of students, faculty, and staff, chances are that a crisis will involve the actions of one person, as it did in the Bateman case. We believe in preparing for the contingency of a crisis, but do not have a formal crisis plan. Our method consists primarily of assembling the crisis team and preparing a statement, whether we issue it or not. The preparation itself clarifies thinking about the crisis.

We did learn several lessons that might help others in dealing with a crisis:

• Put student welfare first, everything else second.

• Communicate with your stakeholder audiences first. They are the people who really need to know.

• Your stakeholder communications (to students, parents, etc.) will make news in themselves, so be prepared to deal with these publicly almost as soon as they are issued privately.

• Strike a balance with the media between cooperation and the privacy interests of your internal audiences and community members, even the person or persons who caused the crisis.

• As the crisis winds down, work toward closure with all audiences, including the media. Stories may just go away, but it helps if they have a conclusion.

Phillips Exeter Academy

July 20, 1992

Dear Exonian,

As you may well have heard by now, something extremely serious has happened here in the last few days. My usual summer letters need now to give place to a far different message.

Faculty member Lane Bateman was arrested on Thursday, July 16, on charges of possession of child pornography. School authorities knew nothing of the investigation until the arrest was made. We understand that the investigation is ongoing and we are fully cooperating with the authorities. At the time of this writing we do not know what further information the police may be pursuing or what actions they are contemplating. The school has terminated Mr. Bateman's employment and asked him to leave campus no later than August 1. This decision took into account the information that led to Mr. Bateman's arrest and consultation with legal counsel and was based on my evaluation of the effectiveness of his employment as an appropriate role model.

I can imagine from my own feelings that you are struggling to come to terms with the substance and the seriousness of this information, whether or not you know Mr. Bateman. The anxiety alone is hard to accept. It is difficult, too, that those of us who will make up the school community come September are scattered now and so must wait some period of time before we are together and can share our reactions. I hope that students will talk with parents and friends. Students may want to call advisers and/or other adult friends at the Academy. The Health Services has a confidential help line at extension 527 for students who have questions or concerns they wish to address to counselors. I am here, too, should you want to talk to me.

This is a strong school, drawing its strength from a long tradition of excellence and integrity and from the intelligence and caring of the many people, young and older, charged with the stewardship of the institution. As a boarding school we have a special responsibility for the welfare of our students. I'd like to assure those of you who offer support from a distance that we here now will do our best to take care of the school and to take care of each other, with particular attention to student concerns. Wherever this incident leads us, I am confident that we will emerge whole. I am grateful for your support; thank you.

Sincerely,

Kendra S. O'Donnell

Kendra Stearns O'Donnell
Principal

Exeter, New Hampshire 03833-1104   Tel (603) 772-4311   Fax (603) 778-9563

Phillips Exeter Academy

February 10, 1993

Dear Exonian,

I am writing to let you know that the legal process arising from the arrest and conviction of former faculty member Lane Bateman on charges of possessing and shipping child pornography is at last over. On January 11th of this year, Mr. Bateman was sentenced to five years in federal prison with an additional three years' probation. This event concludes a process that began July 16th with Mr. Bateman's arrest. As you know, I terminated Mr. Bateman's employment the day after his arrest, following an interview with him by a senior member of the administration.

Late in December the United States Attorney released information he believed relevant to sentencing. Because my first concern continues to be for the students, I addressed the school community in Assembly our first day back from vacation. I spoke frankly about the information in the public documents, what the students might read in the papers, and how they might feel. I felt that it was important to tell the students that Mr. Bateman's actions violated the trust that we depend upon in order to function as a community, and that while individuals may find ways to explain or forgive his conduct, there was no way, in my view, to excuse it. It was simply wrong. Then I urged the students not to let their anger or shock affect their trust in other adult members of the community and in each other.

Remarkably enough, there has been, I think, only a minimum of disruption to the ordinary business of the school year. From our observations, the experience of students and faculty in general has not been altered or overshadowed by this episode. I am happy to say that our admissions inquiries and Annual Fund giving continue to be very strong this year. If you feel that the school is not addressing an aspect of this situation which troubles you, please let me know.

Let me assure you that life for all of us at Exeter continues to be busy, challenging, and productive. Our usual expectations and our characteristic energy have carried us along, and even our more routine crises have kept us growing. I have every confidence that we have weathered a difficult time, thanks in large part to your support.

Sincerely,

Kendra S. O'Donnell

Kendra S. O'Donnell, Principal

Exeter, New Hampshire 03833-1104   Tel (603) 772-4311   Fax (603) 778-9563

From the Editor

These have been harsh days at the Academy. As a former journalist who still writes for publications from time to time, I believed that pack journalism had disappeared. Not so. This summer, we were buried under an avalanche of media who came to investigate circumstances surrounding the arrest of a faculty member on child pornography charges. L. Lane Bateman, a 12-year teacher at Exeter, was tried in Federal District Court in Concord, New Hampshire, in early October, and was found guilty of one count of possession of child pornography, two counts of transporting child pornography, and a forfeiture count which turns over equipment seized in a raid on his Academy residence to the government. He was dismissed by the Academy shortly after his arrest.

What do alumni and alumnae want to know? One of the most pressing questions at Alumni/ae Council Weekend in late September was whether students were involved. If so, how many? The most controversial story appeared in the *New York Times* of August 4, citing involvement of 10 former students. In October, when the trial began, this number was repeated by CNN. We objected to such an unsubstantiated report, while attempting to learn from law enforcement officials what these allegations were all about. As it emerged in the trial, the truth was that one former student had been involved in one of the films seized by police at the time of Mr. Bateman's arrest. This was a serious enough concern.

Upon learning the outcome of the trial, the Academy issued a statement: "The jury has given its verdict on the evidence presented to it. From the beginning, this case has been between the United States government and Lane Bateman. Throughout this situation, the Academy's main concern has been the welfare of all of its students and former students. Phillips Exeter Academy has not been a party to the legal proceedings and is not prepared to speculate on the reasons for the jury decision."

Simply put, the Bateman case has been a nightmare for the Academy. Media arrived in force the day after the arrest, and were doing wrap-up stories well into October. *Vanity Fair* magazine will—by the time you read this—have published a lengthy feature offering one view of the situation, largely based on an interview with the defendant before the trial judge issued a gag order. Elements of privilege and scandal in the story fit right in with what is a disconcerting media emphasis on what one critic calls "soft shock."

Alumni and alumnae should know that the Academy's posture toward the media has been one of openness and cooperation, while at the same time maintaining the privacy interests of those at the Academy and Mr. Bateman himself. Our belief was that we had nothing to hide, and that it was in the long-term best interests of the Academy to allow the media to speak with students, faculty, and others as long as reporters did not interfere with the educational process. Principal O'Donnell devoted herself to running the Academy during this crisis; the Communications Office handled most of the media visits and queries. An exception was the interview Mrs. O'Donnell granted to the *New York Times* in August, on the condition that she discuss matters of school policy and not the details of the Bateman case. Unfortunately, the truncated version of this interview which appeared seemed an attempt to link school policy on health education with the former faculty member's behavior. For the record, Mrs. O'Donnell feels her remarks, while accurately quoted to the extent they were reported, were misused.

The *Times's* sensationalism in its major story about the Bateman situation was both hurtful and disappointing to us. Compounding this was the reliance of several other major media outlets—notably *Time* magazine and CNN—on this one newspaper report. You may have seen our letter to *Time* taking them to task for writing an account of what was happening at the school without ever having made even a token effort to contact us. As a person who still, literally, carries a press card in his wallet, I was shocked at the sloppy journalism in evidence all around the Bateman situation. By contrast, several reporters and news organizations stood out in their attempts to report all sides of a complex issue: Laura A. Kiernan of the *Boston Globe*, Boston's WBZ-TV (Channel 4), and radio station WBUR at Boston University, where reporter David Wright's sensitivity to issues raised by the arrest and trial was commendable.

Given the Academy's direct communications with its students and former students, parents, and many friends, we hope your questions regarding the arrest and trial—and the Academy's position during both events—have been answered. If not, please feel free to call or write. Principal O'Donnell has been addressing alumni and alumnae all fall, Dean of Students David T. Swift is willing to discuss the matter with parents, and Alumni/ae Affairs Director Harold Brown would be happy to talk to all alumni and alumnae, too. The Communications Office can address itself to any concerns raised by the media coverage or the Academy's posture toward the media.

—*David W. Johnson*

From the Editor

It is snowing, and the campus is peaceful. These spitting snowflakes of January follow a major storm on Wednesday, which was also the day L. Lane Bateman was sentenced. Our former drama teacher received a sentence of five years in prison, followed by three years' probation. The federal charges were possession and shipping of child pornography. The day of the sentencing concluded a six-month ordeal for many at the Academy. We are not in a position to comment on Mr. Bateman's personal ordeal. According to the *New York Times*, he said this just before sentence was passed: "I have broken laws of my community, broken taboos in my community, and I realize I will be and deserve to be punished. I want to apologize publicly to my family, my friends, my students for all the pain I brought them. I hope I can...become a healed man."

In its own short statement following the sentencing, the Academy said: "From the outset, the Academy's primary concern has been for the welfare of its students and former students. We are outraged, shocked, and saddened that Mr. Bateman's behavior has violated the trust inherent in the teacher-student relationship. Such behavior is inexcusable and wrong."

Media coverage was intense on the Monday before the final sentencing, when the United States Attorney introduced in court of two tapes Mr. Bateman had assembled. One interspersed student projects with child pornography, and the other was a "peeping Tom" tape taken from his dorm room of students in another dorm without their knowledge. On the day of the sentencing itself, the United States bombed Iraq and one of the season's largest snowstorms arrived in New Hampshire. The roads were clogged with powder; the land-scape was quiet. The worst was over. Now is the time the Academy must come to terms with the emotional issues aroused by the arrest, trial, and sentencing of a former faculty member on serious criminal charges of particular repugnance to those who value children. Such a process will take time. Many of us need time to heal.

* * *

My most vivid memory of the fall term — other than the above — is of standing at the sidelines during the final minute of the Exeter-Andover football game. They had a 6-0 lead. We had the ball with a first and goal situation. The excitement was as tangible as the students pressing into my back on the sidelines. I had staked out a good spot so that my 13-year-old son Geoffrey could see the action. Our four plays failed, and Andover once again claimed victory. On the field, several Exeter players were in tears produced by equal parts of effort and frustration. Victory over Andover has been elusive for six years now. I walked up to one of the players and said, "It's OK. You played your heart out. You did your best." A defensive back, he had come up with an important interception. This was a good, proud team. There will be plenty of big victories in the players' futures.

* * *

Tartuffe was terrific. The fall performance featuring Brent Yoshikami in the title role brought lively farce and satire to the main stage of Fisher Theater. Directed by drama instructor Peter King, this well-costumed production had a professional feel for much of it. This viewer thought that Catharina Wrede's characterization of the sassy maid Dorine was outstanding. Congratulations to all involved.

* * *

Teaching and learning are what Exeter do best. That is why we de-cided to devote the next two issues of the *Bulletin* to what we have called "the cutting edge" of teaching — that is, what is new in the many disciplines represented in the Academy's curriculum. Our original idea was to have a single issue on the subject, but the response of various departments gave us so much good material that we felt we should publish as much of it as we could.

In this issue, we have a feature by our own staff member Janice Reiter on the new Exeter Mathematics Institute — a wonderful collaboration between the Academy and teachers everywhere. From the English Department, we have examples of the changing canon of literature now assigned and read. Our Classics Department invokes the power of the computer, though reaffirming the importance of the human teacher. Two mathematics instructors explain the changes the graphing calculator has brought to their discipline.

The Academy Library's array of electronic learning and referencing systems is a far cry from thumbing through titles in the Amen Room of the former Davis Library. The Art Department implemented a new course in basic design to introduce students to several skills and technologies. In our next issue, we will hear from a number of other areas: VCRs and laser disks in modern languages; off-campus programs; and a moment in which East meets West in a religion class, with both philosophies gaining from the encounter.

The excitement of teaching and learning is still as real at Exeter as the coming of spring. In this issue and the next, each discipline—like each spring—will bring us something new and fresh.

—*David W. Johnson*

Chapter • 10

Getting Beyond the Grief
University of Iowa

Joanne Fritz

The crisis at a glance

Late in the afternoon on Friday, November 1, 1991, a graduate of the University of Iowa's distinguished physics department, disgruntled over not receiving a coveted award, fatally shot three physics professors, a fellow graduate student, and an associate vice president. He also shot a young female student filling in for a secretary in the vice president's office. She became paralyzed from the neck down.

The shootings started in a conference room of the physics building where three of the victims were killed and the office of the chairman of the department who was killed instantly. The gunman then ran the two blocks to the main administrative building where he killed another victim and wounded another. He went up one floor, into an empty classroom, and killed himself. The shootings took approximately 20 minutes.

Confusion ensued. The first emergency call from the physics building summoned police and ambulances, only to be followed minutes later by similar calls from the administration building. The first alerts sweeping the campus were that a random gunman was loose and people rushed to lock buildings and office suites. Several professors and students who were in that first conference room and witnessed the shootings were in shock, as were the witnesses to the aftermath at the administration building.

A few minutes after the shootings, police discovered the body of the gunman, identification was made, files were checked, and the story started to come together. The gunman, Gang Lu, had targeted those people who he was convinced had treated him unfairly. The only random victim was the secretary who just happened to be in the way. There was a record of Gang Lu's complaint that had worked its way through the graduate school, the physics department, and the office for academic affairs. Letters came to light—one written to the *Des Moines Register* sometime earlier, and several copies of another meant for major news outlets such as the *New York Times* were found that explained in painful detail the disintegration of Gang Lu's mind and his growing paranoia about the university.

Far from being a random shooting enacted spontaneously, Gang Lu had nurtured his

Joanne Fritz is director of university relations at the University of Iowa.

complaints for months and planned and carried out what amounted to an execution of his perceived enemies.

The crisis team

Our crisis team was headed by the vice president for university relations, director of university relations, news service director, university counsel, dean of student affairs, head of counseling services, the university hospital's public information officer, chief of security, chief of Iowa City police, Johnson County prosecutor, vice president for finance, and the university's president and provost. Those who were immediately available assembled in the president's suite within a half hour of the end of the shootings. The initial meeting and a number of activities initiated at that point lasted well into the evening. Various members of the group met the following two mornings and then less formally for the next several days.

The communication mix

On the communication front, our first concern was informing the families of the victims. Administrative teams of two (an example was the associate vice president for academic affairs and assistant vice president for finance) went to each of the victim's family homes to personally deliver the news. In some cases this was the first notification for the family. One spouse of a victim had to be tracked down by long-distance phone and informed of the situation by the university counsel.

We relied on the mass media to get the news out to our other audiences. In reality, we had no time for any other form of communication. Within minutes of the shootings local and national news sources were on the phone to us. Several reporters had monitored and responded to the first police radio calls and, in fact, knew more than we did when they first contacted us. At first we could only confirm that something had happened and we were piecing together the facts as quickly as possible. Within two hours we held a media briefing that was carried live by one TV station and attended by virtually all media within a 100-mile radius. Simultaneously, one person handled calls from the national media and regional markets across the nation. At 10 p.m. that same evening we held a second briefing where we were able to release the names of the victims.

Briefings were held the following Saturday morning and again on Sunday morning. After that they were held on an as-needed basis. During this week after the incident we began to turn our attention to more personal communications with our on-campus constituents. Because the gunman and one of his victims were Chinese, for example, we reached out to our international students. We wanted to console them, give them an opportunity to speak, and reassure them that the international community was not to blame in any way. We also arranged a community gathering in the student union on Monday morning where the provost spoke and we introduced a network of university and community mental health workers who had volunteered to provide individual and group counseling.

There was only one public funeral during this week but the office of university relations handled the overwhelming media attention and attendance. On Thursday a memorial service was held at the university arena that drew some 4,000 people who came to grieve and pay their respects to the families of the victims.

Words to the wise

1. *Imagine the worst.* Be prepared for crises before they strike. Gather your institutional relations staff members and make a list of potential crises—and responses. Take time now—when you have it—to assign specific staff members to specific jobs so you won't lose valuable time during your next crisis.

2. *Work fast.* Take advantage of quick internal communication vehicles, such as electronic mail or your campus TV or radio station. We found, as a result of this crisis, that we did not have good channels to quickly alert our university community of 42,000 people. With a decentralized campus, this is difficult to do but we are working on assembling a number of options that we can use in the future.

3. *Develop a network of support across campus beforehand.* Know people in key positions who can help get things done, serve as an early-warning system, and serve as "expert" spokespeople on various aspects of a crisis (e.g., a housing director on emergency procedures that are followed in case of a fire or bomb threat).

4. *Provide media training to key administrators.* We use a consultant once a year to give a workshop on media relations. This has been extremely popular and genuinely helpful.

5. *Establish one voice or spokesperson for the university.* This will be the consistent voice/face seen/heard by the public.

6. *Establish a policy of openness to the media and public.* Provide all information that can be provided as quickly as possible. The facts, bad as they might be, are far better than rumors. Media in an information vacuum will find ways to create stories.

7. *When the institution is at fault, admit mistake, and take action to correct it and to make sure it doesn't happen again.* Avoid defensiveness, denial, and minimizing.

NEWS

THE UNIVERSITY OF IOWA
IOWA CITY, IOWA 52242

EXHIBIT 3

Release: Immediate   General News   Contact: Ann Rhodes
                            307 E. College   or Joanne Fritz
                                                             319 335-0293

EDITORS AND NEWS DIRECTORS: The next news briefing will be at noon Sunday,
Nov. 3 at 307 E. College.

BROADCASTERS: Miya Sonya Rodolpho-Sioson is pronounced
               Mee-yah Sown-ya Row-dol-fo See-yo-sown
               Linhua Shan is pronounced Lin-wah Shawn

(Sixth victim dies in University of Iowa shootings)

        IOWA CITY, Iowa -- T. Anne Cleary, associate vice president for
academic affairs and professor in the College of Education, died at
1:42 p.m. Saturday, Nov. 2 at the University of Iowa Hospitals and Clinics.
She was 56 years old.

        Cleary died after life support systems were removed at the request of
her three brothers. Cleary was one of six people shot late Friday afternoon
by a former graduate student at the University of Iowa.

        Gang Lu, who recently received his Ph.D. in physics, also shot and
killed four members of the department of physics and astronomy before
killing himself. Those killed were: Christoph K. Goertz, 47, professor;
Dwight R. Nicholson, 44, professor and department chair; Linhua Shan,
research investigator; and Robert Alan Smith, associate professor.

        A sixth shooting victim remains in critical condition at University of
Iowa Hospitals and Clinics. She is Miya Rodolfo-Sioson, a member of the
academic affairs support staff.

        Speaking on behalf of the University of Iowa faculty and staff,
University of Iowa President Hunter R. Rawlings III said, "I extend our
deepest sympathy to Anne's family. She and the others who have been lost in
this tragedy leave us with a profound loss of magnificent professional
talent and treasured friendships."

        In a news briefing Saturday morning, Rawlings announced that
University counselors will be meeting Saturday and Sunday with people
closely affected by the shooting. Classes will be cancelled Monday to allow
others in the University community to participate in counseling sessions.

        Although classes will be cancelled, University offices and patient
clinics at the College of Dentistry and at University of Iowa Hospitals and
Clinics will remain open on Monday.

                        -30-   11/2/91

NEWS

THE UNIVERSITY OF IOWA
IOWA CITY, IOWA 52242

EXHIBIT 5

Release: Immediate   General News   Contact: Steve Maravetz
                         307 E. College   319 335-3901

(UI deals with sadness and grief at loss of colleagues and friends)

IOWA CITY, Iowa -- On the campus of the University of Iowa Monday, members of the university community expressed their sadness and sympathy in the aftermath of Friday's shootings, which left six persons dead and another seriously wounded.

The campus was quiet. Classes had been canceled in memory of the victims and out of sympathy for their families.

A meeting, attended by several hundred persons, was held at 9:30 a.m. in the main lounge of the Iowa Memorial Union on the UI campus. At the meeting, which was called by the university administration to provide information about counseling services available to persons seeking such help, University President Hunter R. Rawlings III summed up the feelings of many on campus:

"This has been a week of deep and terrible sadness," Rawlings said. "The injuries we have suffered are devastating."

Rawlings went on to encourage members of the university community to come together to share their feelings.

"We must now begin the long and very difficult process of healing. We must turn to each other for comfort."

A university-wide gathering will be held for the victims Thursday, Nov. 7 at 7 p.m. in Carver-Hawkeye arena.

Small group counseling sessions began this afternoon and will continue as long as they are needed. The UI International Center is providing ongoing counseling and support to foreign students. The counseling is being provided by UI staff members, along with private practitioners, ministers and priests from the local area.

"We have made arrangements to provide help for as long as it takes," said Peter Nathan, UI vice president for academic affairs.

Groups within the campus community expressed their feelings in various ways. In the chilly morning wind, two wreaths adorned the doors of Phillips Hall, home of the College of Business Administration. Their black ribbons fluttered in the breeze.

Just down the street, at Van Allen Hall where four of the fatal shootings took place, several hundred people gathered at noon. A group of

                         (more)   11/4/91

(UI deals with sadness and grief at loss of colleagues and friends--2)

engineering students represented by Henry McGill, a junior from Marion,
S.C., placed a black and gold wreath near the west entrance to the building.
The crowd bowed their heads in a spontaneous moment of silence.

Earlier, a handlettered sign had been placed in front of the building
by an anonymous person. It read: What's it going to take to get a handgun
law if this can happen in a small Iowa pacifist community?

St. Patrick's Catholic Church was filled with mourners for the 11 a.m.
funeral services for T. Anne Cleary, associate vice president for academic
affairs. Cleary was shot in her office in Jessup Hall, two blocks down the
street from Van Allen Hall. She was buried at St. Joseph's Cemetery.

Another person shot in Cleary's office, Miya Sioson, 23, a senior
global studies major and a member of the department's support staff,
remained in serious condition in University Hospitals.

Letters, telegrams and telephone calls of sympathy poured into the
university and to the families of the victims from around the world. A
group of Chinese students and scholars issued a statement expressing their
shock and grief, and extending their sympathy to the families of the
victims.

The statement also thanked the university and the Iowa City community.
"Their support, either by acts or by words, touched and inspired us.
This is America. We will never be the same," the statement concluded.

At the Monday meeting at the IMU, Rawlings announced that the
university would handle the funeral of Linhua Shan, whose doctoral
dissertation won the prestigious D.C. Spriestersbach award. Shan was killed
by Gang Lu, who apparently believed he should have received the award.

Financial assistance funds have been established for Sioson and for
Linhua Shan's widow. Contributions for Sioson and Shan's widow may be made
in care of the Iowa State Bank and Trust Co., 102 South Clinton, Iowa City
52240. Questions about the funds should be directed to Char Terrell or Eric
Nilausen at the bank. The telephone number is (319)356-5800.

Members of Cleary's family have established the Dr. T. Anne Cleary
Psychology Scholarship for International Students in her memory.
Contributions may be made through the University of Iowa Foundation, P.O.
Box 4550, Iowa City 52242-4550.

(UI deals with sadness and grief at loss of colleagues and friends--3)

Contributions in memory of any of the victims may be made to the UI
Foundation. The use of those funds will be related to the university's
mission and will be determined by family members and others later.

-30-   11/4/91

CHAPTER 11

Treading Softly as You Go Coed

Wheaton College

Gail Berson

The crisis at a glance

Although no one would argue that an institutional change wracks the same havoc as a natural disaster or campus murder, the sometimes bumpy transition can result in challenges of crisis proportion. And any advancement professional involved in the move from a single-sex to a coeducational institution knows that this transition ranks among the most dramatic institutional changes imaginable.

At noon, January 28, 1987, Wheaton College President Alice F. Emerson convened the college community in Cole Chapel to make a historic announcement. The board of trustees had decided—in principle—that Wheaton would admit men as degree candidates beginning in the fall of 1988. But that was just the half of it. To allow for wide consultation with members of the Wheaton family, the board agreed that it would not finalize its decision until May.

Within minutes, a challenge of enormous magnitude ensued. The admission staff adopted a new vocabulary, embraced an expanded mission statement, and accepted the challenge to generate applications from young men and women to enroll in Wheaton's first coeducational class. What's more, the interval between January and May left only five months to solicit and win converts to the prospect of a coeducational Wheaton.

The crisis team

Our crisis team consisted of the president, the provost, vice president of college relations, dean of students, dean of admission and student aid, and the trustees.

The audiences

Obviously, the transition to coeducation affected our entire campus community of faculty, staff, students, as well as Wheaton alumnae, parents, prospective families, and secondary school guidance counselors who recommended Wheaton.

Gail Berson is dean of admission and student aid at Wheaton College in Massachusetts.

The communication mix

During the five-month consultation period, Wheaton gave equal opportunity to voices against and voices in favor of coeducation. The emotional intensity of that time was matched only by the intensity of our outreach.

Armed with facts and figures, complemented by patience and understanding, Wheaton trustees and staff members traveled to meet with alumnae groups and parents of current and prospective students. Each meeting allowed for sometimes heated but more often productive exchanges of view. Most of all, travel across these constituencies kept the college profile highly visible.

To get the word out to our 14,000 alumni, we sent letters to alumnae, current parents, and friends of the college from the president and the chair of the board of trustees. Complementary letters from the admission office accompanied the standard letters and were mailed to the guidance community, prospective students, and their families.

Staff members from the admission and institutional advancement offices also set up a telephone hotline to deal directly with constituent concerns.

Words to the wise

1. *Encourage campus community involvement.* At Wheaton, it was essential that everyone on campus understand the rationale for the institutional change. Involving students, staff, and faculty assured us shared information and support.

2. *Don't discourage media attention.* While it is true that you can't control what the media say about you, I think the old adage that "any press is good press, as long as they spell the name right" is also true. Media coverage may be uneven in quality and substance, but one could never buy the amount of attention the media give a "hot" story. To be sure, we may have wished for a different spin when the *Boston Globe* covered Wheaton's transition to coeducation as a protest story. But the fact that Wheaton had become a household name was undeniable.

3. *Develop talking points.* Our hotline taught us the value of anticipating tough questions—and developing straightforward answers. Hotline operators met regularly to compare notes, update the top 20 questions, and refine their responses.

4. *Reward team efforts.* After the trustee vote in favor of coeducation, our president took the lead role in thanking members of the campus community for their efforts. Supervisors across campus sponsored celebratory events to recognize the end of one phase of the coeducational campaign before embarking on another. Whether in the form of letters, flowers, or dinners, each "thanks" helped us create additional good will and strengthen morale.

5. *Accentuate the positive.* Change is often upsetting. The challenge is to make change energizing and positive. Here at Wheaton, we think our successful transition to coeducation stands as an example of how "managed crisis" can produce positive results.

CHAPTER • 12

Recovering from an AIDS Death

The Johns Hopkins Medical Institutions

Joann Ellison Rodgers

The crisis at a glance

In the fall of 1990, several patients and their support groups contacted the Johns Hopkins Hospital demanding information about a breast cancer surgeon's HIV status and confirmation that he had AIDS. Prohibited by Maryland law from requiring HIV status or releasing such information if we had it—and faced with the "no comment" from the surgeon and his lawyer—Hopkins officials did what they could to reassure women of the extremely low risk of physician-to-patient HIV transmission. We also explained the hospital's universal precautions that would protect them if, in fact, an infected surgeon had operated on them.

At the time, the American public was emotionally and politically distracted and distressed by the news of the Florida dentist AIDS case and the raging debate over mandatory disclosure of HIV status by patients and health care workers.

After the surgeon's death in December 1990, some patients and their support groups went to the press, notably the *Baltimore Sun*, and won the paper's advocacy for full disclosure. During this period, reporters and editors with whom we had built a long-term working relationship tried relentlessly—and mostly reasonably—to get confirmation from us. Reporters interviewed patients and friends of the surgeon but were careful not to print the story until the late surgeon's attorney finally confirmed the facts in writing to the *Sun* and the hospital's chief counsel.

Within hours after the public confirmation, The Johns Hopkins Hospital notified by mail every one of the surgeon's patients that the physician had died of AIDS. The hospital offered them confidential counseling and testing for those who remained concerned. Hopkins also sought a collaborative "look back" study, conducted by the Maryland State Health Department, the U.S. Centers for Disease Control and Prevention, and the Hospital staff. Results of the study, published in the April 14, 1993, *Journal of the American Medical Association*, added further evidence of the extremely low risk of transmission to that found in previous studies of more than 35 health care workers and 19,000 patients.

The firestorm that subsequently broke was no surprise. The hospital faced a spate of

Joann Ellison Rodgers is deputy director of public affairs and director of media relations at The Johns Hopkins Medical Institutions.

lawsuits from women seeking financial compensation for the emotional distress they suffered when the hospital failed to inform them of the surgeon's HIV status—even though it would be against the law in Maryland to do so. None of the women were HIV positive. We had begun to anticipate escalation of an already inflamed and emotional debate and to prepare, as Jefferson exhorted the press, to "inform the discretion of the public" with a proactive and reactive communications program.

Negative fallout surrounding a previous AIDS case, in great part, drove Hopkins' decision to undertake open communications of this complicated situation and the set of thorny issues it generated. In 1983, a cardiology resident contracted HIV infection during a puncture accident. In that case, in the absence of federal, state, or institutional precedents or policies, Hopkins officials were unprepared for the social, legal, ethical, financial, and practical consequences of house staff, fellows, faculty, and others who developed AIDS. The officials elected to mostly decline comment, ignore the public uproar, and rely on standard, legalistic responses to the doctor's and family's demands for financial help and employment. By the time public affairs was brought into the story, the communications situation was in crisis—complete with lawsuits, gag orders, a defiant and dying physician, faculty divisiveness over the institution's handling of the case, and relentlessly negative press. This is a story that still haunts us.

The crisis team

In the public affairs department, the following staff members served on our crisis team: our public affairs director, associate director for media relations, and our media representative who covers AIDS. The following Medical Institutions' administrators also served as members of the hospital's crisis team: the vice president for medical affairs, director of medical affairs, chief counsel, and the senior epidemiologist. Because these administrators were already knowledgeable about the issues, plugged in to state health department policies, collegial with state officials, and willing to work with public affairs before the crisis actually broke, their contributions to our communication efforts were invaluable. An outside media trainer helped hospital administrators prepare to meet the press during the crisis.

The audiences

The crisis touched the lives of a wide variety of constituents, including the surgeon's patients and their families; other patients and women in general; public health officials at the local and federal levels; Hopkins internal audiences; lawyers, judges, and policy makers; and the general public.

The communication mix

Despite some early official misgivings, Hopkins enjoys a long history of relative openness and proactive media relations about AIDS, the care of AIDS patients, and AIDS research. As an academic medical center, Hopkins receives more federal AIDS research dollars than any other institution in the United States. What's more, with some of its faculty among the pioneers of AIDS research and patient care, Hopkins is committed to the public health approach to AIDS control, community advocacy, and rational, science-based AIDS policy. In short, there exists at Hopkins a high level of comfort in communicating about AIDS.

During the crisis, we relied on a variety of communication vehicles to keep all concerned parties informed. Among the communication tools we used were:
- letters to patients, the CDC, and local newspapers;
- press releases and fact sheets sent to local and national media;
- press conferences with well-trained hospital spokespersons;
- telephone conference calls with reporters;
- quick response to any errors of fact or misleading information reported by the press;
- coverage of the crisis in internal periodicals and special "hotline" publications;
- op-ed columns in the *Baltimore Sun;* and
- meetings with the *Sun*'s editorial board.

Words to the wise

1. *Gather the troops.* Do whatever you can to develop a core crisis team within your communications office and with your institutional leadership. Position yourselves as contributors and managers of messages—not just stenographers or suppliers of press releases.

2. *Put it in writing.* Prepare formal written materials including a communications plan, press releases, and fact sheets, as well as daily or regular contingency statements to respond to emergent issues and questions.

3. *Get the facts straight.* Gather all the facts, rumors, and speculation from all concerned parties. Write each piece of information down, identify its source, and confirm its accuracy.

4. *Spread the word.* Set up a consistent means of delivering crisis updates to internal and external audiences quickly and accurately.

5. *Plan what you say.* Make sure your official spokespersons can speak for themselves—and your institution. That means rehearsing, reading, asking questions, and being as comfortable with the technical, legal, and scientific facts as your experts are. Whether you enlist campus or outside media trainers, provide them with crisis background materials and encourage your own staff to participate in the training sessions, too.

6. *Monitor media attention.* We tracked our coverage on a daily—and sometimes even hourly—basis.

7. *Put it in perspective.* Once the immediate crisis has passed, move to more proactively seek stories that move the issues from an institutional focus to the wider debate, such as Hopkins did with the issue of CDC responsibility.

8. *Evaluate your progress.* We did it mostly informally but were quick to circulate supportive stories, editorials, and legislative developments, as well as problem stories we needed to address quickly.

9. *Multiply by two—or more.* Be prepared to spend at least twice as much time as you scheduled to deal with any kind of communications crisis.

The
Johns Hopkins
Hospital

600 North Wolfe Street Administration 125
Baltimore, MD 21205
(301) 955-2491

Hamilton Moses III, M.D.
Vice President Medical Affairs

December 3, 1990

Dear Patient:

Because our patients' well-being is the first priority at The Johns Hopkins Hospital, I am writing to you with some information that may be important for your peace of mind.

We have learned that a physician who was on the Hospital staff and who participated in your care here had the Acquired Immune Deficiency Syndrome (AIDS). Recently a number of patients who heard the rumor contacted the Hospital. We made numerous attempts to obtain confirmation or denial, including contact with the physician's family and the Maryland Department of Health and Mental Hygiene. We obtained confirmation today. You may have seen news about this over the weekend.

You should be reassured by knowing that there is very little chance that you could have become infected. The Hospital's physicians and other workers follow many precautions that are designed to prevent the transmission of all infections, including AIDS. To date, there is only one reported case in the United States in which it is suspected that a health care worker transmitted HIV to a patient. The facts in that case are very unclear and remain in dispute. Also, as more information is gained about the AIDS epidemic, it has been very reassuring to learn that the transmission from physician or worker to patients has not elsewhere occurred. Nevertheless, the Hospital appreciates the concern that even the smallest possibility of transmission of HIV can cause.

If you or your physician have questions or concerns, please call Timothy Townsend, M.D., Senior Director of Medical Affairs at the Hospital at 301-955-0620. If you or your physician desire counselling about the possibilities of transmission of HIV, or would like to be tested for HIV, Dr. Townsend will arrange this for you.

In closing, let me re-emphasize that the best medical and scientific judgment is that there is negligible risk of your having been infected. Because of the implication of HIV infection and AIDS, the Hospital wishes to assure that you have the best information available to make decisions about your health.

Sincerely yours,

Hamilton Moses, III, M.D.

HMIII:mvh

JOHNS
HOPKINS
HEALTH
SYSTEM

THE JOHNS HOPKINS MEDICAL INSTITUTIONS

FOR RELEASE ON RECEIPT

HOPKINS CALLS ON CDC AND OTHERS TO SPEED POLICY, JOIN STUDY

Johns Hopkins Hospital officials today called on the U.S. Centers for Disease Control (CDC) to expedite plans to issue new HIV testing and disclosure policies for hospitals, physicians and patients. At the same time, the Hospital announced that Maryland Department of Health and Mental Hygiene and CDC experts will join Hopkins specialists to study the risk of HIV-1 infection in more than 600 women who have sought testing after learning they were patients of a surgeon who died of AIDS.

In a letter to William Roper, M.D., director of the CDC, Hopkins asked that critical questions be answered by any new policies issued by the CDC.

"We want answers to these questions because we are in a policy vacuum," said Hamilton Moses III, M.D., vice president for medical affairs of the Hospital. "And we're dealing with an infectious disease that has been politicized to such a degree that rational decisions on behalf of the public's health and health care workers are impossible," he added.

Among the questions:

o The CDC announced the first -- and only -- case of suspected health care worker-to-patient transmission (the Florida dentist's case) in August 1990. No revision of previous CDC guidelines has yet been issued. When can hospitals and health care workers expect more specific guidance?

o If a physician, nurse or other health care worker discovers that he or she is HIV-1 positive, is there an obligation to report that fact to his or her employer or hospital?

o What are the specific medical procedures -- if any -- that pose a higher degree of risk for transmission from health care workers to patients?

o Does infection with HIV-1 warrant the curtailment of a health care worker's career?

o If curtailment of practice is not warranted, are there circumstances that warrant advising patients of a health care worker's positive status before treatment is given?

o What studies need to be done to quantify better the degree of risk of physician or worker to patient and patient to worker transmission?

(more)

The Johns Hopkins Hospital   School of Medicine   School of Public Health   School of Nursing

Office of Public Affairs   Suite 1100   550 North Broadway   Baltimore, Maryland 21205   (301) 955-6680

JHMI--CDC--2

o If a hospital or employer learns of the HIV-positive status of a member of the staff, what action is required?

o What steps beyond universal precautions need to be taken to minimize any risks identified?

o Extremely restrictive laws are now in place in Maryland and the laws across the nation for getting informed consent to do HIV testing vary greatly. When, then, should a physician or other health worker do to get knowledge of a patient's HIV status when the worker is stuck with a needle contaminated with the patient's blood and consent from the patient cannot be obtained?

o Given rapid development of new knowledge about AIDS and HIV, what agency or agencies should lead the way in setting policies and standards that are clear and useful? And how can the CDC or other lead agency accelerate the evaluation and development of policy?

o Should there be a consistent, national approach in policy for physicians and laboratories with respect to reporting an HIV-positive test result?

o If risk is identified, what restrictions can hospitals legally place on health care workers who are known to be HIV positive or have AIDS.

At a news briefing in Baltimore, Hopkins officials said that clear, practical policies must be set by responsible agencies soon in order to meet the needs and expectations of patients and health care workers.

"We are currently operating in a policy vacuum, a vacuum that exposes all hospitals, doctors and patients to unnecessary fear and anxiety," Moses said.

"What policy exists is hopelessly vague," said Moses. "It's time to take some firm steps, but we cannot do that without guidance, cooperation and commitment from the CDC, state health departments and physician specialty groups," he added. "We've been willing to face our situation here at Hopkins in an open, public way, but we must ask others to fulfill their responsibilities, too."

The situation to which Moses referred involves a Hopkins-affiliated surgeon who died of AIDS in November. The surgeon told neither the hospital nor his patients of his disease, despite repeated attempts by Hopkins to obtain confirmation or denial of rumors about the physician's physical condition.

Newspaper stories generated by patients' calls to the media have since resulted in hundreds of calls to Hopkins. Hopkins has offered to arrange counseling and testing (at no cost to patients) either through patients' private physicians, the health department, the Red Cross or a special facility at Hopkins to all who ask. And Hopkins sent letters to more than 1,800 patients of the surgeon, outlining the offer and reassuring them of their very low risk.

(more)

JHMI--CDC--3

Infectious disease specialists at Hopkins will work with the Maryland State Department of Health and Mental Hygiene and the CDC to evaluate results of the HIV-1 tests and the risk of HIV-1 infection posed by having been patients of a surgeon with AIDS. Hopkins officials said the study will take several months to complete and details of results will not be made public until all of the data are available and subjected to critical scientific analysis.

Based on the general prevalence of the disease, the specialists emphasized that in any population of 1,000 people -- whether or not operated on by a doctor with AIDS -- two to four are likely to be HIV positive. "The important thing to remember is that there could be a few positive tests in this study, but that does not mean the surgeon transmitted the virus," said Timothy Townsend, M.D., senior director of medical affairs for the Hospital. "Each HIV-1 positive person must be thoroughly evaluated. The value of this study, as in a similar study in Nashville, is that we will get much needed, hard information about risk. We already know it's very low. But we don't know how low," he said.

At the briefing, Hopkins' general counsel Paul Rosenberg also sharply criticized lawyers who are soliciting groundless suits against the estate of the surgeon, who has since died of AIDS, and against the hospital.

"By exploiting undue fear among patients whom we know from the evidence are at very, very low risk of infection from their treatment, these lawyers are creating both panic and false expectations," Rosenberg said. "The litigation that follows will simply divert resources from health care of the desperately ill and needy patients who seek health care at Hopkins," he added.

###

(For press inquiries only, call Carol Pearson or Joann Rodgers at (301) 955-6680.) 12/14/90

CURRENTS
On Crises

CHAPTER • 13

Beyond the Crystal Ball

Forget about relying on your sixth sense. Issues management requires a system, a strategy, and plenty of self-discipline

Richard B. Heydinger

In 1986 the University of Minnesota experienced its first animal rights demonstration. As our administrative team huddled to devise a response strategy, it was obvious that we were reacting differently to this protest than we had to others in the past.

Our security measures were in place. The university had already developed a comprehensive policy to assure our responsible use of animals in research. We had the facts ready to present to the media. We knew who would be our chief spokesperson. And we were able to put forth our side of the story forcefully. Things were different for this demonstration because we were, in fact, prepared.

Upon reflection I realized that this did not happen by chance. Two years earlier we had begun an experiment in issues management, which had set in motion those activities that helped us respond to the concerns of animal rights activists. We were "managing" the issue—and, indeed, it was working.

Cynics might view the word *management* pejoratively; they may interpret this approach as an attempt to manipulate, block, or put spin on problematic issues. Although there's always the potential for such a reaction, the approach deserves a more enthusiastic response.

A systematic issues management program ensures that your short-range crises do not drive out your need for longer-range discipline. And if you handle this program properly, you can improve communication on and off campus, help present a complete picture of your institution's policies, and thus become more responsive to all your constituencies.

Expanding your vision

Managing tough issues has long been the responsibility of communications professionals. Think of such legendary PR coups as Tylenol's strategy following the cyanide poisonings, McDonald's response after a child swallowed a giveaway toy, and Kaiser Aluminum's move

Richard B. Heydinger is senior fellow and executive director of the Alliance for Higher Education Strategies at the University of Minnesota. At the time he wrote this article for the January 1992 CURRENTS, he was the University of Minnesota's vice president of external relations.

to ride the recycling wave to defend its production of cans.

Reputations rise and fall according to our ability to get our institutions out of difficult situations. Yet the quickly developed response plan is no longer enough; today's effective communications professional anticipates issues.

Over the past 15 years, advocates of strategic planning and futures research have developed a number of ways to do this—including issues management. The term came from W. Howard Chase, who in 1984 wrote the seminal work on this topic, *Issue Management: Origins of the Future*. He saw that PR had an arsenal of techniques for defending yesterday's actions but few approaches to risk assessment or strategic planning. Chase noted that developing such approaches would increase the PR profession's credibility with senior management. By being out in front of an issue, he reasoned, you could become an actor in the development of public policy—not just a member of the audience watching events unfold on stage.

Effective communications professionals have always done this. But our planning has relied on our sixth sense—or as Chase said, it has been visceral rather than disciplined.

Issues management moves the process from the instinctive to the systematic. Based on the premise that forewarned is forearmed, it's a tool for expanding our vision and enhancing our strategic thinking. However, it's not a prediction device; it's a coping device. After all, the future is unpredictable—or we'd all be making our living at the horse track.

Issues managers don't exactly buy into the crystal ball concept. But they do follow the assumption that our crystal balls are not entirely blank; indeed, we can see fuzzy outlines of approaching issues. The key is deciphering these outlines to get the best possible results for our campuses.

From theory to practice

Issues management, like most aspects of public relations, is more art than science. Yet the process does follow a logical theory: If you identify issues early, you can debate alternative responses, decide on the best approach, and carry out an action plan. The following five-part framework explains how to put the premise to work.

• *Stage 1: Identify issues and trends*. To spot the issues, begin by examining as many factors as possible that could affect your institution. These include social, technological, economic, environmental, and political trends.

In doing so, don't limit yourself to those with an immediate and direct bearing on your institution (like demographic shifts). Also consider longer-range, less precise factors (such as the expanding use of video technology in K-12 education). Envision your activities as a radar screen, scanning 360 degrees of the horizon for approaching changes in your environment.

The most common approach to scanning has been a systematic reading program. Typically, institutions ask a diverse group of broad thinkers to monitor emerging issues by reading periodicals with a variety of viewpoints. At Minnesota, we hired three graduate assistants part time to help us scan newspapers, magazines, journals, reports, and speeches ranging from congressional briefings to *Mother Jones*.

Formal reading programs can work; however, I know from experience that they can also be time consuming and difficult to manage. Consider two other possibilities.

First, most campus PR professionals are curious and monitor a wide variety of publications on their own. So try a twice-yearly retreat for your PR staff to develop a comprehensive list of issues. This may be all you need to initiate a formal issues management program. At the retreat you can brainstorm in a group setting, and subgroups can then develop more detailed definitions of each issue.

Alternatively, a structured set of interviews with on-campus experts may be just as productive. On almost all campuses, for example, there are faculty members who watch societal trends as part of their research. At Minnesota, faculty in geography, political science, agricultural economics, and health policy offer their perspective. By interviewing such a group, you can build on the scanning they do in their work.

The most difficult aspect of stage 1 is describing these complex, sometimes diffuse trends in convincing, credible terms. Reducing broad topics to a few sentences leaves your effort open to criticism, particularly in academe. But if issues management is to be a useful management tool, you have no choice. Your team will have neither the expertise nor the time to describe an issue in the same level of detail as they would in a research report.

Framing the issues is also a most important step. Once you've identified a trend, you must put it in the context of your own institution. For example, your team might identify young people's growing use of computing and video technology as a trend to monitor. You could then frame this trend in two quite distinct ways.

1. Is our institution keeping abreast of the developments in computing technologies to accommodate students' expectations?

2. Are we monitoring the curriculum innovations in high schools so that we are aware of the changing experiences and skills of teenagers?

Although this step may seem trivial, it is one of the most important in gauging the effectiveness of your program. It will determine the focus and direction of the institutional alternatives that you develop in stages 2 and 3.

• *Stage 2: Evaluate the impact of the issues and set priorities.* Fans of issues management have discovered something that journalists and PR pros have known for ages: There is a development cycle for each issue. Issues move sequentially through stages—emerging, developing, maturing, and declining.

This is a useful framework for sorting through and setting priorities for the issues you need to monitor. In setting these priorities, you should ask several key questions. The U.S. House of Representatives' Committee on Energy and Commerce—in its January 1993 document—"Foresight in the Private Sector: How Can Government Use It?"—came up with this helpful series.

1. What is the probability that a given trend, event, or development will become a major issue?

2. How great will the eventual impact on the institution be?

3. Will the impact focus on the campus or affect the entire community?

4. When is the issue likely to peak—in the short term, medium term, or long term?

5. Who are the major players, and what positions are they likely to adopt?

6. What can the institution do to deal effectively with the issue?

These questions help gauge two things: the potential impact the issues could have on your institution and when the issue is likely to peak. If the likelihood is *high* and the potential impact is *great*, your institution should put some resources into developing a response strategy. After you've asked these questions, present your findings to your senior management team for review.

• *Stage 3: Establish the position.* On many issues, your institution's desired position may be obvious. But when it comes to choosing the points to emphasize, there may be considerable debate. Your administrators and perhaps even your Board of Trustees may want to be involved in developing your institution's position.

Keep in mind that not all issues are crises or cause problems. Because certain trends (such as smaller high school graduation classes) may be consistent with your institution's long-term objectives (like downsizing the undergraduate student body), your position can build on these trends and thus further your institution's goals.

• *Stage 4: Design an action and response plan.* Once you know what position your institution wants to take, you can pull together issues teams with a variety of expertise to propose strategies for senior managers. Candidates for the team include faculty members, administrators, alumni, and others interested in your institution's future.

With a disciplined program, you'll have time to discuss alternative responses and agree on strategy. You can deal with the issue when and how you—not the media or an activist group—would like to. For example, you can frame the animal rights issue to focus on the importance of human health.

As part of your plan, you should consider timing strategies. Two sample questions to ask: Do we pre-empt our critics by calling attention to the issue now on our own terms? Or do we wait, then come prepared with our response after others have brought the issue to the forefront? Such questions will help you develop the best plan for you.

• *Stage 5: Implement the action plan.* In this stage, you'll execute the plan. However, remember that a short-term crisis can drive out your longer-range strategies. So again, you need self-discipline to ensure that you take advantage of all your planning.

As you implement your program, remember that issues management is not a panacea; it is only one tool in the PR professional's tool box. Also keep in mind three guidelines.

1. You need discipline to keep your program on schedule. It's easy to postpone this longer-range work for the current crisis; it's not easy at all to envision the payoff.

2. Issues management is hard work. Because you're dealing with myriad unknown factors, deciding which issues to monitor and which strategies to develop can be extremely frustrating. For the PR officer who thrives on the stress of the momentary crisis, issues management is not always rewarding.

3. Your program must be focused, efficient, and manageable. You can succeed if you schedule periodic examinations of issues. But if you try to identify all the issues that could possibly affect you, your program will collapse under its own weight.

20-20 hindsight

Our pilot test of issues management at the University of Minnesota ended in 1984, nine months after it started. By that time, I personally had become skeptical about its value.

I wondered, among other things, how our group could ensure that we were covering all the relevant issues for the university. And I questioned how, as only casual observers of societal trends, we could accurately assess their potential impact on the campus.

My skepticism about issues management soon faded, however, and I began to understand its value when our PR office reacted calmly and confidently during that 1986 animal rights demonstration. A more recent experience has made me even more sure of its merit.

Last summer, I rediscovered a paper our issues management team had written in 1984. It summarized the technological, economic, political, and social trends at work in our state and their implications for our university.

The emerging trends we identified were hauntingly accurate. To take just one example, our description of the university's 1990 populations (with many more part-time students and returning adults) looked as if we'd written them from today's data.

Certainly we were not clairvoyant. Although we were in fact looking into the future, there was a method to our so-called madness—and we can now say our efforts were worthwhile.

In the last few months, we've begun our second issues management pilot program at the university. Retired faculty members are helping us identify and monitor trends. And a graduate student is working part time to make sure we have the support necessary to keep our effort moving ahead.

Our goals are the same as in 1984. We seek to identify important issues, develop an institutional response strategy, and frame the issues on our own terms. What's different is that we begin this second test better prepared and more confident about the theory and practice of issues management. We know our success depends on having the discipline to stay with it—even in the face of day-to-day demands.

CHAPTER 14

Here Comes Trouble

During an emergency, a run-of-the-mill crisis plan isn't enough. There's a better method for coping and communicating

Matthew Maguire

Quick: It's 6:30 a.m., and you just got off the line with the director of public safety. She gave you what little information she had on a rape reported in a dorm last night. She also warned you that she'd already referred three reporters to you.

As you try to decipher your notes, the first reporter calls and demands a comment for his top-of-the-hour newscast. He wants to know if your campus does anything specific to prevent rape and help victims—because he's already interviewed enraged students who say your institution does nothing of the sort.

Now, tell the truth. Which of the following do you wish you had at that moment?

1. A standard crisis plan—the soothing, one-size-fits-all security blanket that spells out policies and procedures for crisis communications, lists key contacts' home phone numbers, and supposedly guides you through any emergency.

2. A network of well-cultivated campus contacts—key players in every campus office who know you, respect you, and understand your vital role in gathering and disseminating complete and accurate information at times like this.

3. A complete background on campus safety—one that details your rape awareness programs, your counseling services for victims, and everything else your institution does to prevent such tragedies.

The first might be helpful. The second is essential. But the third supplies what you really need—*information*, the most precious commodity in crisis communications. In most emergencies, your on- and off-campus constituencies crave it. But in too many cases, for reasons as varied as the crises themselves, PR professionals can't get their hands on the right information at the right time.

That's why the best-prepared crisis communicators go beyond plan writing and network building. They add to those tactics with the "What are you waiting for?" approach. They foresee crises. And they compile information—now—on what the campus does to ward off and cope with troubled times.

Matthew Maguire is assistant director of foundation relations at Rensselaer Polytechnic Institute. At the time he wrote this article for the March 1993 CURRENTS, he was RPI's director of news services.

The plan isn't everything

The written instructions so many campuses rely on during a crisis vary widely in length, style, and content from institution to institution. Generally, though, plans spell out who does what and how in an emergency: If it's this kind of crisis, call this person first. For that disaster, so-and-so chairs the committee. This is who speaks to the media. The flashlights are there. Here's our philosophy of responding.

True, this kind of information is useful whether the crisis is a one-day flare-up over a controversial speaker or a national ruckus over slayings on campus. But many PR people pooh-pooh written crisis plans by saying they waste time and effort. Indeed, even professionals who have plans acknowledge limits to them—particularly these three.

1. *All crises are different.* "It's not as though a 747 is losing altitude and you have to go through a checklist," says Bill Tyson, a partner at Morrison & Tyson Communications in Walpole, New Hampshire. "There are no 10 steps that you adhere to religiously and that always work."

Don Hale agrees. "There are too many differences and nuances to each crisis," says Carnegie Mellon University's vice president for university relations. "It's hard to imagine that you can write something that encompasses all the procedures for every kind of crisis. Or that when a crisis happens, someone reaches into a drawer, dusts off the plan, and says, 'Now, what do we do here?' "

PR professionals at institutions with good, detailed instructions cite cases in which a crisis outflanked their plan.

After Hurricane Andrew, the University of Miami found itself without power—and thus without the computers and fax machines that would've helped put the plan into effect. Printers, mail houses, and courier services were nonexistent. "This was considered the worst natural disaster in U.S. history," says Susan Bonnett, associate vice president for university relations. "There was no way we could have anticipated the severity of its impact on south Dade County and the ramifications for the university."

Loss of power also nullified much of DePaul University's plan during a serious flood in downtown Chicago in April 1992. Says Leda Hanin, associate vice president for university relations: "The crisis plan gave us a backbone—but frankly, it didn't apply."

2. *Plans create a false sense of security.* "Process-oriented plans are valuable, but they make you think, 'I've done it, I can put it in the drawer, and I don't have to think about it anymore,' " says consultant Tyson. "Plans are nice for review, but you then need to set them aside and respond to the situation."

Especially difficult to predict and control will be the flow of information—in other words, who says what to whom and when.

"If a fire breaks out, reporters at the scene will be able and inclined to get feedback from any of dozens of bystanders," says David Piker, director of college relations at Rose-Hulman Institute of Technology. "If you think you can control all the information, you're being naive."

3. *Crises happen too fast.* Conventional plans often reflect much deliberation by the PR officers and others, including the campus safety staff, the physical plant staff, the dean

of students, and lawyers. People developing such slow-to-evolve plans can wrongly assume that crisis management will unfold at the same relatively leisurely pace.

But reality may be too fast for your plan. Joseph A. Distefano, director of public relations at Metropolitan Community College, puts it this way: "You can't sit down and read 25 pages of verbiage while your gut's roiling and you're wondering, 'Now what?' "

The I's have it

The problems with plans demand a revised attitude toward crisis communication. Think of it as a four-part process: developing *instructions*, becoming an *insider*, gathering *information* in advance, and using your *instincts*. You should do the first three long before the trouble arises.

Develop instructions

The material in conventional plans may not be sufficient, but it is necessary. You need information about your campus and how it should operate in an emergency.

A short list of fundamental facts would include key campus players in student affairs, risk management, public safety, legal affairs, and so on. Record their office, fax, home, and beeper phone numbers as well as their electronic mail addresses.

You should also be able to reach local media—fast. You obviously need a good list of addresses and phone numbers. But to move even faster, buy a fax board for your computer and program into it the fax numbers of all local newsrooms. This will let you send simultaneous releases directly from your computer. An alternative is to hire an outside service to distribute your news releases electronically.

Many institutions with vast crisis experience have plans that provide even more detailed knowledge.

For example, the University of Florida's policy needed updating when media swarmed the campus after five Gainesville murders in the fall of 1990. Linda Gray, assistant vice president for university and government relations, later developed a list of campus rooms suitable for a large press conference and a list of sites big enough for a flotilla of television satellite trucks.

The earthquake of 1989 had a similar effect on the California Institute of Technology. The campus now uses a detailed earthquake plan that describes all PR staff members' duties and work sites. Such planning is essential for coping with the inevitable media aftershock, says Robert O'Rourke, assistant vice president for public relations.

Be an insider

Regardless of how detailed your instructions and your institutional knowledge, you must also be well-connected on campus to be an effective crisis communicator.

"No crisis plan can take the place of being involved with the issues right from the beginning," says Debra Townsend, director of news and communications here at Rensselaer Polytechnic Institute.

The first step in cultivating those connections is to start at the top. Build credibility, for yourself and your whole office, with your president or school head. In a crisis, the CEO will base vital decisions on advice from influential campus leaders. You'll wield no clout in crisis management if you simply crank out publications and craft releases, no matter how creative they are.

To earn this respect, demand a place with top management. "No crisis plan can be instituted by a PR office that isn't represented at the table when decisions are being made, and too many decisions are made without such representation," says Terry Denbow, vice president for university relations at Michigan State University.

As Caltech's O'Rourke points out, that means having the head communicator not only on the leadership council but also on any crisis management team: "If you leave the chief communications person or his representative out of that committee, that's a crisis right there."

Once you've earned the CEO's ear, keep it—by providing frequent updates during a crisis. Just as the press craves information about the emergency, the president wants to know what's happening, what problems you see, what your advice is, and what you're saying to the media. Florida's Gray communicates with her president by e-mail because she knows he's a daily user regardless of his schedule.

To complement your connections at the top, develop a broad network of contacts throughout campus. A good list is not enough; you need relationships.

"For anything that happens on this campus, I've got a personal relationship with the key people built on mutual respect," says Hale of Carnegie Mellon. "They're going to work with me, and we're going to do it together."

Many professionals say good contacts are especially important at large institutions. Ohio State University has 52,000 students and several PR offices in a decentralized, complicated, statewide bureaucracy, says Steve Sterrett, director of news services. "That's one reason I haven't attempted to develop more detailed plans—because it is so big and so diverse that you're better off knowing who the key contacts are."

Gather information

Once you've written instructions and you're an established player, don't stop there. No matter how good your rapport with your campus contacts, you shouldn't assume they'll be able to give you or the media the necessary information during a crisis.

For one thing, the contacts themselves will be mired in crisis management. The director of public safety might be unable or unwilling to explain, in 15 different interviews, the nuances of campus lighting and the escort service. For another, it takes PR expertise—which the safety official probably doesn't have—to know what facts will best meet reporters' needs and what strategy will best represent the institution's interests.

Granted, you don't know which type of crisis is next or when it will strike. And yes, some crises are so bizarre that no one could predict them. If a meteor strikes your campus, no one will ask for your meteor-emergency plan or your meteor-safety backgrounder.

Likewise, communications director David Johnson never would have thought 12-year Phillips Exeter Academy faculty member Lane Bateman would be arrested last July 16 for possessing child pornography. He also never could have predicted the barrage of media interviews and articles, including a prominent one in the December *Vanity Fair*, or the way the story seemed to get more scandalous by the day. Bit by bit, the police—and the press—discovered that Bateman not only possessed pornography but also that an Exeter student had been involved in one of the videos and that the teacher had secretly filmed other students near a bathroom on campus.

Through it all, the school's response was decisive and open: Exeter fired Bateman on July 17, the principal described the situation in a July 20 letter to parents and friends, and more details came in Johnson's editor's note in the Winter 1992 alumni magazine. Exeter's approach was straightforward in part because of the lessons learned from a 1985 crisis, when alumnus Edmund Perry was shot and killed in New York City 10 days after graduation.

The Perry and Bateman cases combined to teach Johnson another lesson: "What I'm acutely aware of is that we're a school of nearly 1,000 students, 160 faculty members, and 350 or so full-time staff members," he says. "Given the nature and size of that community, bad news is going to happen from time to time, and it's largely going to be in the human tragedy area."

Taking that philosophy into account, he is now working with others at the school to develop a new crisis plan to cover as many contingencies as possible. He says the procedures the school has adopted in its two most publicized crises—both human tragedies—have worked well enough to become a basis for dealing with future situations, whether or not they involve students, faculty, and staff.

You too can try to prepare for what I call "sooner-or-later crises"—troubles that inevitably arise on almost every campus. Even if you can't pinpoint the precise date, you can identify general areas—such as alcohol or safety—that will one day give rise to an emergency.

Dan Forbush, associate vice president for public relations at SUNY Stony Brook, does just that. Each year, he confers with his media relations director to identify 50 issues that may become crises. He also schedules a weekly meeting of a "sensitive issues planning group" at which professionals from university affairs, legislative relations, community relations, and other areas can discuss brewing problems.

At Rensselaer, we decided last spring to gather information on every crisis we could imagine. Half a dozen PR professionals had a team nightmare to list everything that could possibly go wrong. Then we interviewed the key contacts responsible for preventing those crises. We asked what they do now to head off such disasters, what they'd do if the crisis happened, and whether they had other concerns that we hadn't mentioned.

The result was a 126-page crisis preparation manual. It outlines—in just two pages—general steps we'd take in any crisis. The rest of the document includes 33 detailed backgrounders on Rensselaer's programs and activities in such areas as chemical safety, radiation safety, dormitory safety, public safety, animal research, tenure, academic fraud, athletics, Greek life, and research overhead. We completed the first draft only about three months after we started.

The project began a long struggle to gather essential information for reporters covering an alleged date rape. Though our campus contacts were cooperative, they couldn't cope with the nature, number, and velocity of questions.

"We spent too much time reporting on our judicial procedures when we probably should have been strategizing," says Rensselaer's Townsend, who says she's already used the new document to handle media calls during several subsequent crises.

"With our new crisis plan, if you spend three or four minutes reading through it or highlighting it before taking any calls, you've already got a bank of background knowledge in your head and in front of you," she says. "And most of the questions you get are background questions."

Use your instincts

None of these preparations—developing a plan, contacts, relationships, or backgrounders— is a substitute for thinking creatively and instinctively when the crisis erupts.

To do that, first follow basic public relations principles. Crisis communications should be the same as everyday communications—which means you deliver accurate information as promptly and as truthfully as possible. Michigan State's Denbow, an outspoken opponent of temporal crisis plans, uses a media action plan that spells out the university's commitment to candor year round—not just during a crisis.

And second, simply do what's right. Remember that public relations has wisely been defined as "doing the right thing and getting caught at it."

"Nothing is a substitute for doing the right thing," says Florida's Gray. When her campus was paralyzed by terror after the five murders, the university offered students a safe place to stay, allowed free phone calls to worried families, and changed the rules for dropping and adding courses so no one suffered financially or academically. No crisis plan directed UF's leaders to take these measures—but they're what students needed at that particular time. Not to mention, says Gray, "we also got some great publicity."

As you contemplate how a similar approach will serve you during your next disaster, remember that crisis communication is an art, not a science. And it's more like jazz than classical music. You need knowledge, skill, technique, and the ability to work with your colleagues. But when you're under the lights, your audiences won't expect you to read a pre-orchestrated score. Instead, they'll measure your virtuosity largely by how well you improvise.

CHAPTER • 15

Getting Out the Inside Story

When crisis strikes, internal audiences need accurate information. Here's how to predict, prevent, and prepare for troubled times

Sally Ann Flecker

Just after 6 p.m. on December 6, 1989, a 25-year-old man in hunting clothes stormed into the engineering school at the University of Montreal. He stalked from room to room with a semi-automatic weapon, shouting about his hatred for feminists. Within a few minutes, he had murdered 14 female students, wounded 13 others, and killed himself.

The massacre—the deadliest in Canadian history—caught the world, the University of Montreal, and the communications department off guard. The university's principal and the engineering school's director were in France. Director of Communications Raymond Carbonneau had left campus for the evening. And there was no crisis plan to follow.

Carbonneau remembers the chaos that followed the attack. He sped back to the university and immediately began working to calm the hordes of alarmed people on campus. His top priorities were to cooperate with the police and the media, but he didn't forget internal audiences. He realized the importance of getting accurate information to them as well as reassuring them that the shooting spree was over.

Carbonneau's office worked with the engineering school's PR department to get the word out quickly and effectively. They answered phone calls from shocked parents and students, broadcast the news over campus radio and TV stations, and conducted emergency meetings with deans and vice principals.

For the next several days, PR staff members learned to put their feelings on hold. "We often worked 20 hours a day and showed no emotion," Carbonneau says. "We just had to work." Their grief came later—after the funerals ended and the story disappeared from the front page. "That was the difficult time for our staff. We had a hard time working after that."

The University of Montreal's experience serves as a frightening reminder of the emotional and logistical challenges any PR office can face. Whether your crisis centers on the loss of lives or a governance scandal, communicating with faculty, staff, and students is just as vital as dealing with the media and outside publics.

Campus professionals, industry officials, and PR consultants agree: Successful internal communication during a crisis depends on the groundwork you lay when times are good.

Sally Ann Flecker is the editor of Pitt Magazine *at the University of Pittsburgh in Pennsylvania. At the time she wrote this article for the October 1990 CURRENTS, she was* Pitt's *senior editor.*

"There's only one thing you can control," says Patrick Jackson, public relations consultant and editor of *PR Reporter* newsletter, "and that's what you do before the crisis occurs."

In communicating with internal audiences during troubled times, keep three key words in mind: predict, prevent, and prepare.

PREDICT

If you can spot a disaster before it happens, you'll be better able to head it off. Here's advice on how to read the warning signs.

Keep your ear to the ground

The most obvious indicators are often right in front of you. When Director of Public Information Roselyn Hiebert walks through the University of Maryland College Park campus, she's on the alert for graffiti on the walls and posters on the telephone poles.

"Keep a finger on the pulse of student life," she recommends. "When you see graffiti—like 'Crush the Jewish Student Union' or 'Crush the Black Student Union'—alert your top administrators there's apt to be a problem." You've got to be especially worried if someone such as Louis Farrakhan, the black orator and controversial Nation of Islam leader, is scheduled to speak on your campus.

Develop good relations with the student newspaper staff

Again, students are often the best source of information on crises waiting to happen. Hiebert's routine schedule includes a weekly, hour-long meeting with the university president and representatives from the student media—radio, newspaper, and lately even television. All sides benefit from these sessions.

Not only do students have access to the president for comments on specific issues like how the health center is responding to a meningitis scare, but Hiebert can get a feel for what's bubbling under the surface on campus.

"These kids can tell you what's going to break next week," she says. "For example, they let me know about a rumor that was going around that some university employees had been jabbed with contaminated hypodermic needles mixed in with the trash. That gave me a chance to prepare before the story actually broke with local media."

Respecting student journalists can help ensure that they'll respect you during hard times, as Pima Community College learned last year during a three-part crisis.

The trouble started in February 1989, when a regional accrediting agency placed the college on probation because of governance problems. Then in March, Pima's board removed the college's president from office after discovering he had falsified his resume. And from February to July, four out of five members of the Board of Governors left office for reasons ranging from misuse of college property to illegal campaign practices.

Because the media relations office had routinely treated the students as professionals, the *Aztec Press* acted as an independent voice in covering the college's woes. "We treated them just like we treated other reporters," says Krista Neis, acting director of media relation. "They knew I would neither withhold information from them nor give them special treatment. As it turned out, we got thorough coverage, and the students got some scoops."

Look at the rest of the world

You need to be in touch with issues off campus, too. "Keep your antennae way up," suggests Mary Ann Aug, assistant vice president for university relations at the University of Pittsburgh. "Pay attention to the general issues around the country."

Aug recalls a phone conversation with her counterpart at a small college on the East Coast not too long after AIDS began making inroads into public awareness. Her colleague was on her way to deal with a demonstration: A professor had AIDS and the students didn't want to go to class.

"I got off the phone and said, 'We've got to have an AIDS policy,' then formed a task force that produced one," Aug says. Any issue that stirs up controversy at other campuses has a good chance of coming to yours.

Set up an issue-anticipation team

A group of alert people can often accomplish more than you can alone.

Consultant Jackson suggests uniting a "cross section of the campus community—students, faculty, administration, alumni, maybe even a neighbor." Then assign the team an issue—say, racism. Have members examine what's happening in society and on other campuses. And finally, have them look into the likelihood of such a problem erupting on your campus. Ask yourself: Are conditions here similar to places where there's been a problem? Does our campus have the same attitudes? Are there any warning signs, like a letter in the campus paper?

"Two things happen," says Jackson. "You will find a lot of stuff that you can stop before it explodes. Secondly, this cross section of people works together and emphasizes a common interest in the institution. They're actually practicing teamwork, starting the process of campus unity."

PREVENT

Let's say you do see the handwriting on the wall. (Literally.) What next?

You'll need to act fast to prevent a potential crisis from becoming a full-blown one. To do this, institutions and corporations take a variety of different approaches.

Walk into the lion's den

"Where we often make our biggest mistakes in internal communications is that we fail to communicate with our critics," says Langley. You can't deal well with opposing opinions if you've made no effort to learn what they are.

Take the University of Cincinnati, Langley's former post. In the mid-'80s, the administration routinely learned the faculty union's position on collective bargaining discussions only when the press called for an official response. Langley turned this potentially disastrous situation into a less divisive one with a simple act. He walked over to the head of the union's office and introduced himself.

"Too often when you come under criticism, your tendency is to duck," he says. "I don't confront. I just go over and say, 'Here I am. Since we seem to be talking about each other in the press, I'd like you to know who I am.' I've noticed when I've done it how disarming it is."

By communicating with the union head before releasing any statement to the press, Langley lessened the chance for misunderstanding. "Something wonderful happened in the process," he says. "What I was saying was not misinterpreted by the press or by others outside. The union representatives were less likely to react in a prickly way if they knew what my approach was and why I felt the need to communicate certain facts to them."

Convene a focus group

You can also learn from the experience of industry executives. Before Motorola, Inc., decided to develop a universal drug-testing policy, the company conducted a series of focus groups with a demographic mix of employees throughout the country. The objective of the focus groups, conducted from October 1989 to April 1990, was to find out what employees thought about drugs in the workplace and whether Motorola should develop a testing policy, says Steve Biedermann, the Schaumburg, Illinois-based corporate director of employee communication.

Some 80 percent of participants supported the idea of an expanded policy. Some, however, struggled with the issue of invasion of privacy.

Biedermann used information from the focus groups to construct a communication plan centered on employee awareness and education. In addition to supervisory and employee training, the plan mapped out communications before, during, and after the announcement. The plan also provided for a briefing book and videotapes to help managers explain the policy. Managers and supervisors received the word about the imminent policy in mid-May, and the entire corporation got the announcement two weeks later. "So far there's been very little noise," Biedermann says.

Langley recommends a similar approach on campus. At Georgia Tech, the director of human relations and members of the external affairs staff sit down with students at the beginning of every semester, find out their concerns, and then have the president respond to the larger student population. This works for two reasons: Students appreciate being asked how they feel and tend to be impressed when the president proves he or she has taken the time to try to solve a problem.

"Whether it's acquaintance rape or another difficult issue, all students really want to know is, are you aware? Are you doing something about it? Are you trying?" Langley says.

"What they're most worried about is indifference. If they're not reassured, they tend to think the worst. Actively seeking out the issues is important."

Bringing opposing factions together *before* trouble erupts

"If you can't avoid a crisis, you can minimize it in many ways," says Hiebert at Maryland. "For instance, when Louis Farrakhan visited campus last spring, we knew there might be racial tensions between black and Jewish groups because we had encountered volatile situations when Kwame Toure, another controversial black speaker, came to campus."

Among her suggestions for preventing a crisis: Bring together the appropriate groups for mutual planning and discussion, establish rules, and mediate if necessary. It's more difficult to dismiss another's point of view when you've met face to face many times. As a result of Hiebert's intensive planning sessions, Farrakhan's visit was peaceful. What's more, in an evaluation session afterward, the planning group discussed ways to create greater harmony among black and Jewish students in the future.

Provide a retreat

Sometimes you can avert a crisis by producing a place to communicate with each other.

That's what Oregon Episcopal School discovered in March 1990 when the campus community was reminded of an earlier tragedy. In 1986, seven students and two faculty died in a mountain-climbing accident. One parent sued for negligence, and the suit came to trial this spring. Sensing that the trial and sensational media coverage would take a toll on the school, PR Director Mariann Koop set up a "safe room" in a small reading room in the middle of campus for troubled faculty, staff, parents, and trustees.

Throughout the four-week trial, the room provided conversation, information, and nourishment. People went there to talk to each other and receive news of the trial from a designated courtroom observer. Koop also made dessert, fruit, and coffee available at all times—"food for comfort and caffeine for energy," she says.

This welcoming atmosphere allowed faculty and staff to relax and in turn provided needed support to students. "We gave people a safe place to be together with others who had lived through the initial horror of the accident," Koop says. "What could have been an extremely painful time was instead calm and nurturing."

PREPARE

For every potential crisis you can foresee and forestall, there will always be one that you can't see coming. But if you have a plan to help you get out the right messages, you'll have less chance of being caught off guard—and your communications will go more smoothly. Consider these elements when you're developing or revising your plan.

Identify your internal audiences

Consider current students, faculty, staff, parents, alumni, friends, and neighbors of the institution, and prospective students.

Langley at Georgia Tech suggests taking this step further. "Think in clear terms about the audience and don't generalize," he says. "Segment as much as possible. Think about specific organizations within any campus community. Identify minority groups. Identify opinion leaders—people who are outspoken but highly regarded by their colleagues, although not necessarily by the administration." For example, Langley has identified the minority affairs committee and faculty senate committees and subcommittees.

Pinpoint the people who are responsible for communicating with key internal constituencies

The University of Pittsburgh's plan builds in a fail-safe communications tree. It designates not only senior administrators on the front line but also first and second alternates. In the university relations department, Aug is first in the chain, then the director of media relations, then the director of publications.

Aug also takes advantage of pre-programmed fax dialing for instant updates to inform those who are involved. For example, when a recent oil spill on nearby rivers threatened Pitt's water supply, Aug's office was able to fax hourly water usage bulletins to managers in all 56 campus buildings.

You might want to make key names available to others, too. Every year at the University of Maryland, Hiebert gives senior administrators a wallet-sized laminated card. The card includes the office and home phone numbers of important leaders—the president and the directors of environmental safety, student affairs, health services, and so on. A handy tool at 2 a.m., it precludes the problem of unlisted numbers.

Make a good-faith effort to inform your internal audience first

Clarke College had to act on instinct when fire destroyed four of 10 buildings, including the main administration building, in May 1984.

Clarke placed such a high premium on this, in fact, that during the fire the president herself went up and down the street with a bullhorn saying that Clarke would remain open, emphasizing that exams would take place, and telling employees to report for work the next morning.

Pima Community College, too, placed its highest priority on internal audiences. "Without a doubt, our greatest concern was making sure faculty, staff, and students understood the implications of the various events," Neis says. "We reassured them whenever possible that we were making progress at the college."

The marketing and media relations offices took several vital steps to accomplish this. In February 1989, when the accrediting agency put Pima on probation, the college bought space in the student paper to run a letter from the president. The letter explained the terms of the agency's decision but also emphasized the positive: The probation would affect neither academic credits nor financial aid. The same letter went to every student in every class on Pima's three campuses.

Neis also worked with the president's office to get the word out to faculty and staff. Special editions of the Bulletin, Pima's weekly internal news sheet, reiterated that the probation would not affect academics. In addition, the president's office sent letters to faculty members' homes to keep them up to date through the summer.

Pima took a different tack after the board of governors removed the president from office. Within a week, a 10-minute videotape announcing the appointment of the acting president was broadcast via the internal TV network to cafeterias and student centers on the college's three campuses. The tape, which featured the new president explaining the steps she was taking to stabilize the institution, also appeared on the channel designated for students taking courses off campus via television.

Neis says these varied communication techniques helped the campus community to not only survive the turmoil but also to thrive: "There's nothing like a crisis to get people to rally around a cause." Pima is still on probation, but enrollment has held steady, faculty members have not deserted the institution, and a new board of governors is functioning well. Best of all, the college has a new president—one with impeccable credentials.

In the event of an accident, designate an information site

Clarke College had to establish a way to communicate quickly after the fire. "One of the critical things we did was set up a central area to provide information, even if it meant putting up large bulletin boards and keeping them up to date by the hour," says Jane Daly Seaberg, then director of public relations at Clarke and now assistant executive director of PR at Georgetown University.

In deciding where to set this up, Seaberg recommends that you know and use campus traffic patterns. "In our case, our hub was destroyed," she says. "So we used the building that then housed the cafeteria, campus post offices, and (as a result of the fire) all administrative offices."

Langley at Georgia Tech points out why this step is so necessary on a college campus. "What we lose going from high school to a university is homeroom, a session every day where you learned what was going on," he says. Some institutions respond to that need with electronic methods.

In addition to helping get out information, Seaberg identifies a hidden benefit of a central communications area: "A main, centralized place seems to draw people together. That community-building process is very important."

Work the phones

Rumor spreads faster than fire. "The switchboard is the initial point of rumor and gossip in a crisis," says Hiebert. "If you have a good working relationship with your key switchboard operators, they know to call you immediately when someone says three women have been abducted from the dorm. You can stop the rumor at the switchboard."

Hiebert also recommends using an answering machine in the public information office to quell rumors or efficiently pass along information to faculty, staff, students, and parents. "If you have an answering machine, you can immediately record a message: 'No, there was no fire in the student union at 8:40 p.m.' Operators can transfer calls to the answering machine to increase the number of people they can respond to quickly."

A phone bank—perhaps in the alumni phonathon center—can be another useful tool. In some situations, it may be wise to choose your best people to answer the phones. Says Seaberg, "We picked the people who had the most experience—people in admissions, senior administrators, front people, directors. You have to project as strong an image as possible."

If you can, route calls from the campus community to people who are prepared to deal with the special needs of faculty, staff, and students. To make sure you pass along a consistent message, provide a script as well as up-to-date fact and information sheets.

Make your emergency plan widely available

Consultant Jackson recommends printing a version of it on the one tool *everyone* on campus uses—the internal phone book. "Spell it out. Have it where everyone keeps bumping into it," he says. "Include an outline of the average person's responsibility. Provide a number to call if people hear rumors or if the siren goes off."

In the end, evaluate

"Crises are not the easiest things to live through," says Hiebert. "But they're interesting. The more you're prepared and the more you evaluate what happened when it's over, the better you'll do the next time. And you can always count on a next time. The situations may change, but crises will never go away."

Hiebert's words apply at the University of Montreal, where the effects of last year's rampage linger. Faculty, staff, and students continue to talk about the murders. Some women are still angry and fearful. Students of both sexes are more conscious of violence against women.

The tragedy also catapulted the PR office into action: Carbonneau is developing a plan to guide his office in the event of another emergency. Not only will the plan make crisis communication easier, but also it will act as a reminder of what the future may hold.

"We thought an incident like this could never happen in Canada," Carbonneau says. "We hope nothing like this will ever happen again. But we know it is possible."

CHAPTER • 16

Communicating in a Crisis

The good news is that candor, credibility, and cool heads can keep the bad news from getting worse

Lindy Keane Carter

Last year's news coverage of the turmoil at Southern Methodist University was *so* heavy that the *New York Times* ran a story on how heavy the coverage was. At times SMU was swarming with as many as a hundred national and local reporters and technical personnel. Many camped out in the Office of News and Information for hours at a stretch. They clamored for facts, interviews, photo opportunities, parking spaces, phones, and aspirin.

The stories unfolded in tantalizing episodes. First a former football player claimed that he received improper benefits while playing for SMU. Nine days later, the president retired. Next the Board of Trustees launched an investigation into the leadership of SMU, and the NCAA suspended the football program until 1988. Then Texas' governor, who had served as chair of the SMU Board of Governors, revealed that he knew about the payments to football players. The board of governors voluntarily disbanded.

And if all that weren't enough to make the SMU public relations staff wish for a nice quiet job at PTL, there was the unrelated departure of the vice president for university relations for a position across town and the dismantling of the Office of University Relations. Consequently Pat Sites, then director of news and information, found herself reporting directly to the interim president and his special assistant just when the first negative stories began to surface.

"None of us recommends that office structure," says Sites. But she handled each development as it came up and thanked her stars for the positive image her staff had been quietly helping to build over the years.

"Bryant Gumbel and Ted Koppel aired our problems, that's true," she says. "But they prefaced their stories with 'How can something like this happen to such a fine institution?'" On balance, Sites believes SMU fared as well as she could have hoped.

Although most campus controversies don't grow into such tempests, a little turmoil is a normal part of the college PR office. This isn't surprising, given the fact that campuses are places where opinions collide, teenagers experiment, and millions of public and private

Lindy Keane Carter is assistant director of the capital campaign at Loyola College in Maryland. At the time she wrote this article for the November/December 1987 CURRENTS, she was the magazine's assistant editor.

dollars get spent. Campus PR directors should wake up each morning ready for unpleasant surprises.

And in fact, many do. To find out how some senior PR professionals prepare to deal with negative publicity, CURRENTS asked several to share the principles by which they operate. Virtually all pointed out that the best measures are preventive. Still, most acknowledge that some problems are impossible to predict. Here's how to handle them in a way that will help you remain in control.

Keep cool

Remember that negative publicity isn't the end of the world. (And find a tactful way to get that message across to anxious higher-ups.) Even SMU has spotted no discernible damage to its academic health. Although the total number of applicants was down last spring, entering students' SAT scores were up. Furthermore, faculty recruitment was unimpaired and student retention held up well. Gifts were down by $8 million from the previous year's record high of $29 million, but Sites points out that Texas' soft economy may be equally at fault.

It also helps to remember that reporting controversy is a journalist's job. To stress this fact, Ed Meek, director of public relations at the University of Mississippi, refers staff members and his journalism students to the textbook *Four Theories of the Press* by Fred Siebert, Theodore Peterson, and Wilbur Schamm.

As Meek sees it, America's mass media currently operate on the social responsibility theory, which says that the reporter's duty is to "raise a controversy to the level of public discussion." That's why, Meek says, "we shouldn't be defensive when a reporter calls asking probing questions."

Finally, say the pros, keep your sense of humor, use your manners, and get enough rest. You may not be able to control the story, but you can to a large extent control the climate in which everyone operates.

Take charge of the story

If you're fortunate enough to avoid being blindsided by a negative story, you'll have time to gather the facts and plot your course of action. Contemplating how you would answer certain questions may convince you it's best to take a wait-and-see approach. (Many PR directors have successfully gambled that their negative stories would never get out, but they stress that each situation is different.)

Sometimes you may not be able to release any facts—such as private information about employees or students, or facts pertaining to a case under litigation. But whenever you can, put yourself in a proactive position. Then you can control the story.

"Bad news is bad, but it's worse if you let the media take control," Meek points out. "If you call a news conference, you're being responsible, maintaining credibility, and getting out accurate information."

Lt. Col. Ben Legare, director of public relations at the Citadel in South Carolina, knew he had to move fast when he heard that Charleston television stations were receiving anonymous calls about an incident between five white cadets and a black cadet. The callers were saying that during the night the five had entered the black cadet's room and harassed him with racial slurs.

Within a few hours, Citadel's president gathered Legare, the cadets, and appropriate commanders for a frank assessment of what actually occurred. Then Legare called the local newspaper (which hadn't yet received the tip-offs) and read the facts over the phone so the paper could meet its deadline. Next, Legare's staff wrote a story for release and read that over the phone to the TV reporters.

Designate credible sources

"If there is not one voice, there will be babble," says Richard Conklin. As assistant vice president for university relations at the University of Notre Dame, he teaches a course on crisis communication at the annual CASE Summer Institute in Communications.

Meek says that in an emergency only a single source—usually the senior PR official—can provide the big picture. Even so, other situations may require responses from hospital directors, deans, and academic authorities, for example. Certainly you've given high-level administrators such as these media training already. But have you thought of everyone you might ever need to call upon?

After a murder-suicide stemming from a domestic quarrel between two Virginia Commonwealth University employees, Stephanie Halloran, acting director of media relations, found out the hard way that a key security officer had not attended any of the PR office's media training workshops. At the news conference he answered yes or no—and that's all.

Says Halloran, "If it hadn't been for the physician who was also answering questions, that conference would've been a disaster. I'll never again use someone who doesn't have a proven track record."

While the multiple spokesperson approach can sometimes create confusion, it does have at least one advantage: You protect your speakers from burnout. This is especially important if your controversy stretches on for weeks or months.

"Watch for the fatigue factor," says Sites of SMU. "If I could've done something differently, I would've shared the load among more people."

In fact, you must always keep in mind your responsibility to protect your spokespersons. They have certain rights—including the right to get back to work after making a statement, points out Mary Still, director of news services at the University of Missouri-Columbia. "Issue a statement that gives the facts and allows the president to continue his or her day," she says. A news release may also prevent the spokesperson's being misquoted and eliminate the media's opportunity to shoot videotape—thereby lessening the story.

Hide nothing

"If the truth hurts, then that's tough," says Matthew Maguire, director of news services at

Rensselaer Polytechnic Institute. "If a story is true, then even the appearance of trying to worm out of it can compound the negative consequences."

Legare agrees. Even when reporters and crew from CBS' "West 57th Street" called, the Citadel PR staff invited them to film anything and interview anyone. Their candor paid off. When the black cadet refused to speak to them (or any other members of the media, for that matter), "they respected that because they knew we'd been open about everything else," says Legare.

Besides strengthening your credibility, baring all from the beginning has another advantage: You prevent reporters from slowly unearthing facts that can keep a story alive forever. To make reports about SMU as accurate as possible, Sites produced a warts-and-all media packet that the staff updated throughout the academic year.

React carefully to errors

Nearly all PR pros agree that reporting mistakes are more common than they'd like. What you do about them will depend on the source of the error, its impact, its size, and your relationship with the reporter. Usually, many professionals say, it's best to let sleeping dogs lie.

"You can make a minor story major by commenting on an error," says Meek of the University of Mississippi. "I've never called a newspaper or TV station to complain. But I have called and given additional information. And I can't recall a situation where we couldn't get the correct information picked up when we called with a pleasant attitude."

RPI's Maguire says you have to ask yourself what's to be gained by securing a correction. "It will give another day's life to the story and make people wonder why the university is approaching this problem in such a nit-picky way."

Legare found one story so biased, though, that he just couldn't let go. A reporter from a major Southern newspaper had interviewed one black cadet and based a lengthy article solely on this cadet's negative comments about the Citadel.

"We didn't back off from that newspaper," says Legare. "We commented in various interviews that some out-of-state newspapers were not fair in their reporting. This caused the editors to review their analysis of the Citadel incident and begin more factual and objective coverage."

After Legare eventually won the editors over with his candor, the editors concluded that the paper needed to talk with other cadets. Later the paper ran several favorable stories and editorials. It also launched an investigation into the writer's reporting methods.

Every once in a while, however, a story comes out that makes a public relations director not only want to wake up sleeping dogs but also to use a cattle prod to do it.

Sharon Kha, director of the Office of Public Information at the University of Arizona, isn't the first PR officer to open the newspaper over breakfast and see a front-page story that kills her appetite. But she may be the only one who saw a same-size headline the next day that said, "The Star Was Wrong!"

The *Arizona Daily Star* reported in March 1985 that the University of Arizona bought its basketball uniforms from a manufacturer that paid UA's head coach a consulting fee. The university's attorney, who had been interviewed by the reporter who filed this story, immediately knew that the reporter had misused his quote and built an incorrect case on it.

By the time Kha hit her office and began gathering the facts, the attorney had already called the *Star*'s editor ("on a personal basis," says Kha) and objected to the way his information had been used. An investigation by the editors proved the story was wrong—and the sports editor and the reporter, faced with reassignments, quickly resigned.

Watch for reporting trends

As reporters search for local angles on hot national topics, many may find just the scandal they're looking for on your campus. As PR pros at institutions with large athletic programs know, these days campus sports are making news on the front page as well as the sports page. One recent example: The *Macon Telegraph-News*' 18-article series on the graduating rates of athletes at the University of Georgia and Georgia Tech, which won a Pulitzer Prize in 1985.

At the March 1986 Investigative Reporters and Editors conference for journalism students, a seminar called "Sports Scandals: The Big Payoff of Big-time College Sports" was led by Chuck Cook of the *Memphis Commercial Appeal*. As in Memphis, the home of Memphis State University. As in the paper that in 1985 ran front-page articles for 30 straight days about the MSU basketball coach's involvement with people under investigation by a federal grand jury for gambling.

Charles Holmes, director of university and community relations at MSU, says he was caught off-guard by the local media's clamor for information. "In retrospect," he says, "I can see it was the result of this new thrust of sports reporting."

To grapple with all the attention, Holmes called PR officials at other institutions that had dealt with sports scandals: Clemson University and the universities of Georgia and Kentucky, among others. He learned that negative publicity was unpleasant but not fatal to an institution. This helped him and his staff continue their usual policy of communicating openly and frequently with the press.

"That was tough sometimes," he allows. "But once you go to 'no comment,' your publics only become more confused."

Take advantage of the attention

As long as your institution is news, make sure you establish relationships with reporters you've only dreamed of meeting, sell your good news, and pitch future stories.

"Build your credibility while you're in the spotlight," advises Sites of SMU. "If you can be thorough when it's not to your advantage, then they'll believe you when it is."

Throughout last year, SMU's PR staff constantly inserted positive angles as they answered the media's negative questions. They did this by using bridging mechanisms. For example, when answering a call about campus dissent over football, the staff member would say,

"Yes, it's true that factions have arisen. But you need to know that faculty and students are working together on a town meeting next week to air the differences."

"But you've got to have your facts at hand," advises Sites. "Reporters won't wait for a follow-up call."

SMU also invited media to come back and cover the campus during 1987-88—and they're coming. Sites says the *Chronicle of Higher Education* is scheduled to attend this month's homecoming events: a soccer game and other sports activities. "I'll bet that's the first time the *Chronicle* ever covered anybody's homecoming!" she laughs.

A few months ago the University of Missouri found itself at the center of attention because of a journalism professor's racial slur and the resulting outcry from minority students. News Services Director Still capitalized on the situation by making sure all news of minority scholarships, apprenticeship programs, and faculty accomplishments got out. To her delight, several media outlets picked up her releases—especially in St. Louis, which is one of the university's prime minority recruitment areas.

Conklin tells of the time a public interest group stirred up students and reporters by distributing material saying that Notre Dame was conducting hazardous research on recombinant DNA. After establishing that the claims were false and calming students, PR staff members took advantage of the community's sudden interest in biological research. With the help of a Notre Dame scientist, they organized a public forum at which campus researchers and ethicists discussed the field's ethical implications.

"It was standing room only," says Conklin. And the local media covered the event thoroughly.

Communicate with constituents

You can give the media facts, but you can't write the stories for them. That's why it's imperative that you take advantage of the one medium you can control: your internal communication. Which vehicles you use depend on the situation.

From November 1986 to February 1987, while SMU awaited the NCAA rulings, Sites and other advancement officers prepared and carried out a constituency relations plan. They anticipated various reactions, identified the most important constituencies and their concerns, and discussed the best ways to reach the groups.

These ways included letters from the interim president, meetings with campus groups, in-depth coverage in the quarterly alumni magazine, and the introduction of a four-page, fact-filled newsletter called *SMU Update*, which fully reported developments in the athletic/governance controversies. The university mailed the first *Update* as soon as the NCAA levied its sanctions and later published two more issues. The newsletter, which went to alumni, donors, students, and parents, was well received, Sites says.

A similar newsletter worked well for the University of Missouri when students launched antiapartheid demonstrations and called for the university to divest its investments in South Africa. Originally designed to communicate with important alumni, legislators, and business leaders, the *Chancellor's Update* turned out to be popular on campus as well. News services director Still used it to explain why university police arrested students during demonstrations and why it allowed the student-erected shanty to remain on campus. The four-page, one-color newsletter, produced on a word processor, was easy to turn out overnight when necessary, says Still.

The Citadel inserted into an alumni newsletter a president's letter that gave the facts of the racial incident. Memphis State booked its president to speak at alumni meetings and distributed a letter to key supporters with background on what MSU was doing to investigate the charges against the basketball coach. MSU also sent the letter to the *Memphis Commercial Appeal*, which ran it in full.

And if you have a message that's student-related, send newsworthy reports to high school guidance counselors, suggests Maguire of RPI.

Weathering the story

"Bad news is like rain—inevitable and passing," says Conklin of Notre Dame.

There are bound to be times when controversy is as uncontrollable as the weather, such as when the faculty give the chancellor a vote of no confidence or fraternities disrupt the neighbors with one wild party too many. But as a professional, you must nonetheless try to at least set up an effective crisis intervention center, limit the damage, and line those clouds with as much silver as possible.

And, most important, keep your perspective. When it all blows over, your institution may not have taken such a bath after all.

An ounce of prevention

Read campus graffiti. Talk to the janitors. Schmooze with members of the chamber of commerce. Do whatever it takes to keep in touch with the word on campus and around town, for PR pros agree: The best way to keep from getting burned by bad news is to prevent things from getting too hot in the first place.

Here are some of the ways you can anticipate potential problems:

1. *Set up a system for monitoring what's happening on campus.* Your beat system is probably already telling you a lot. But have you trained yourself and your staff to really listen for trouble?

The key is to cultivate all kinds of sources. Let everyone from the president to the physical plant workers know that your PR staff wants to know what's going on and that you respect their opinions. Because the chief of police at one university notified the PR director when an animal-rights group applied for a demonstration permit, the director was able to brief the appropriate people and cut the demonstration short. Coverage was minor because there wasn't much of a story.

Get on every mailing list on campus. Charles Holmes, director of university and community relations at Memphis State University, regularly reads the schedules of upcoming guest speakers. That's how he knew that atheist Madalyn Murray O'Hair was coming to speak on campus. By the time local religious leaders started objecting, the PR office was ready to explain who sponsored her visit and why it was important for a university to examine a variety of viewpoints.

2. *Anticipate trouble.* Matthew Maguire, director of news services at Rensselaer Poly-technic Institute, watches for scribbled comments on bulletin boards or entered in the campus's computer bulletin board. "If some dissatisfaction has made its way into this type of campus media," he says, "it may make its way to the general media eventually."

For example, if Maguire saw a snide remark next to an announcement of a lecture on how to avoid sexual harassment, he'd call security personnel and the dean of women, ask if they were aware of recent reports of harassment, and prepare for possible media calls.

Also pay attention to the calendar, Maguire advises. During exam week and job recruit-ment time, for example, students are under a lot of stress. If your conversations with coun-selors or the job placement director lead you to believe you could be dealing with a suicide soon, one of your moves before any such tragedy occurs should be to prepare information on what your institution does to help students cope with stress. Other seasonal headaches: rush week or an annual wild party.

Stay in touch with students. Several years ago a PR director at a large Southern university learned through his student contacts that black students were going to demonstrate to object to the use of the Confederate flag on campus. Unfortunately, the chancellor failed to act on the PR director's advice, and the inevitable fistfight ended up in the international press. But that's another article.

Assume that problems plaguing peer institutions will spread to your campus. For example, the University of Pennsylvania and Temple University are located in Philadelphia and do medical research. When Penn began having problems with animal-rights activists, Emilie Mulholland, Temple's associate vice president for university relations, advised admin-istrators to review the campus animal policy and determine whether researchers were adhering to it.

3. *Make sure a senior PR official has access to top decision makers.* It's imperative that you make top academic administrators aware of the public consequences of their actions. Some PR officials are fortunate enough to attend board meetings; others meet regularly with vice chancellors or the president for briefings on their board's decisions.

If your attempts to gain access are spurned, at least put your advice in writing and persist in submitting it to the higher-ups. Mary Still, director of news services at the University of Missouri-Columbia, says her office has been bold about asking about board decisions. "When we're on the front page, it is our business," she says.

CHAPTER • 17

At Odds Over Openness

Corporate and campus PR pros tell how they fight closed minds and mouths during a crisis

Jan Michelsen

The time: The 1960s.
The place: Brown University.
The crisis: The university's black students walk out, demanding that the university increase the number of black students and faculty.

The PR strategy: The university releases no information, no statement, no comment.

The results: The reporters get the story themselves. And, as far as the university is concerned, they get the story wrong.

That was then. This is now. As PR professionals dealing with crises at our institutions, we've come a long way.

Or have we? Despite volumes of testimonials by media relations veterans, despite sterling examples of just how well crisis management principles work, people still have trouble applying them. And the reason is unchanged: You can lead administrators to a press conference, but you can't make them speak.

"Many of my colleagues say they knew what they would have done *if* they had the proper authority, the proper support, and the ear of the right people," says Bob Roseth, director of information services at the University of Washington. But that's a big if. And that tiny word can mean a huge difference between public support and public humiliation.

The chasm between crisis management theory and practice has been the downfall of many an institution. Why do the problems arise and how can you, the PR professional, prevent them? To find out, CURRENTS asked senior professionals in corporate and institutional PR about their strategies for convincing top management to release information during a crisis. After all, one of the first steps toward uncorking reluctant executives is understanding why such reluctance occurs.

Why the beef?

Here are some possible explanations for high-level resistance.

Jan Michelsen is now attending law school at Indiana University. At the time she wrote this article for the October 1988 CURRENTS, she was director of hospital relations at Indiana University Medical Center.

• *Short-term views.* "Most errors in logic are made by viewing things in the short term," says Bob Reichley, vice president for university relations at Brown University. "Some top managers feel that if they withhold information today, the situation will disappear tomorrow. It takes only one crisis to learn that nothing is gained and a great deal is lost by sitting mute while a crisis erupts around you."

Many executives refuse to acknowledge that a problem exists. But denial just prolongs the agony. Ford Motor Co. operated under a siege mentality for years as it fought allegations that the gas tank on its Pinto was poorly designed and therefore dangerous.

• *Problem personalities.* Some executives are more committed to openness than others, notes Joe Hopkins, media relations manager for United Airlines. "It may boil down to an individual management style."

Certainly it's easier to obtain and release information in an environment where minds are already open. If you aren't in such an environment, take time to assess the attitudes of the people to whom you'll have to appeal for authority during a crisis. Then think about how you can convince them that a crisis calls for flexibility, spontaneity, and forthrightness.

• *Paranoia.* Hostility toward the media or unwillingness to "come clean" may be the result of a bad experience. Or it may be the result of no experience at all—just fear of the unknown. CEOs without a lot of exposure to crisis management may be uninformed about which are the best approaches to take.

• *High stakes.* If top management feels there is blood to be shed or face to be lost by speaking up, the risk may seem too great to bear, politically or personally. Many executives hope that staying silent will help cut the losses—especially in sticky situations where the person responsible for the crisis is part of the executive team.

The three steps to cultivating trust

Despite such fear and loathing in some organizations, others come through a crisis relatively unscathed. In many cases this is due to one or more of the following: the PR officer's standing in the organization's hierarchy, an education program for decision makers, and well-publicized crisis planning.

1. The PR person's position

Does it matter where you, as a public relations professional, fit in the organization? Is the title of vice president necessary—or sufficient—for getting cooperation? How do you get access to the people, the facts, and the secrets you need? How can you be sure you're included in the meetings where major decisions take place?

It's not the level you occupy but the confidence top management places in you that really matters, says Susie Fleck, director of public relations for the University of Indianapolis. "It sometimes takes years to earn that credibility. They'll see if you can get the job done before they trust you in an advisory role. It's essential to have the ear of the president."

The PR director's status depends entirely on the relationship between the PR executive and the CEO, say Ed Meek, director of public relations at the University of Mississippi. "The CEO must have confidence in my reading of the tea leaves, my ability to deal with problems before they become public issues."

The key is to ensure that your skills are more than adequate, he says. "The burden is on you to seek respect and involvement. Being seen as top management is something that has to be earned."

Of course, all the skills in the world won't help you if your CEO simply won't acknowledge the place of good public relations. Save yourself some grief by finding out up front where you'll stand, suggests Reichley of Brown. "When you take a job, have some understanding of what your fundamental position will be in an inevitable crisis."

2. The CEO's education

Unfortunately, no sure-fire argument will convince all presidents. A lot depends on the situation, the institution, and the history and predisposition of the chief executive. But some strategies seemed to work for those we interviewed. They're worth a try if you are battling a "no comment" mentality.

• *Raise awareness.* "Make sure that everyone understands what a crisis is—and how swiftly one can occur," says Steven Fink, president of Los Angeles-based Lexicon Communications, a crisis management firm that has counseled academic and corporate clients around the world.

• *Deal with feelings*. No matter how finely tuned a plan, how dramatic a role-playing session, the real thing feels different. Plan for that.

Lexicon Communications has a staff psychologist who trains participants to make decisions under stress. "When a crisis has erupted, an organization may find that management is incapable of making decisions," Fink explains. This "analysis paralysis" may mean lost time and lost opportunities for action. In those cases, you may need to have ready an in-house crisis management team or even an outside expert who can be available to offer the much-needed objectivity.

• *Learn from your mistakes.* Better yet, learn from others'. Make a current crisis your opportunity to plan for future crises.

After your institution or another has made a mistake, point it out. Say, "if we/they had only done this, such and such might not have happened." For example, when colleagues on another campus are despairing because they're forced to provide inaccurate or inadequate information, mention the problem to your CEO and remark that things don't have to be that way. This will lay the groundwork for openness when your time comes.

• *Appeal to ego.* In the corporate world, media relations is part of a CEO's training. After all, highly educated, highly motivated business managers usually make the best decisions—including PR decisions, says Ted Smyth, director of corporate affairs for H.J. Heinz. Most top executives would no more ignore the rules of good crisis PR than they would ignore proven wisdom on finance, marketing, or operational principles.

Subtly challenge campus executives who are roadblocks to meet the business world's standards. Convince your CEO that, as successful corporate leaders know, it's in his or her best interest as well as the institution's to disclose any necessary information.

• *Explain the value of telling your side of the story.* Says Reichley, "The argument that information will get out anyway—and that it's better to give your side of it—is a convincing one."

Remind top managers of this basic rule of good media relations: If you want the media to report on the good things, you have to be candid with them about the bad.

• *Share the burden.* Managers may be more willing to go public with news if they're not the only source of information—or blame.

For example, when the University of Indianapolis held a news conference during a devastating dormitory fire, the state fire marshal accompanied the president to the news conference to answer questions about probable cause and the structural safety of other campus buildings. And when a stadium collapsed at the University of Washington, the institution was careful to act only as a conduit of information to the contractor, who was responsible.

• *Help higher-ups gain perspective.* Unlike those in the corporate or political arena, managers in the nonprofit world aren't so accustomed to knocks and shakes from the media. Loosely defined, a crisis might include any event that draws intense media attention or any situations that carry the potential for making very public mistakes. College administrators may overreact to any negatives or single out criticisms and bad news without seeing the whole picture. That's why you have to show them that not all crises are necessarily bad.

For example, when CBS approached United Airlines about sitting under the hot lights for the news program "48 Hours," the airline decided to take a different tack from one of its competitors and give reporters access to United's entire operation. Company officials were pleased with the results, and their competitors lost a golden opportunity.

• *Reassert that crises will happen.* What's more, you, as a public relations person, have the expertise needed to make them go as smoothly as possible.

"It's your job to help position your team and enlighten them as to the realities they will face in certain situations," says Blake Lewis, who was PR director at St. Luke's Hospital in Davenport, Iowa, when Cary Grant died there. As macabre as it may sound, hospital PR offices (and others) have to plan for the inevitability of death.

"Don't be afraid to discuss the unthinkable with senior management," Lewis told *Communication World* magazine, "even though they don't want to think about who will be reading statements at 2 on a Sunday morning."

3. A well-publicized plan

Although crises in the corporate world may be grueling, at least you can anticipate to some extent how they could happen. Utilities inevitably experience blackouts, restaurants face the scrutiny of the health department, and airlines are subject to crashes and hijackings.

In a university, as in a small city, crises can arise from almost any arena. They can run the gamut from a stadium collapse to a personnel matter, such as the firing of a coach or a faculty sex scandal. With such a variety of crises possible, can planning help you prevent the last-minute clam-up?

"Yes!" says Fink of Lexicon Communications. "Anyone who says you can't plan for a crisis doesn't have a good grasp of the concept." He suggests that rules for responding to crises become part of the corporate discipline.

Johnson & Johnson did just that in perhaps the most famous crisis success story of the '80s. When seven people died from cyanide-laced Tylenol capsules in Chicago in 1982, company officials had already been thoroughly indoctrinated with a 40-year-old corporate philosophy that customers are the No. 1 concern. Working from this solid foundation, officials could quickly set priorities and divided up responsibility.

Says CEO and Board Chair James E. Burke, "Crisis planning didn't see us through the tragedy as much as the credo that prompted the decisions that enabled us to make the right early decisions." The company's first crucial decision, which the PR staff made immediately with management's full support, was to cooperate with the news media. "Every one of us knew what we had to do," says Burke. "There was no need to meet. We had the credo to guide us."

The true measure of success: Despite worldwide publicity that linked Tylenol with product tampering, Johnson & Johnson had recaptured 90 percent of Tylenol's U.S. market share five months after the tragedy.

In preparing a crisis plan for your institution, you may be able to raise administrators' awareness of potential problems and discern who your opponents might be. The following tips aren't a complete guide to how to set up a crisis plan. But these basics will help get you and your colleagues thinking about how your institution will respond in the next crisis.

• *Do your homework.* Put everyday campus information into written form, ready to hand to reporters. These might include bios of the president and other prominent faculty and staff, up-to-date lists of trustees, background sheets on campus issues that come up often, and so on.

When the PR staff at the University of Indianapolis heard about the dormitory fire, "I knew we'd have everyone on our doorstep," Fleck says. "So my secretary and I worked quickly to get the history of the building together immediately."

• *Anticipate the worst.* Good crisis management is proactive. Unfortunately, most plans are reactive because people don't like to think about, and therefore don't plan for, adversity.

Many corporations, such as United Airlines, have an elaborate crisis plan that they review quarterly. At United everyone knows beforehand what his or her job is, says Media Relations Manager Hopkins. "There's an orderly process for getting information cleared and people designated to provide the information in certain situations." This saves time, eliminates confusion when order is most important, and gets everyone to commit to a plan of action and division of responsibility.

• *Be prepared.* A tenet that's served the Boy Scouts for decades is also simple but effective wisdom for crisis planning. "The key to crisis communication—in the corporate or nonprofit area—is to make sure you have cemented managerial buy-in before things go down," says Al Orendorff, communications specialist at Allstate Insurance. "Cover all possible scenarios and prepare a persuasive enough case before the fact." Set it in stone, or at least on paper, in advance, he recommends.

PR pros also say that there's no point in hoping you can establish trust with the media when the crisis is breaking. You have to do that beforehand.

"It's difficult to argue reason in the heart of a crisis," says Reichley of Brown. "Setting the rules then is virtually impossible." He suggests discussing the matter in quieter times—at staff meetings or in management retreats when opinions can be voiced, policies devised, and commitment cultivated. "Look to the long-term effect of actions and policies," Reichley says, "and make the move that conscience and reason tell you are correct."

Fleck agrees that management must take the well-spent time to determine the best answers. "Say, 'Here are the questions they're going to ask—what are we going to answer?'"

Role playing can help with this, Fleck says. A former reporter herself, she can simulate even the most hard-nosed interrogation. She has also succeeded at getting management and faculty members to calm down and realize that in a crisis, as in life, the expectation of doom usually far exceeds the reality.

When discretion is in order

On the other hand, reluctance to divulge everything may sometimes be appropriate. Says United's Hopkins, "It's important to remember that just because the media ask a question, that doesn't mean it has to be answered." For example, he says, it takes about six months to pinpoint the probable cause of an airplane accident. That's why it's not appropriate for an airline to comment on the cause in the first few days—even though reporters want to know.

In the academic world, as in most corporations, PR people are reticent about personnel matters. And when you don't have full information available or can't get it verified—say, in the case of what happened in a rape or murder—you should tell reporters so.

Imposed silence about some facts doesn't mean being uncooperative, however. "Our policy is still to be available to the media, to try our best to get them information, and to communicate as quickly as we are able," Hopkins says.

Building trust today

The November 1987 *PR Journal* included this view of effective crisis management from Anthony Katz, a senior PR officer at D-A-Y/Ogilvy & Mather Public Relations:

"The public relations professional's first and perhaps most important role is to convince top management of the need for detailed preparation—even when business is thriving and a crisis seems unimaginable. Without this top-level commitment, it is difficult to prepare fully. There is no single formula for developing this commitment; know your CEO's personality and your corporate structure and approach the situation accordingly."

So invest time and energy today in ensuring that you have access to top management and they trust you. Start a campaign to educate your top executives. And initiate activities that will prepare your institution for the inevitable. You'll encourage cooperation as well as raise the crisis consciousness of management and staff.

CHAPTER • 18

Learning the Legalities

Prepare yourself and your lawyers to handle campus crises

Victoria Stuart

Your phone rings at 3 a.m. The police have just arrested a student for selling drugs in the dormitories, and the local newspaper's chief investigative reporter wants an interview. Do you need to call the campus lawyer before you comment?

What you, as a representative of your institution, say during a crisis like this has great potential for creating sticky legal problems. But you can help yourself, too—by becoming familiar ahead of time with the basics of media law.

When to call in the lawyers

Certain types of crises almost cry out for help. According to Paul Dee, who has had six years' experience as legal counsel for the University of Miami, these crises involve:
- litigation or potential litigation;
- a violation of a law or regulation (or even the suggestion of it); or
- incidents with any hint of liability, such as murder, rape, burglary, accident, or injury.

Dee cautions you, however, to avoid hiding behind your lawyers; they don't have to be involved in every crisis. Use your own judgment, but also seek advice from the campus officials who administer the area in question, such as your athletic director, provost, or dean of students. Their expertise will guide you.

The three types of general crises mentioned above could apply to anyone. Andrew Schaffer, vice president and general counsel of New York University, goes on to name some crises specific to schools, colleges, and universities. He says you will probably need legal advice when:
- your institution is named in a major lawsuit;
- a student gets into trouble on or off campus and the media call for an official comment;
- your Board of Trustees is working on an important issue and reporters get wind of it; or
- legislative developments are affecting your institution or higher education in general.

Victoria Stuart is director of public relations at St. Thomas University. At the time she wrote this article for the November/December 1987 CURRENTS, she was assistant director of media relations at the University of Miami.

(An example of this occurred at Miami when classes taken under tuition-remission benefit plans became taxable income in Florida.)

If you're still not sure whether to get your lawyers involved, call and ask, Schaffer advises. If you are sure, call them—and call them fast.

Becoming acquainted

Of course, it's best to know your lawyers before trouble strikes. By establishing a good working relationship and educating each other on your respective needs, you'll help ensure smooth dealings. Remember: It's much easier to work out a hypothetical situation than a real emergency.

Larry Thompson, special assistant to the president at Ohio State University, suggests meeting with lawyers informally to discuss issues and problems. Include staff members (both yours and your lawyers') so that both groups understand the other's perspective.

"If communication is not established ahead of time, the lawyers' response may well be one that the communicator cannot live with," Thompson says.

Avoiding legalese

Lawyers are often cautious and highly specific about what they advise you to say simply because those words could come back to haunt you in court.

That's why you and your lawyers should discuss your comments and work together to state them in a way that will communicate your position most effectively. This will help you come up with safe but clear statements for the press.

Miami's Dee reminds us that the lawyer's role is to give advice and counsel, not necessarily to make policy decisions. Ideally, he says, your lawyers should tell you what verbal pitfalls to avoid.

Getting background in media law

Basic knowledge of media law is vital to making snap decisions in a crisis. Specific areas to bone up on include:

• *First Amendment rights.* These include freedom of speech and freedom of the press. Because the U.S. Constitution allows for varied interpretations, the greatest controversy surrounding this amendment involves the conflict between the right to a fair trial and the rights of a free press. If your institution becomes embroiled in a major court case, you might want to read the American Bar Association's book *The Rights of Fair Trial and Free Press*, which details specific guidelines for lawyers, police, court personnel, jurors, litigants, witnesses, and members of the media.

• *Libel.* This is a false statement printed or broadcast about someone that tends to bring that person into public hatred, contempt, or ridicule, or injures him or her in his or her business or occupation. Libel laws vary in each state, so become familiar with your own state's laws.

• *Slander.* Similar to libel, this involves spoken defamation.

• *Privacy.* Who's a "public figure" and who's a "private individual"? This is a more complex question than you might think simply because there are no hard-and-fast rules. However, Bruce W. Sanford, a partner with the Washington, DC, office of Baker and Hostetler (the national law firm that serves as general counsel for the Scripps-Howard newspaper chain), offers good guidelines to follow in his book *Synopsis of the Law of Libel and the Right of Privacy.*

Although written primarily for journalists, the book is helpful to PR people as well. It explains that the Supreme Court has defined two general kinds of public figures: (1) people who occupy positions of such persuasive power and influence that they are deemed public figures for all purposes, and (2) otherwise private individuals who have voluntarily thrust themselves into a significant public controversy in order to influence the issue's outcome.

Examples of public figures with "persuasive power and influence" could include book authors and college football coaches. Public figures by reason of participation in "public controversy" might include a college athlete who, for instance, takes it upon himself to speak out against an institution's athletic program.

And examples of nonpublic figures could include fund raisers for charities, major corporate stockholders, research scientists working on government grants, and criminal defendants.

Again, these definitions are subject to debate—as evidenced by the number of court cases that have grown up around them. Generally speaking, though, you can usually assume that someone is a public figure if:

1. To a large extent the individual has voluntarily sought the limelight or gotten involved in a particular public controversy;

2. A genuine public controversy exists (as opposed to a flap created by a publisher or broadcaster); and

3. The person has access to the media to rebut accusations.

• *Open records.* Each state has laws specifying which records are public or private. Your state press association is a good place to learn about state laws and the outcome of recent court cases involving access to public records.

• *The Buckley Amendment.* This is the popular name for the Family Educational Rights and Privacy Act, a federal law that protects the privacy of student records. Basically it covers two types of information: directory information (name, address, phone number, etc.), which is a matter of public record; and academic and student disciplinary records, which are private.

Sometimes, though, it's difficult to determine what is and isn't considered private information. For example, what if an alumnus dies and the local paper wants to publish a photo from an old yearbook? Yearbook photos aren't restricted by the amendment because the yearbook is considered published—and therefore public—information. But you shouldn't leave decisions like this to guesswork; seek legal advice before releasing anything questionable.

The Department of Education publishes regulations that further explain its policy for enforcing the Buckley Amendment. Failure to comply carries the potential of substantial penalties, including the withdrawal of federal funds from your institution. Many states have additional privacy laws, so consult your own state statutes as well. You can find all these regulations in law libraries and local law offices.

Where to look for help

If you want to brush up on media law or find out more about legal issues in higher education, there are several sources to which you can look.

For more background on media law, Martin L. Reeder, chair of the Media and Communications Law Committee of the Florida Bar Association, recommends the textbook *Mass Media Law*, Fourth Edition, by Donald R. Pember (William C. Brown, Dubuque, Iowa, 1987), and *The Journalist's Handbook on Libel and Privacy* by Barbara Dill (The Free Press, a division of Macmillan, Inc., 1986).

In addition, the American Bar Association's Forum Committee on Communications Law publishes a quarterly newsletter that you can order by subscription. Or you can write to the ABA for booklets on specific subjects, such as *Synopsis of the Law of Libel and the Right of Privacy* by Bruce W. Sanford (Scripps-Howard Newspapers, 1984), and *The Rights of Fair Trial and Free Press: The American Bar Association Standards*, prepared and published by the Standing Committee on Association Communications of the ABA (ABA Press, 1981).

If you need more than books, the American Bar Association hosts an annual media law conference. The conference is designed primarily as an issues forum for lawyers and members of the media, but it also can help the lay person. Other state bar associations and the National Association of College and University Attorneys offer conferences as well.

To learn more about current legal issues specific to higher education, Ohio State's Thompson suggests keeping up with the *Chronicle of Higher Education,* which he says is the best nontechnical source. He also recommends an article called "The Role of University Counsel" by Roderick Daane in the winter 1985 Special Symposium Issue of the *Journal of College and University Law*.

Make your own decisions

So the next time a reporter calls in the wee hours to ask about a campus controversy, you'll know what your choices are: Either you have enough information to make a brief comment and go back to sleep, or you have to call your lawyers for advice.

If you choose to call, don't worry about waking your lawyers up. Later all of you will rest easier, knowing that good relations between you kept the crisis from growing worse.

CHAPTER • 19

Keeping Your Cool

Here's how to stay in control under the hot lights

Kay Miller and Michael J. Baxter

The scene that spring morning in 1986 was nothing less than chaotic. The president of the University of Georgia, the state's flagship university, was set for what the media had billed as a showdown with the Board of Regents, the governing body of Georgia's university system.

The dispute began when developmental studies professor Jan Kemp successfully sued the University of Georgia for firing her for exercising her First Amendment rights in exposing preferential treatment of athletes. The controversy reached a climax after a systemwide audit of remedial studies departments led to what looked to be a heated face-off between the regents and Fred C. Davison, president of the University of Georgia.

On that day Davison's supporters, dressed in the school colors of red and black, lined the narrow hallway leading to the regents' board room. Reporters mobbed the doorway. Camera crews jockeyed for position. Spectators milled around the elevator.

From an office around the corner, members of the board of regents marched single file to the meeting room. Minutes later, President Davison appeared, sporting a bright red blazer and trailing an entourage. The supporters in red and black erupted into a spirited rendition of "Glory, Glory to Old Georgia." Videocams whirred, flashes popped, questions flew. The moment had come.

A mere 15 minutes later, it was all over. Instead of clashing with the regents, President Davison resigned—signaling the end of one of the biggest crises in the university's 200-year history and of the most intense media scrutiny we'd ever experienced.

Coping with crisis

Even if such a conflict had occurred a few decades ago, chances are it never would have gotten the all-out coverage it has in this age of live-at-5 broadcasts and 24-hour newspapers.

Kay Miller is director of system advancement and assistant to the chancellor, and Michael J. Baxter is director of publications for the University System of Georgia Board of Regents. The board of regents is the governing body for Georgia's 34 public colleges and universities. When they wrote this article for the November/December 1987 CURRENTS, Miller was assistant to the chancellor and Baxter was public relations specialist/editor for the board of regents.

Along with this increased attention has come the vital need for better public relations in higher education.

To be sure, some campus public information officers have been heard to mutter prayers of diversion. "Please, God," they'd whisper, "just one little hijacking or assassination to get us off the front page." Without downplaying the value of prayer, however, the staffs of the Georgia system office and of other institutions we've surveyed have found that a good crisis strategy can do much to keep a difficult situation from becoming impossible.

Our crisis plan, per se, didn't exist in the form of voluminous white pages in black spiral notebooks. But it existed nonetheless—a coherent strategy borne out of years of discussions, meetings, and a general spirit of cooperation among the PR staff and higher-ups in the central office.

After conferring with other institutions on crisis communications, we learned just how much carefully considered rules and practices can help keep you from tripping over yourself as you deal with everyone from the *Gwinnett Daily News* to "60 Minutes." Some important points:

1. *Make sure the staff speaks one language.* You or someone else in authority must see to it that the chief players get briefed on the facts as you have them. Depending on the size of your institution and the magnitude of your crisis, you may also want to designate a single representative to handle all questions.

An example: Georgia Southwestern College in Americus has a press emergency plan that allows for consistent communication. Key college officials each have a copy of the plan, which outlines where to go, whom to contact, even which telephones to use. No one—not even the college president—issues any statement to the media without the knowledge and input of Director of Public Information Patty Plotnick.

Plotnick says the plan was especially helpful in 1986, when two local men drowned in the campus lake and two students were charged with raping a 16-year-old girl. Like most towns, Americus had an abundance of "young, eager reporters," Plotnick says, who could be kept at bay only when a strong, central voice was speaking for the college.

2. *Review with officials what can and cannot be said.* The middle of a storm is no place to set policy. If you haven't already, determine now what sorts of information you can legally give out about arrests, accidents, injuries, or lawsuits. Then be sure to communicate it to others on campus—before questions come up.

For example, when the son of a former vice presidential candidate Geraldine Ferraro was charged with drug dealing last year at Middlebury College, the college's public affairs office was besieged by press inquiries. "Our office policy was to give directory information only," says director Ron Nief. "That means the name, the class year, the hometown." He felt it was a good policy because the federal Family Educational Rights and Privacy Act prohibits much more from being disclosed about a student.

3. *Help reporters out.* By establishing rapport with members of the media, you can offset some of the rumors that so often find their way into morning editions and nightly broadcasts.

Such a philosophy has worked well for David Parkman, public relations director at West Georgia College. "Reporters don't always want to talk with the PR guy," Parkman says, "so I just try to assist them."

For example, when an accident occurred in a chemistry lab at West Georgia a couple of years ago, Parkman knew reporters wanted to talk with someone in the chemistry department. So he arranged for them to speak with the person in charge of the lab at the time, and he set up other interviews on request. He says that giving reporter access to campus phones added to the spirit of cooperation.

Of course, cooperation has its limits. Says Middlebury College's Nief: "Our campus was open to [reporters] with the exceptions that they couldn't go into the dorms or dining halls, or into a classroom without the invitation of a faculty member. We assume that the students' homes are here—that the dorms are their bedrooms and the dining hall is their dining room."

4. *Treat reporters fairly.* Don't play favorites. No doubt you'll hear all sorts of excuses such as, "This is just for background" or "I have a longer lead time." During the Jan Kemp controversy the *Red and Black*, a student newspaper, begged for an advance copy of an audit of the University of Georgia's developmental studies department. We declined. Later, "60 Minutes" called to ask for the same information. Again we said no. Both may hate us today, but they can't accuse us of having a double standard.

5. *Be accessible.* Since a crisis knows no hours, you need to be on call day and night. It helps to keep reporters' home phone numbers with you so you can reach them if they couldn't find you earlier. This kind of preparation also helps to cut down on published rumors.

Accessibility can be difficult, especially when members of the media just can't seem to get enough, says Roselyn Hiebert, director of public information at the University of Maryland College Park. A good example is the uproar over the cocaine-related death of basketball star Len Bias.

"There were so many reporters camped out in my hallway that I couldn't get out the door without being bombarded," she recalls. "One time I had to go out a seldom-used exit and literally climb over some large ice cream machines to get to the chancellor's office."

6. *Avoid the words "no comment."* It sounds as if you're hiding something. When you simply cannot disclose certain information, say something like, "I'll be frank with you: We just can't say right now."

But be prepared for the press to treat "no comment" as a story in itself. One television station in Atlanta shot the "Information" sign on our door with the voiceover, "Information. This is what the board of regents' office wasn't giving today."

7. *Pounce on misinformation immediately.* Many public relations professionals think it's better not to wrangle with reporters over small errors. Big errors, however, may be another matter entirely.

For example, several members of the media reported last year that a prostitution ring was operating out of Brown University. In fact, those reports sprang from wrong information released by the chief of Providence police.

Of 46 women involved in an alleged Providence-centered ring, only six were current or former Brown students, says Eric Broudy, director of the university's news and information services. "The media placed the focus of the investigation at Brown when, in fact, it was a much broader, Providence-based of which Brown was only a small part."

When truly scandalous information is incorrectly reported, you've got to stand up for the truth, Broudy now says—even if it occasionally means retaliating against the media. But you must do so promptly and with absolute accuracy.

The day after the news from the police chief's news conference hit the papers, Brown held its own press conference, with the vice president for university relations presiding. "We corrected the errors and took certain media to task for sensationalizing the story and misleading their readers," Broudy says. The strategy appeared to work, because later stories shifted the focus from a Brown-centered ring to a Providence ring, and erroneous numbers no longer appeared.

Broudy says Brown missed the mark on another recent crisis: when students took a vote on stocking "suicide pills" in the campus infirmary in case of nuclear war.

"We waited too long to respond," he says. "Many in the media assumed that if the students voted to stock the suicide pill, we would have stocked it. We should have stated clearly from the start that the university had no intention of stocking such pills and that, in our view, the vote was a symbolic expression dramatizing the threat of nuclear holocaust.

"We eventually did say that, but our position would have been clearer had we stated it sooner."

8. *Never lie.* If your back is to the wall, follow the advice in Rule No. 6.

9. *Beware of the "other media."* Not all journalists work on the up-and-up. Reporters from sensational grocery-rack tabloids are especially notorious.

"One thing that was unnerving during our crisis," says Nief of Middlebury, "was the quasi-media presence from some of the less-respected newspapers. They don't function under the same set of rules the legitimate media use. They use tricks such as threats and false names."

Nief adds that one of these papers misquoted him or took his quotes out of context so often that he refused to return the reporters' calls. "And if they did get me on the phone, I just hung up. That's the only way to handle those people."

10. *Don't forget the public.* During the Kemp trial, we didn't foresee the flood of calls that came from John and Jill Q. Citizen. The fact is, there are plenty of people out there who want you to know what they think about your crisis. Common sense and good public relations dictate that you deal with these people courteously. If they took the time to call, then you or someone in your office should try to take the time to treat them as if their opinions matter—which, incidentally, they do.

Look on the light side

Not all the rules of crisis communication are so grim.

For example, Maryland's Hiebert advises against wearing a white jacket and high heels to work. She did one day and found herself clambering all over a campus construction site that had been the scene of an accident.

And then there's the counsel of another education official:

"Handle a crisis as you would mayonnaise. Keep cool, but don't freeze."

CHAPTER 20

Media Training Checklist

The top 25 tips for faculty and administrators who deal with journalists

Annette Hannon Lee

When a reporter calls

1. Return the call as quickly as possible; you can't influence a story once its deadline has passed.

2. Ask what the interview is about; what information the reporter needs; the news affiliation of the interviewer; who else the reporter is contacting; the location, time, and estimated length of the interview; the caller's phone number; and the deadline.

3. Keep in mind that radio reporters may ask to tape an interview over the phone. If you want to collect your thoughts first, say you'll call back—and do so before their deadline.

Before the interview

4. Determine your message with three to five key points.

5. Practice getting them across.

6. Think about difficult questions and how to answer them.

7. Gather facts, statistics, or background information.

8. For cameras, check your appearance. To look your best, avoid flashy jewelry and wear comfortable clothes in solid colors or soft shades.

9. Contact your communications office if you need assistance.

During the interview

10. Answer truthfully, even if it hurts. Don't lie, guess, or exaggerate.

11. State important facts first.

12. Be sure to make your points.

13. Avoid complex explanations.

14. Don't use jargon; speak in conversational terms.

15. Be brief. Deliver responses in 20 seconds or less for print or broadcast. Keep in

---

Annette Hannon Lee is director of media relations at Florida State University. She wrote this article for the March 1992 CURRENTS.

mind that 10-second sound bites are the building blocks of TV news stories.

16. Remember that the reporter is a conduit; speak to the public, not the reporter.

17. Use examples, comparisons, or statistics as back-up information for follow-up questions.

18. If possible, provide illustrations, visual aids, or a demonstration for photographers or videographers.

19. If you don't know the answer to a question, admit it. Offer to call back or refer the reporter elsewhere—to the media relations office if you're unsure.

20. Never speak off the record. If you don't want to have a statement quoted, don't make it.

21. Correct the record if the reporter has wrong information.

22. If something is truly too controversial to discuss, explain as much as you can. "No comment" sounds as though you're hiding something.

23. Beware of the reporter who remains silent, thus encouraging you to ramble or dilute your message. Don't fill those lulls with conversation.

24. Keep your cool; don't argue with the reporter.

25. Always maintain a positive attitude.

CHAPTER • 21

Why Crisis Plans Fail

Some situations—and people—resist good crisis management strategy

Bob Roseth

The November/December 1987 CURRENTS restated the basic tenets of what has become known as crisis management. These tenets, of which most public relations professionals are aware, can be summarized in three principles. Have a plan, speak with one voice, and—most important—tell the truth, the whole truth, as soon as you can.

If these principles are widely known and accepted in the public relations community, why do my colleagues and I bear so many scars on our toes from having shot ourselves in the feet?

Deep down, we PR professionals may know the "right way" to handle a crisis. But newspaper headlines and off-the-record conversations with my colleagues suggest that a sizable gap exists between theory and practice.

In analyzing our role as campus PR professionals, we must remember that we're not entirely masters of our institutional fates. Too often we discuss our role as advisers and advocates as if we were the *only* advisers and advocates. Powerful institutional forces exist that we can't influence. Sometimes these forces work to our advantage; at other times they frustrate our efforts. We may propose policies, but the ultimate decision regarding their adoption rests with others at the institution.

For instance, some situations by nature resist good crisis management strategy. In my experience, the worst cases often arise from personnel actions. By custom and sometimes by law, institutions usually won't discuss why a person was fired. If the hiring or firing becomes a *cause celebre*, the critics get center stage and can make whatever claims or charges they wish. If these critics get public support— from the community, from students, or from faculty— news accounts can go on for weeks and even months. The university's reluctance to explain its actions— the "mystery," if you will— becomes the story itself.

A crisis plan offers small solace in the face of personnel problems. If we, as public relations professionals, have good rapport with individual journalists, we can help tone down some of the controversy. But the best strategy in this case appears to be to tighten your chin strap, keep your head down, and avoid stray bullets.

Another major obstacle to good crisis management comes from the campus adminis-

Bob Roseth is director of news and information at the University of Washington. At the time he wrote this article for the March 1988 CURRENTS, he was the University of Washington's director of information services.

trator or faculty member whose program or decision is being held up to public scrutiny (and often ridicule). Such a person is apt to become defensive, hostile, and finally, uncommunicative. If this individual is also a key institutional decision maker, he or she can effectively block any crisis management effort.

It's easy to be too critical of people who thwart your crisis plans. But we in PR need to be realistic. In my 38 years on the planet, I've encountered only a handful of people who are able to so detach themselves from their ideas that they can look at their work impartially.

The tendency to defend one's own work is only human; we can't change that. Add to it the administrator or faculty member's view that public scrutiny is unwarranted and disruptive. Then, on top of that, add aggressive reporters who leave no leads unexplored and who incessantly call the person and his or her colleagues at home and at work. Should we be surprised when our arguments for a "proactive" posture fall upon deaf ears?

Although full disclosure may be a wise practice, the idea prompts in the average administrator many of the same anxieties a new driver feels when told to steer in the direction of a skid. It may work, but understanding why won't come by instinct.

To advancement professionals with less-than-perfect records in convincing their institutions to adopt sound crisis management strategies, take heart. Your task is not an easy one. Many of your colleagues, both inside education and outside, have had the same problems you have. And remember: Even Hall-of-Famer Mickey Mantle only batted about .300.

CASE Issues Papers: Communicating Controversies on Campus

CASE Issues Papers

Author Updates and Ordering Information

Since CASE originally published these Issues Papers, the following authors have changed positions. Details of their new posts follow.

Bill Johnson, director of marketing communications, Lehigh University

Michael Lawrence, assistant director for news, University of Texas Health Science Center at San Antonio

Margaret Simon Lutherer, director of university news and publications, Texas Tech University

Connie Stewart, former associate vice president for university relations, Emory University

William Walker, director of university relations, College of William and Mary

Every year the Council for Advancement and Support of Education publishes numerous *Issues Papers* on communicating about sensitive campus concerns. Each advice-filled paper offers campus communications professionals valuable insights into how they can success-fully spread the word about tough and timely topics on their campus.

For information on how to subscribe or contribute to upcoming *Issues Papers*, call (202) 328-5979. Or write to:

CASE Communications
Suite 400, 11 Dupont Circle
Washington DC 20036-1261

Is your *Issues Paper* library complete and up-to-date? Are you missing some of the earlier papers? Now you can have every *Issues Paper* at close hand. CASE is offering digests of previously published *Issues Papers* for sale. Each digest comes in a convenient binder for easy reference and filing. The $10 price per digest ($15, nonmembers) includes shipping and handling (though there is an additional charge for foreign orders), and orders must be prepaid. Prices are subject to change without notice. Purchase orders, VISA, and Mastercard are accepted. For more information or to order, call: CASE Publications Order Department, (800) 554-8536; or write: PO Box 90386, Washington, DC 20090-0386; or fax: (301) 206-9789 (if paying by credit card or purchase order).

RACIAL INCIDENTS ON CAMPUS

July 1990   A CASE Issues Paper for Communications Professionals   No.1

According to the U.S. Department of Justice, in 1989 alone, 77 colleges and universities reported racial incidents on their campuses—an increase of almost 50 percent over the pervious year. The National Institute Against Prejudice & Violence reports that racial incidents occurred at 300 colleges and universities since the Fall of 1986. The rise in recent years of racial incidents on college and university campuses demands quick and efficient decision-making and action from campus public relations officers. **James Langley**, vice president for external affairs at Georgia Institute of Technology, has been a communications professional in higher education for over 10 years and has had significant experience handling racial incidents on campuses. His most recent experience includes handling racial incidents at the University of Massachusetts at Amherst. We asked Jim to give us his top ten tips for communicating effectively during a racial incident on campus.

1 **Beware of the "shame factor" which leads to denial of racial problems.** There's no need to be ashamed of having a problem; some of the most progressive institutions in the country have been afflicted by racial incidents. The only real shame comes from failing to address the problem. Approach communications—internal and external—as an appeal to friends to help solve a societal problem that has found its way to your campus.

2 **Establish multiple lines of communication.** Don't rely on the administrative chain of command. Messages can be filtered by administrators seeking to protect their turf. As a result, senior administrators become removed from the real campus concerns. Analyze reports of racial incidents on campus. Did they come up a white-to-white chain of command? Was a minority perspective introduced somewhere along the way? If not, call upon your contacts in the minority community to get a broader view. Remember, housing all senior administrators in one building may increase bureaucratic efficiency, but it also increases isolation from the rest of the campus. Your job is to help overcome that obstacle.

3 **Think about outcome. When it's all said and done, what kind of community do you want to have?** In the heat of controversy, don't say or do anything that will make it difficult to achieve a sense of community in the future. If you know what you want to achieve, you'll create a light at the end of the tunnel of controversy. Make sure the actions of the administration move you steadily toward that light. Persevering and enhancing a sense of community are the most important goals. Silencing your moist strident critic is not. Appeal to the reasonable majority.

4 **Don't respond to emotional concerns with intellectual answers.** If members of a minority community fear for their safety because of an attack on a member of that community, respond to their emotions. Offer reassurance. Show how you plan to improve safety on campus or prosecute offenders. Don't provide statistics or goals to prove you are a progressive institution. If emotions are running high, don't rely on printed communications. Make sure that senior administrators are visible on campus. Set up forums where senior administrators can listen and ask for suggestions. Tell these administrators that they don't have to have all the answers or provide all the solutions.

5 **Beware of discrepancies between word and deed.** There's no point in professing noble sentiments if they are not consistent with actions. What good editors say about writing is true of all communications: show don't tell. Show in a way that is meaningful to your constituencies. For instance, there's no point in telling minority students that you are committed to multiculturalism if the multicultural center on campus is in constant disrepair. The center will be seen by students as a very real expression of administrative neglect. Try to see the world from the students' point of view and make the changes necessary to bring words in line with deeds.

6 **Make sure that all vehicles of communication deal openly and candidly with the problem and include all viewpoints.** Air your controversies out, don't try to contain them. If you don't provide venues and vehicles on campus for all points of view to be expressed, they will seek expression in the outside media and the controversy will widen.

7 **Don't appeal to the press as the final arbiter.** Don't become obsessed with telling the administration's side of the story. Members of the press will respond favorably if they see the administration working openly and actively with faculty and students to resolve the problems. Seek common ground (i.e. deploring racism, empathizing with concerns of minorities) with your critics.

8 **Help the press see that there are more than two sides to every story.** Don't let them oversimplify, i.e. black vs. white, administration vs. students. Show that there are fifty sides to every controversy, that they can't make glib assumptions about the "black community" or the "Asian community." Show that your campus is a collection of interesting individuals with a variety of viewpoints on any given issue.

9 **Establish context.** For example, if you are successful in heightening awareness of and sensitivity to racial misdeeds, reports of racial incidents on campus will increase as more and more people recognize and respond to the problem. If you don't explain that increased reports can mean more, not less progress, the press may unintentionally misrepresent you.

10 **Understand that controversies are like weeds. If you don't get to the roots, they keep coming back. Don't just hope they will go away.**

We've listed below campus public relations officers from institutions of higher education across the country who have handled racial incidents on college campuses. They represent an array of institutions and are willing to share their expertise and strategies with other campus communications professionals.

Robert E. Freelen, Vice President for Public Affairs
Stanford University (CA)   (415) 723-2862

Karen Grava-Williams, Assistant Vice President for External Affairs
 University of Connecticut (Storrs, CT)   (203) 486-3530

Greg Hand, Assistant Vice President, Public Affairs
University of Cincinnati (OH)   (513) 556-1822

Walt Harrison, Executive Director of University Relations
University of Michigan, Ann Arbor (MI)   (313) 764-1817

James Langley, Vice President for External Affairs
Georgia Institute of Technology (Atlanta, GA)   (404) 894-5070

Tom Montiegel, Vice President for Development and University Relations
Northern Illinois University (DeKalb, IL)   (815) 753-0283

Robert A. Reichley, Vice President, University Relations
Brown University (Providence, RI)   (401) 863-2453

Roger Williams, Assistant Vice President and Executive Director of University Relations
Pennsylvania State University (University Park, PA)   (814) 863-1028

ANIMAL RIGHTS BREAK-INS AND DEMONSTRATIONS

October 1990   A CASE Issues Paper for Campus Communications Professionals   No. 2

The traditional function of a university public relations department is woefully inadequate in dealing with an animal rights break-in or demonstration. Strategic planning in advance, a major public education campaign both on and off campus, and a crisis management plan that involves all key players are essential in planning for animal rights activity. Should an attack occur, the institution will be involved in a long-term public information campaign and the public relations office will be command central for the battle against the animal rights movement. Should your institution never experience disruptive animal rights activity, as an academic institution dedicated to serving humanity and educating the public, you still have a responsibility to explain the benefits of biomedical and agricultural research to your community. **Margaret Simon, director of news and publications at Texas Tech University** -- the scene of some of the nation's most aggressive animal rights activity -- is currently writing a book on the topic. She offers the following guidelines:

1   **Do your homework on the animal rights movement.** Very different in philosophy from animal welfare groups, animal rights groups believe that man has no right to keep or use animals for any reason, including research, agriculture, clothing, or even pet ownership. Some animal rights groups are quite militant and have been responsible for over 70 acts of terrorism on college campuses and research institutions in the last 10 years. Background reading as well as perusal of animal rights publications is essential to understand the movement. The "Bible" of the movement is Peter Singer's Animal Liberation (New York: Random House, 1975).

2   **Prepare a briefing package on the movement and related history of university break-ins and demonstrations over animal-based research for all senior administrators.** There is a tendency to believe that a break-in could never occur on your campus. Thus, your president and senior officials may not be well informed about this complex issue. However, every campus where any type of animal research is conducted is a potential target, according to security officials at the National Institutes of Health. Briefing material should include: 1) a police description of Animal Liberation Front (ALF)-related terrorism, 2) news clips of recent demonstrations and break-ins, 3) white papers from the scientific community (such as the American Medical Association White Paper), 4) a listing of the membership of your Animal Care and Use Committee, and 5) an evaluation of security problems in your research labs from your campus police force, and 6) an assessment of local animal rights activity.

3   **Become involved with the biomedical support network.** The National Association for Biomedical Research, Washington, D.C. and the many state biomedical research organizations can provide resource materials -- from legislative updates to training tapes for public education about the value of biomedical research. Institutions where break-ins have occurred are also invaluable resources should you need information quick.

4   **Learn about your institution's animal care and use program.** Under Federal law, every research institution must have an Institutional Animal Care and Use Committee (IACUC), made up of university faculty as well as members of the community. The IACUC reviews and approves protocol of every experiment involving animals on your campus. If they are doing their jobs well, your first line of defense and information after a break-in is the IACUC. Their records can quickly help you assess the experiments in question.

5   **Know the local animal rights and animal welfare scene.** Virtually all campus animal rights incidents in the last decade were preceded by a sudden burst of interest and activity by a local animal rights group. A prominent member of the movement has appeared on campus a few months before many recent break-ins.

6 **Educate your community about the value of animal-based research.** The animal rights movement is a powerful propaganda machine that spreads misinformation and misleading interpretation of data. They have been successful thus far because the scientific and academic community has not been interested in public education on the issue. A research scientist is not always the best spokesperson in your university, but the public relations office should work with the research office to identify effective public speakers on this issue who can appear before civic groups, public school groups, and internal faculty and staff meetings.

7 **Educate the media.** The general assignments reporter is likely to believe the sensationalistic claims of the animal rights movement, especially if he/she has no medical or scientific background. Arrange a tour of your vivarium and animal labs for the media -- from the general assignment reporter to news director. Because of the turnover in television personnel, plan to repeat the tour once a year. Have researchers and veterinarians available to answer their questions and explain the benefits of their research. Should a break-in occur, a reporter who has visited your facility and seen first-hand that your animals are well cared for will be much less likely to believe any unfounded claims that the perpetrators of the crime may release about you.

8 **Be proactive in your dealings with the movement.** Should a break-in occur, be the first to the media with a prepared statement and the full support of your administration. Commonly, the terrorists will arrange for an animal rights public relations network to release information charging the institution and investigator with horrible cruelty. Unless you are first to explain what happened to the media, your institution may become the accused instead of the victim of criminal activity.

9 **Involve your police department, legal counsel, IACUC, public relations/information office, and administrators involved with research in a network to discuss the animal rights issue.** Be sure that these key staff members are constantly updated about any activity on your campus and throughout the nation.

10 **Above all, formulate a crisis communications plan to deal with the eventuality of an attack.** Circulate the plan to all key players, so that should an attack occur, you can assemble the crisis team as quickly as possible to respond with a cohesive institutional plan. The aftermath of an attack can last for years, through demonstrations and vicious letter-writing campaigns against the university to prolonged court battles. Your crisis communications plan should take the long term aftermath of an animal rights siege into consideration. It should also deal with the problems inherent in fighting a propaganda attack. For example, the animal rights movement will turn the attack into an emotional debate. The height of emotion involved will determine that you cannot respond to the claims made against your institution with scientific explanation alone. The crisis communications plan must be based upon the premise that the real emotional issue involved is man's desire to advance knowledge to improve the human condition.

The individuals and organizations listed below are willing to share their expertise and strategies to campus communications professionals confronted with animal rights break-ins or demonstrations.

Claire Basset, Director of Communications, Baylor College of Medicine (Houston, TX) 713-798-4712

Mary Brennan, Assistant Director, National Association of Biomedical Research (Washington, DC) 202-457-0654

Carol Farnsworth, Assistant Vice President of University Relations, University of Pennsylvania (Philadelphia, PA) 215-898-7798

Daniel Forbush, Associate Vice President for Public Relations and Creative Services, SUNY, Stony Brook (NY) 516-632-6308

Christine Helwick, University Counsel, University of California System (Oakland, CA) 415-987-9736

Larry Horton, Associate Vice President for Public Affairs, Stanford University (CA) 415-723-2862

Sharon Kha, Director, Office of Public Information, University of Arizona (Tucson, AZ) 602-621-1877

Joan Hartman Moore, Director of Public Relations, Association of American Medical Colleges (Washington, DC) 202-828-0455

Kay Rodriguez, Director of Health Science News and Information Services, University of Washington (Seattle, WA) 206-543-3620

Margaret Simon, Director of News and Publications, Texas Tech University (Lubbock, TX) 806-742-2136

CRIME INCIDENTS ON CAMPUS

December 1990   A CASE Issues Paper for Communications Professionals   No. 3

Campus crime is one of the most serious issues confronting colleges and universities today. Comminications professionals must play a key role in educating all concerned publics about crime at their institution. **Bill Johnson**, university information director at Lehigh University, has had significant experience dealing with crime on campus and suggests the following guidelines for communicating about a major violent crime incident. Senior communications and campus security experts from a wide variety of other campuses met at a recent special CASE forum to discuss the topic and review Johnson's suggestions.

The most important requirement for effective communications about a serious crime is providing timely, accurate, and consistent information to all those concerned. During a crisis, your effectiveness as a communicator is dependent on having strong relationships with local law enforcement officials, crisis intervention professionals, and the media. Most critically, you need to have the trust and confidence of your colleagues in student affairs, campus safety and security, legal affairs, and senior administration. You need to be a full-fledged member of a campus crisis response team to be an effective communicator during a serious crime incident. As the communications professional on that team, you may want to consider the following points:

BEFORE A CRIME OCCURS

1   **Prepare information about your institution's security and safety policies**. Also have available information on drug and alcohol abuse programs, rape prevention programs, and other materials to educate key publics and document that your institution takes crime seriously and has prevention programs in place.

2   **Plan how the public information office will operate**. At least one communications person should be part of the crisis response team. Depending upon the size of your public information operation, you may need to line up additional staffing during an emergency. Don't forget to plan such small details as notifying your campus telephone operators where they should switch various calls.

3   **Identify student, faculty, and other campus leaders who can serve as volunteers to help communications efforts during a crisis.**

4   **Discuss with community leaders, local law enforcement officials, and members of your campus crisis team how you can effectively work together during a crime incident**. Indentify, for instance, community groups you should alert if a crime occurs. Make sure you know the laws about releasing specific information about crimes. Determine campus policies and procedures for allowing the media to photograph or film on-campus sites such as residence halls.

5   **Identify your campus' most knowledgeable spokespersons and provide media training for these individuals.** The individuals who can most effectively serve as spokespersons may vary depending on the specifics of a crime. In some cases, it may be most appropriate for a communications professional to serve as a spokesperson; at other times, your campus law enforcement or student affaris officials can provide greater expertise and credibility. In all cases, the spokespersons should provide accurate information, quickly and consistently.

6   **Select and equip sites for news conferences and media use during an emergency.**

WHEN A CRIME OCCURS

Outline your audience's short- and long-term communications needs. Your audiences will need varying degrees of information: some will need a personal approach; others will require frequent updates; still others will want information long after the crime has occurred. How personal and frequent your communications will be depends on the type and nature of the crime, the size of your campus, and the resources available to you. You and others on the crisis response team will need to communicate with the following audiences to varying degrees, depending on your specific situation:

1   **The victim's family**. Your president and other top officals should visit or contact the victim's family members as soon as possible after a violent crime. Quite likely they will be angry at whoever calls. Respond as sympathetically as possible. Do not challenge their assertions. This is a time for outreach and compassion. At a later time, you can discuss with them suggestions for possible change.

2   **Students**. Student affairs personnel must communicate face-to-face with students early and often. Support these efforts by working closely with campus newspapers, radio, and television stations to make sure they are kept abreast of key information and are aware of the steps you are taking to ease students' fears. If possible, establish a hotline for students to call and provide round-the-clock religious and professional counseling. Meet with student groups and individual students as often as possible to address their fears. The students, faculty, and other volunteers you previously identified can help communicate with students.

3   **Parents**. As soon as possible, your president and other top administrators should send a personal letter, or series of letters, to parents detailing your continuing efforts to address campus safety and their children's reactions to the crime. If you can, set up a separate hotline for parents and appoint knowledgeable individuals to field incoming calls.

4   **Alumni**. A serious, violent crime is likely to evoke feelings of shock and hurt from alumni. Keep alumni staff members fully informed. Help them explain that your campus is safe, but not a haven from the real world. Cite measures the institution is planning to improve safety and security. Address alumni concerns at club meetings by bringing your president or student affairs official to report on the incident and your response. Send materials prepared for external media to alumni periodicals editors.

5   **The community**. If a student commits a crime against another student, the focus of communications will not be on the community. However, if an outsider commits a crime against a student or a suspect has yet to be arrested, you need to stay in close contact with community leaders. If appropriate, phone calls, letters, and personal visits to neighborhood organizations and individuals can supplement news media accounts and quash rumors. Also, if a student commits a crime against a member of the community, you need to respond to community concerns by providing a forum for airing those concerns. For instance, you might establish a task force of student leaders, city government and community group representatives, and law enforcement officials to help evaluate the situation and develop solutions.

6   **Faculty and staff**. Campus communicators often overlook this group after a serious crime. Make counseling available to faculty and staff members, too. Keep them informed through campus-wide memos and regular phone calls to deans, department heads, and other faculty leaders. A well-informed internal audience can correct erroneous information and quell rumors that invariably circulate on campus and in the community.

7   **The media**. Use one media-trained spokesperson. This person's comments and all releases to the media and other audiences must be consistent with communications to your other audiences. If the crime is receiving significant media attention, you should hold a formal news conference. State all the facts you know up to that time—even if you repeat previous reports—to correct any rumors. Help media representatives do their jobs by providing them with frequent updates on the crime and supplying answers to questions before their deadlines.

8 **Trustees and friends**. The president or other appropriate top officials need to keep these groups personally up-to-date with regular phone calls and letters. Send them copies of news releases, internal memos, and media reports. They need to know that the institution's response to and communications about the crime are effective.

SOME CRITICAL ISSUES TO CONSIDER

Depending on your circumstances, you and the crisis team may also need to consider several other issues when focusing your communications efforts:

1 **Drugs and alcohol**. Statistics show drugs and alcohol play a significant role in campus crime. Clearly communicate your institution's policies toward drug and alcohol abuse. Ground issues in the larger context that drug and alcohol abuse is not unique to your campus or any campus but is a pervasive social problem. Don't overdo this, however; you may appear to be avoiding responsibility.

2 **Racial aspects**. Any racial overtones of a crime need to be treated honestly. On the other hand, if a crime could be construed as racially motivated but is not, make that clear in all your communications. Meet with various groups to address any real or perceived racial aspects of a crime, and communicate the results of these discussions to other audiences.

3 **Student-to-student crimes**. These crimes require somewhat different communications approaches from crimes by outsiders. Provide information that encourages respect for others' safety, privacy, and property to students and other key audiences. Keep in mind privacy laws that prohibit releasing specific information about students. However, stress that your institution encourages students to report crimes and press charges. Emphasize that when students are victims of date rapes, for instance, they are counseled to report the crime and press charges if they want—and that your institution will fully support them.

The previous points offer general guidelines for responding to a major violent crime. However, crime incidents are complec and vary significantly in nature and degree. The individuals listed attended the CASE forum on crime and helped prepare this document. They are willing to share their expertise in more detail with campus communications professionals confronted with crime incidents on their own campuses.

Mary Ann Aug
Assistant Vice President of University Relations
University of Pittsburgh
3700 Cathedral of Learning
Pittsburgh, PA 15260
(412) 624-3750

Bobby Wayne Clark
Director, Public Information and Publications
Wesleyan University
Middletown, CT 06457
(203) 347-9411

Carol Farnsworth
Assistant Vice President, University Relations
University of Pennsylvania
249 South 36th Street, 410 Logan Hall
Philadelphia, PA 19104-6387
(215) 898-7798

Dan Forbush
Associate Vice President, University Relations
State University of New York at Stony Brook
Stony Brook, NY 11794-0605
(516) 632-6308

Walt Harrison
Executive Director of University Relations
University of Michigan
2064 Fleming Building
Ann Arbor, MI 48109-1340
(313) 763-5800

Bill Johnson
University Information Director
Lehigh University
436 Broadhead Avenue
Bethelehem, PA 18015
(215) 758-3172

Harry Kinne
Director of Public Safety
Wesleyan University
Middletown, CT 06457
(203) 347-9411

Gary Krull
Associate Vice President, Public Relations
Georgetown University
37th & O Streets, NW
Healy Building
Washington, DC 20057
(202) 687-4324

Jim Langley
Vice President for External Affairs
Georgia Institute of Technology
108 Wardlan Center
Atlanta, GA 30332
(404) 894-5070

John Logan
Director of Public Safety
University of Pennsylvania
3914 Locust Walk
Philadelphia, PA 19104
(215) 898-5000

Robert A. Reichley
Executive Vice President, Alumni,
 Public Affairs, and External Relations
Brown University
Box 1920
Providence, RI 02912
(401) 863-2453

Susan Riseling
Assistant Director of Public Safety
State University of New York at Stony Brook
Stony Brook, NY 11794-1501
(516) 689-6000

Wayne Sage
Director of USC News Service
University of Southern California
University Park, KAP 248
Los Angeles, CA 90089-2538
(213) 740-2311

John Smeaton
Associate Vice President, Student Affairs
Lehigh University
Student Affairs Office
Bethlehem, PA 18015
(215) 758-3000

David Stormer
Assistant Vice President for Sagety
 and Environmental Health
Pennsylvania State University
12 Grange Building
University Park, PA 16802
(814) 865-1864

Debra Thomas
Director of Public Information
Bryn Mawr College
Bryn Mawr, PA 19010-2899
(215) 526-5173

Jack Vickery
Chief of Police
Georgia Institute of Technology
Campus Police Office
879 Hemphill Avenue, NW
Atlanta, GA 30332-0440

Johanna Vogel
Assistant Director, News and Public Affairs
University of Pennsylvania
249 South 36th Street, 410 Logan Hall
Philadelphia, PA 19104-6387VOGEL
(215) 898-8658

Ken Wildes
Director of University Relations
Northwestern University
555 Clark Street
Evanston, IL 60208-1230
(708) 491-5000

CLOSING ACADEMIC UNITS

February 1991   A CASE Issues Paper for Advancement Professionals   No. 4

As colleges and universities adjust to the harsh realities of a slowing economy, scarce resources, and declining enrollments, they will face decisions unthinkable in the 1980s. One option is eliminating programs, an action virtually guaranteed to stir great debate on and off campus—a debate that can rage for months and sometimes years. **M. Fredric Volkmann**, vice chancellor for public affairs at Washington University in St. Louis, Missouri, gained first-hand experience when his institution announced the closing of its sociology department and its dental school in 1989. To help other institutions effectively handle closing a program or department, Fred offers the following advice.

1   **Involve as many people as possible**. Or, at least, make sure faculty and students are informed and have had an opportunity for input before the decision is made. Be certain that administrators and trustees have followed appropriate faculty and institutional protocals--possibly forming a special task force to review the programs in question. Make sure your administration has alerted oversight committees, senate councils, and other governing bodies of the faculty. Don't forget to contact key alumni and other interested parties. Then document these efforts. If the process of discontinuing a program appears arbitrary or overlooks an important governing or advising body, the announcement can become an even bigger problem.

2   **Research the past**. Compile a detailed history for yourself, including pros and cons, of the campus program(s) being eliminated or downsized. Your aim is not to gather information for publication as much as to do homework to help you understand the situation. By doing so, you may discover what to expect from those who refuse to accept the decision. You may also unearth evidence that supports the decision.

3   **Anticipate debate on a national scale**. Review the national status of the field of study the program, department, or school represents. Faculty, staff, and students in disciplines that are declining in enrollment, impact, or popularity may see any attempt to downsize or eliminate programs on a single campus as cause for a national effort to alter or reverse the decision. On the other hand, the closing of similar departments at other institutions can often, in fact, buttress your argument and provide a rationale for your actions. Seek advice from colleagues at other institutions who've had similar experiences. Ask permission to use their experiences and to refer reporters to them to broaden the story. (Don't be tempted, however, to try to make your situation look better by implying other institutions are worse off!)

4   **Put your campus community first**. As the decision becomes final, coordinate your announcement so affected faculty and students learn of the situation <u>before</u> it appears in the news media. Your dean, provost, president, and other senior administrators should meet personally with these internal audiences. Although those affected by the announcement may reach the media with their side of the story before you do, you will have taken a professional, above-board, high-road approach. Don't ignore affected subgroups, such as alumni who graduated from the program, parents, secretarial and support staff, and national associations to which the school or department belongs. Meet with or phone leaders of these groups, as well as professionals in your alumni and development offices who are bound to hear questions and reactions from graduates and parents. Follow up as soon as possible with a special mailing of the release before you send it to the media. Your CEO or provost may also want to consider meeting with leaders of nonaffected faculty and students at the time of the announcement or soon after it. You could also send them the news release—or at least make sure internal campus media reach them.

5   **Avoid making finances the only reason for the decision.** You do not want to suggest that the decision is an arbitrary one based solely on financial concerns. On the other hand, you should not imply it stems from substance or quality problems either. Rather, review the changes in enrollment and placement patterns, the evolution of the discipline, and the competition of equally good programs at other nearby or similar institutions as the fundamental reasons for the closing. If possible, place the decision in the context of an overall plan that outlines how the institution will direct its finite resources to achieve its mission in the future. Highlight the specific areas in which the institution has chosen to excel and why. Be prepared to explain the alternatives your administration considered and the logic behind the final decision.

6   **Write a humane, caring news release.** Prepare a written news announcement that is consistent with what your administration is telling faculty, students, and staff--and that is designed, first and foremost, to communicate with them. Remember, your faculty and students have dedicated their education, research, and ideals—not to mention their careers—to this program. When possible, praise those who deserve it.

7   **Develop and communicate programs that help those affected by the decision.** In the news release, describe your efforts to counsel students and ensure they are able to complete their degrees. Emphasize that you are providing placement support, ample time for tenure-track faculty to find new work or to transfer to other departments within the institution, and generous severance packages where appropriate. If agreements with similar departments at other institutions to accept your students and faculty have been arranged, make sure these agreements are known to all concerned parties and the public.

8   **Substantiate with backgrounders.** Beyond writing the basic news release, consider backgrounders on the history of the department, future of the discipline, and rationale for your decision. Besides sending these documents to the media, encourage coverage in your alumni publications and other campus media. Or include these backgrounders in your special mailings to important constituencies. Again, your primary audience is not the news media but those who may believe your decision is a small-minded, mean-spirited plot. Being thorough, fair, and sensitive can help alleviate these fears.

9   **Provide candid, well-briefed sources for the press.** Select key spokespersons from both sides of the issue and realize that others may mount their own media effort, regardless of what you do. Limit speakers to those who have responsibility for the decision and those who lead affected programs. Advise your senior administrators and others on how to refer media queries to you or appropriate spokespersons. As soon as the decision to eliminate a department or program seems probable, prepare a set of likely media questions and suggested responses. Then, brief spokespersons on how to handle themselves in interviews so they will be comfortable with the process as early as possible.

10   **Timing and technique are critical.** Time the news release to be fair to affected students, faculty, and staff. Be sure they all know when you will release the announcement to the press so they can prepare themselves. (Don't wait until the day after finals are over or mid-summer.) For a critical program or one that is likely to generate high interest, consider a press conference attended by your CEO, provost, and a representative of the affected area. (If the decision is made at the trustee level, you may also want to include a member of the board.) While not always the best vehicle, a press conference can help to air the issue in an open forum.

11   **Brace yourself.** Prepare for vocal and aggressive reaction from any and all affected parties, possibly running for the entire phase-out period and beyond. (Some institutions are still hearing about department closings years later!) Anticipate strategies that disgruntled parties could use to embarrass or destabilize the institution. Expect attempts to involve legislators, funding bodies, governmental agencies, alumni, donors, trustees, parents, and faculty organizations.

12 **Do all you can to stay open, accessible, and prompt.** If the situation erupts—or you expect it to—alert the media that the institution is willing and available to respond to legitimate criticisms from affected parties (with the exception of commenting on matters under litigation or confidential personnel matters).

13 **Stay on top of the situation.** As the news announcement stirs reaction, track internal and external information—especially news stories that suggest unanticipated strategies by affected parties. Be certain all potential spokespersons see news stories, video and radio clips, and opinion page reactions as soon as you receive them. Enlist help in monitoring all media in your region, plus national press if you expect a big reaction. However, don't expect media interest to go beyond the announcement itself or any controversy surrounding it. It's unlikely you'll generate much interest in how well your institution is faring over the longer haul as a result of eliminating the department. If conditions warrant, six months or a year after the announcement, you might suggest a feature in your alumni periodical about the positive results of the decision. Suggest it to the external media as well, but don't hold your breath.

14 **Anticipate the best, plan for the worst, and live with the consequences.** You cannot predict the future, especially when it deals with an unpleasant and controversial action. Emotions can take the upper hand. However, you can put your best foot forward by being careful about following decision-making protocols, anticipating news media interest, and monitoring the process as it unfolds.

The previous points offer general guidelines when announcing the closing of an academic unit. However, each institution must decide the most appropriate approach based on its individual structure and circumstances. The following individuals represent a wide range of institutions that have dealt with the closing of academic units. They are willing to share their expertise and strategies with other campus professionals. Also included are the public affairs directors from several major higher education associations who are also excellent resources.

CAMPUS CONTACTS

Bob Freelen
Vice President for Public Affairs
Stanford University
Stanford, CA 94305
(415) 723-2862

Cheryl May
Director, News Services
Kansas State University
Manhattan, KS 66506
(913) 532-6415

Walt Harrison
Executive Director of University Relations
University of Michigan
Ann Arbor, MI 48109
(313) 763-5800

Alice Olick
Assistant Vice President, Public Affairs
Fairleigh Dickinson University
Teaneck, NJ 07666
(201) 692-9711

Fred Knubel
Director, Office of Public Information
Columbia University
New York, NY 10027
(212) 854-5573

Debra Thomas
Director of Public Information
Bryn Mawr College
Bryn Mawr, PA 19010-2899
(215) 526-5137

Gary Krull
Associate Vice President, Public Relations
Georgetown University
Washington, DC 20057
(202) 687-4324

Fred Volkmann
Vice Chancellor for Public Affairs
Washington University in St. Louis
St. Louis, MO 63130
(314) 889-5476

ASSOCIATION CONTACTS

Bob Aaron
Director, Communication Services
National Association of State Universities
and Land Grant Colleges (NASCULGC)
One Dupont Circle, Suite 710
Washington, DC 20036
(202) 778-0818

Gail Raiman
Vice President for Public Affairs
National Association of Independent
Colleges and Universities (NAICU)
122 C Street, NW, Suite 750
Washington, DC 20001
(202) 347-7512

Gay Clyburn
Director of Public Affairs
American Association of State Colleges
and Universities (AASCU)
One Dupont Circle, Suite 700
Washington, DC 20036
(202) 293-7070

Peter Smith
Director of Public Affairs
Association of American Universities (AAU)
One Dupont Circle, Suite 730
Washington, DC 20036
(202) 775-9242

Dave Merkowitz
Director, Office of Public Affairs
American Council on Education (ACE)
One Dupont Circle, Suite 800
Washington, DC 20036
(202) 939-9300

Judy Tomczak
Public Information Officer
American Association of Community and
Junior Colleges (AACJC)
One Dupont Circle, Suite 410
Washington, DC 20036
(202) 728-0200

STUDENT ALCOHOL AND DRUG ABUSE

May 1991   A CASE Issues Paper for Advancement Professionals   No. 5

Substance abuse is the campus life issue of greatest concern to college and university presidents, according to a 1989 national survey by the Carnegie Foundation for the Advancement of Teaching and the American Council on Education. Two-thirds of the presidents surveyed called alcohol and drug abuse a problem on their campuses.

While our society has not reached a consensus on alcohol and drug use, experts agree that extensive informational and educational programs are essential to help combat excessive drinking and other substance abuse among college students. Advancement professionals play a key role in developing and disseminating information about these programs. In addition, we're often among the first called upon to deal with any accidents, crimes, or other crises involving substance abuse. **Connie Stewart**, associate vice president for university relations at Emory University, has had in-depth experience handling issues related to substance abuse on campus and suggests the following guidelines for communicating about them. Senior advancement and student affairs experts from a wide variety of other campuses met at a recent special CASE forum to discuss the topic and review Stewart's suggestions.

As with any major issue, advancement professionals should have a strategic plan for addressing student alcohol and drug abuse. This plan includes (1) the research steps necessary for educating and preparing yourself, (2) ongoing communications activities to inform and educate key constituencies, and (3) a crisis communications plan to handle specific incidents related to alcohol and drug abuse.

RESEARCH

1 **Stay abreast of the national situation.** What's the general climate of opinion toward alcohol and drug abuse on campus? Has a major national story about student alcohol and drug abuse just broken? What was the public reaction? How was it handled in the media? Make sure you examine the situation at your own institution in this larger context. Also, collect comparative information from peer institutions, national education associations, and federal and state agencies. A good source for comprehensive information is the National Clearinghouse on Alcohol and Drug Information, the federal resource of the U.S. Department of Health and Human Services, (800) 487-1447.

2 **Examine your campus culture.** While student alcohol and drug abuse mirrors that of the larger society, each campus has its own social culture. What place do alcohol and drugs have in the social life of students on your campus? Where, when, and how much do students consume? Do they party and drink on campus, or do they go off-campus to drink? Do different student groups on campus have different attitudes toward drinking? You might organize focus groups of students both on and off campus and arrange briefing sessions with student affairs personnel, faculty, and other staff to learn the answers to such questions.

3 **Evaluate your institution's basic position and values.** People have strong individual perceptions about student alcohol and drug abuse. Identify those individuals—your president, deans, alumni director, and others—who are most likely to present a point of view about alcohol and drug abuse to one or more key constituencies. Learn their views and attitudes. Make sure they're in agreement about your institution's guiding philosophy regarding the use of alcohol and drugs. Some institutions have banned alcohol and drugs altogether; others attempt to regulate and control their use. What's your institution's fundamental approach?

4 **Review all relevant policies and procedures to ensure consistency.** Play reporter, and look for discrepancies between word and deed. For instance, does your institution discourage drinking in its formal policies but informally encourage it (or "look the other way") at athletic games and other campus events? Make sure you develop clear, consistent guidelines and that all communications efforts—even the most informal—reinforce your institution's basic values.

5 **Get to know your institution's student affairs staff.** Establish comfortable working relationships and good lines of communication with campus personnel who manage student programs and activities. They can help you understand national data and emerging trends, as well as your campus' policies, procedures, and successful anti-substance abuse programs. They also need to know the questions you face as you interpret and articulate your institution's position on substance abuse.

6 **Learn about your institution's anti-abuse programs.** The Drug-Free Schools and Communities Act Amendments of 1989 require all colleges and universities receiving federal funds to establish anti-drug and alcohol programs. What specific educational, intervention, counseling, and treatment programs has your institution developed? In addition, are there SADD (Students Against Drunk Driving), BAC-CHUS (Boosting Alcohol Consciousness Concerning the Health of University Students), and other national organizations' chapters on your campus? How important and effective are these programs at your institution?

7 **Know the laws and related legal issues.** Laws differ from state to state. Determine the laws and enforcement procedures of your campus and of the surrounding jurisdictions. With your general counsel and campus police, review internal procedures for handling violations and learn about the relationships between campus officials and off-campus law enforcement agencies. In addition, the national Campus Security Act of 1990 requires each institution receiving Title IV student aid assistance to prepare and distribute an annual report that gives statistics on the number of arrests on campus for liquor law and drug-abuse violations. Work with campus police and off-campus enforcement agencies on gathering and disseminating this data.

ONGOING COMMUNICATIONS

1 **Maintain a facts file or briefing book of critical information.** Include in it national and campus data; policies, laws, and enforcement procedures; education, support, and treatment programs; and faculty and staff experts with accurate titles and phone numbers. Keep the file current and in a central location that is accessible to the entire advancement staff.

2 **Identify and communicate regularly with opinion leaders.** Who are the key people within each of your special constituencies you should inform on a continuing basis about your policies and programs? Are there specific parent and student leaders? Trustees and major donors? Also, are there likely critics of your institution's positions, such as outspoken faculty members or community leaders? Build the appropriate network of advancement professionals and other staff who are responsible for communicating with these opinion leaders regularly about your institution's efforts to deal with student alcohol and drug abuse. Don't wait until a crisis hits and you're caught off guard.

3 **Formulate a plan to inform and educate the media.** Encourage the media to cover the national issue and your institution's concerns, policies, and programs before an incident occurs. Think about different ways to examine and portray the problem of alcohol and drug abuse in a broader societal context. Is a professor on your campus researching some of the root causes of substance abuse? Are student groups conducting innovative anti-substance abuse programs to help fellow students? You may want to establish a special "Student Life" beat within your public information office that regularly distributes information about such programs. Furnish journalists with op-ed pieces and national and local statistics; put the media in contact with faculty and staff experts and leaders of student organizations. Don't forget to communicate with established internal media, such as the student newspaper, faculty/staff newsletter, and alumni publications. Encourage them to join you in the education effort.

CRISIS COMMUNICATIONS

1 **Convene a crisis team and assemble the facts.** Include appropriate student life personnel and representatives of the campus police and legal staff on the crisis team. Be sure to think of others who may add valued perspectives, depending upon the crisis. If the incident involves student athletes, for instance, you'll want to include coaches and sports information officers. In addition, students can provide helpful insights as well as effectively communicate with various opinion leaders and the media.

2 **Separate and clarify issues.** Alcohol and drug abuse may be the cause of the incident or only one of several contributing factors. It's extremely important to distinguish the exact role alcohol plays. Is alcohol just one part of a larger problem? If so, you need to acknowledge it as a factor. But don't use it as an excuse for other types of anti-social or illegal behavior, such as racial slurs or sexual assaults.

3 **Develop a basic institutional statement.** This statement provides the essential information to be communicated to the media as well as other key constituencies. Most important, it should express your institution's concern and caring for all the people involved. In addition to the facts, procedures, and plans for dealing with the incident, it should include explanations of any legal restraints on release of information, the institution's philosophy or position on substance abuse, and brief descriptions of your counseling, support, and intervention programs. Acknowledge any problems without being defensive; then tell how you plan to improve the situation.

4 **Relay your institution's perspective to special friends and opinion leaders as soon as possible.** First and foremost, top administrators of your institution should personally contact parents and others directly affected by the incident. Don't let them learn of the crisis from the media. Make sure they know their concerns are among your highest priorities. Also try to reach other friends and opinion leaders before they read about the crisis in the newspaper or see it on the evening news. It's important to have informed people out in the community articulating and reinforcing the institution's position. Get the institutional statement into the hands of the advancement network you've already established—so key administrators can inform trustees and other governing boards, alumni relations staff can contact key alumni, development staff can call major donors, and governmental relations staff can alert appropriate elected officials.

5 **Contact and respond to the national media.** Disseminate the statement to the media and designate a single spokesperson who will make all public statements and to whom all media will be referred. Provide your spokesperson with the appropriate resource people and the statistics and information you've previously compiled. If the situation warrants, arrange a press conference and have members of the student body, student affairs staff, your president, and other senior administrators attend. Again, remember to invite internal media.

6 **Evaluate and follow up.** The chances are good that an alcohol and drug abuse problem will reach the spotlight again. The media may revisit the problem on the anniversary date of the incident or if a major incident happens on another campus. Turn it into an opportunity to set annual goals and monitor your progress. Establish an ongoing evaluation process to prepare for follow-up queries from reporters, to continue to inform and educate, and to prepare for the next crisis—or to assure it never comes.

The individuals listed on the following page attended the CASE forum on alcohol and drug abuse on campus and helped prepare this document. They are willing to share their expertise in more detail with campus advancement professionals confronted with student alcohol and drug abuse.

CAMPUS CONTACTS

Sandy Briscar
Director of Public Information
Berry College
Rome, GA   30149
(404) 232-6825

Tom Goodale
Vice President for Student Affairs
Virginia Polytechnic Institute and State University
112 Burrass Hall
Blacksburg, VA   24061-0250
(703) 231-6272

Sandra Carnet
Director of Public Information
Georgia State University
University Plaza
Atlanta, GA   30303
(404) 651-3570

Jim Langley
Vice President for External Affairs
Georgia Institute of Technology
108 Wardlan Center
Atlanta, GA   30332
(404) 894-5072

Bobby Wayne Clark
Director, Public Information and Publications
Wesleyan University
Middletown, CT   06457
(203) 347-9411

Richard Little
Associate Vice President for University Relations
Miami University
210 Campus Avenue Building
Oxford, OH   45056
(513) 529-7592

Emily Clark
Vice President for Public Affairs
Tulane University
6823 St. Charles Avenue
New Orleans, LA   70118
(504) 865-5123

Carole Pearson
Dean of Student Development
Georgia State University
400 University Center
Atlanta, GA   30303
(404) 651-2206

Terry Denbow
Assistant Vice President, University Relations
Michigan State University
110 Linton Hall
East Lansing, MI   48824-1044
(517) 355-2262

Nancy Seideman
Associate Director, News and Information
Emory University
741 Gatewood Road
Atlanta, GA   30322
(404) 727-6216

Carole Moore
Assistant Vice President of Student Affairs
Georgia Institute of Technology
Atlanta, GA   30332
(404) 894-2000

Connie Stewart
Associate Vice President for University Relations
Emory University
209 Administration Building
Atlanta, GA   30322
(404) 727-4499

SEXUAL HARASSMENT INCIDENTS

November 1991   A CASE Issues Paper for Advancement Professionals   No. 7

University of Oklahoma Professor of Law Anita Hill's accusation that Judge Clarence Thomas sexually harassed her when she worked for him in the early '80s, and the U.S. Senate's public hearing to assess her charges, focused national and international attention on a problem that affects a significant number of people—primarily, but not exclusively, women. Colleges, universities, and independent schools are not immune to this problem. In fact, surveys indicate harassment affects about 35 to 40 percent of the women on a typical college campus. However, because not more than one in 10 of those experiencing harassment actually reports it, the severity of the problem often goes unrecognized.

As the issue of sexual harassment becomes more public and better understood, more harassment victims may seek formal redress. In addition, a growing body of legislation, regulation, and judicial interpretation will better define the problem and bring additional public awareness. No college, university, or school should be lulled into the "it will never happen here" philosophy. Advancement professionals must understand and deal with sexual harassment issues.

Susan Bloch-Nevitte, director of public affairs at the University of Calgary, gained first-hand experience in dealing with such issues when students charged four members of the university's medical faculty with sexual harassment. She offers the following advice to other advancement experts.

BEFORE AN INCIDENT OCCURS

1 **Develop, by consensus, a policy on sexual harassment.** If your institution has established an institutional policy on sexual harassment, review it. If not, encourage your president or school head and other administrators to work together to outline an institutional policy—including both a statement of why it's important to your institution to prevent sexual harassment and procedures to follow during specific incidents of harassment. You need to begin by defining the term, which is harder than it seems in theory. While sexual harassment is defined by law in the United States and judicial precedence in Canada, many areas of ambiguity remain concerning exactly what constitutes sexual harassment. The U.S. courts are still interpreting federal law, for example, on how to more precisely define what is a hostile, offensive, and intimidating environment.

However, it's important to develop as much consensus as possible among faculty, staff, and students. Create a brainstorming committee with representatives from each of these groups. Also consider inviting an influential member of the media; including a representative from outside your institution will give you both perspective and credibility. Don't reinvent the wheel; collect statements and procedures from other similar institutions to see how they've tackled the issue. (Some institutions' procedures encompass other forms of discrimination.) <u>Without fail</u>, make sure your legal counsel reviews the policy before it's final. Your highest governing council should approve it, thereby reinforcing your institution's strong commitment.

2 **Be thorough.** The policy should be as comprehensive as possible and articulate all potential combinations of harassment: student to student (increasing on many campuses today), faculty to student, faculty to faculty, faculty to staff, staff to faculty, staff to staff, even donor/volunteer to staff and vice versa. Be sure to note that staff applies to all levels of staff, including administrators. It's important that your policy takes a strong stand against sexual harassment, includes an educational component to prevent harassment, and clearly defines a grievance procedure with formal routes toward resolution—all based on fairness, promptness, and openness within reason. If your institution establishes a grievance committee, you need to make sure your administration clearly defines who will serve on it, how they will be appointed, and how their findings will be reported back to the community. Also make sure your sexual harassment policy is consistent with your employment policy.

As an advancement professional, you will also want to develop clear guidelines on important communications issues, such as under what circumstances you would inform the public about a case and how much you would disclose. This is an issue of particular importance to public institutions, which must comply with different state laws. It's also important to independent K-12 schools, since they act as *in loco parentis* for minors.

3 **Help important audiences buy into the policy.** Once you've developed the draft policy, run it by every possible constituency group—including the board of trustees and key volunteer groups—to ensure a widespread sense of contribution to and ownership of the product. Look at the draft policy as the public might view it, and make sure it doesn't seem too defensive or overly protective of your institution. Letting a flawed policy get through will only make your institution's life miserable when the first case occurs and damage control is your only option.

4 **Appoint a sexual harassment adviser.** As part of the policy, work with other top administrators to ensure that at least one highly credible individual oversees the policy, serves as the primary grievance resource, and coordinates the educational component. In some cases, your institution may want to appoint more than one person to receive complaints or offer guidance. This is because students, staff, faculty, and other groups may not be comfortable dealing with the same person or office. In fact, some institutions are now appointing a complaint advocate as part of the sexual harassment team. This is to ensure that proper consideration goes not only to the person charged—who can often be a more senior authority figure, such as a faculty member who already enjoys the support of an established professional group or union—but also to the person bringing the charges, such as a student.

5 **Spread the word.** Publicize the existence of the policy and harassment adviser throughout your institution—through special booklets and brochures, and other campus publications—and to external media. Examine regional or national sexual harassment cases to find new angles of publicity for your program. Explore more in-depth stories for your institution's newspaper or magazine; put your adviser on the speaker's circuit. Educating key audiences about the general issue in advance will make communication much easier if, in fact, a specific incidence of sexual harassment occurs at your institution.

6 **Educate.** Work with other administrators to convene campus workshops periodically—for example, during student orientation or throughout the year in residence halls—to educate both men and women about sexual harassment and your institution's policy and programs. It's often best if the president, school head, or other top administrator opens these sessions to reiterate your institution's commitment to the policy. Don't forget to include graduate students and part-time students, as well as staff and faculty. Maintain high visibility for the policy.

7 **Keep current.** Stay in touch with changing state/provincial and national laws on sexual harassment, as well as positions taken by human rights organizations. Your policy should evolve with these changes.

8 **Compile statistics.** Your adviser(s) should keep you abreast of the numbers of, and resolutions to, informal and formal sexual harassment grievances and also make periodic reports to your faculty, staff, and student government. It's important to centralize such statistics so that, if and when you must release information, it will be consistent and accurate. Be prepared to acknowledge that complaints might increase as education on sexual harassment empowers people who might not have filed a grievance in the past.

9 **Designate an external spokesperson.** Know in advance who will speak to the media and other outside audiences if a sexual harassment incident goes public, and provide that person with media training. Make sure he or she is well-acquainted with how to communicate highly sensitive information.

WHEN IT OCCURS

1 **Expect it.** Any community as diverse as a college, university, or school can expect its share of society's ills. So resist the temptation to think that, as a community of great thinkers and leading intellects, you are immune to sexual harassment. In fact, the teacher/student relationship can be particularly fertile ground for such cases.

2 **Don't be defensive.** All members of the institutional community who are involved in handling or communicating about sexual harassment issues must be compassionate—for the accused as well as the victim—while reinforcing that the institution has a comprehensive program in place to handle the matter.

3 **Be prepared.** Few if any institutions are in the habit of issuing press statements on personnel issues—and unless a complainant or respondent takes the case public, now may not be the time. Even so, you should have a clear and concise statement prepared that outlines the complaint, the process, and the educational programs you have in place. Disseminate the statement to any key constituents (board and alumni leaders, donors, and government education officials) who need to understand the situation. If the media contact you, issue the same statement. Make sure this statement clearly spells out any restrictions on information—such as confidentiality clauses in your sexual harassment policy—and stand by them. Your legal counsel should always have his or her stamp of approval on this and other public statements.

4 **Be forthright.** Policy dictates that charges of sexual harassment result in some form of investigation, either by committee or individuals. Once the media are on to a story, be prepared to publicize your findings and recommendations for disciplinary action as forthrightly as possible. Rumors of what did and didn't happen can keep such a story alive in the media for months. Again, it's important to have a previously determined policy defining how much you can disclose about each case; this way you aren't pressured into hasty decisions. Also, if your harassment policy restricts the use of names in any public reports (and most will), expect criticism about "protecting the guilty." There is no agreement on whether to publicize the names of people found guilty of sexual harassment. Legal professionals tend to oppose it; the public tends to demand it. It's a precarious balancing act, and presidents and school heads usually take the advice of their legal counsel.

5 **Be compassionate but firm.** As part of the settlement negotiations, try to establish clear guidelines with the complainant and respondent on what they can and cannot publicly state. Sometimes, during the settlement process, the respondent will negotiate that his or her name not be released. However, an angry complainant--particularly one who feels the grievance policy was faulty or feels the respondent got off too easily--will demand a public hanging in the form of full disclosure, firing, career trashing, or worse. Since this may lead to lawsuits or threats of them, be prepared. If you release further information, double-check every word for accuracy and make sure your legal department or counsel has reviewed it thoroughly. All the while, accept the fact that not everyone will agree with the verdict, communicate your compassion for those involved, and emphasize your confidence in the policy. You <u>must</u> have confidence in the policy.

WHEN THE STORM SUBSIDES

1 **Keep educating.** In communicating the resolution of public cases, be cautious in how you describe the educational process that inevitably follows for all respondents who are found guilty but remain with your institution. The tendency is to describe educational seminars and sensitivity training as a form of punishment. But this attitude could deter others from participating in the ongoing education that is vital to a successful sexual harassment prevention program.

2 **And educate some more.** Work to ensure that your institution runs education programs for the campus community on a host of current workplace issues, such as employment equity, safety and security, and so on. Don't spend all your energy on the hot topic of the day; this creates the perception that you are reactive rather than proactive—or worse, just following the trend.

3 **Rectify policy problems.** If your harassment policy contributed to rather than helped mitigate the problem, suggest that your president or school head appoint a panel of both internal and external representatives to review the policy and make recommendations for improvement. Then publicize the results.

4 **Highlight lessons learned.** If the case received wide publicity, no one has forgotten it after a few months or even a few years. Use your institution's newspaper or magazine for an upbeat story on new programs to improve the work/study environment; at the same time, however, don't shy away from confronting any highly publicized cases. Expect some reluctance from top administrators; you'll have to stand your ground. But recognize that a "what we learned from it" story has remarkable healing potential.

The individuals listed below contributed to this paper and can share their expertise on dealing with sexual harassment issues with other advancement professionals.

Richard Bowman	Jim Collier	Connie Stewart
Director of Information and PR	VP of University Relations	Assoc. VP, University Relations
Queen's University	University of Washington	Emory University
(613) 545-2035	(206) 543-2100	(404) 727-4499
Emily Clark	Sam Pressley	Debra Thomas
VP of Public Affairs	Director of Public Relations	Director of Public Information
Tulane University	Stockton State College	Bryn Mawr College
(504) 865-5000	(609) 652-1776	(215) 526-5137
Cheri Cross	Terry Shepard	Ed Unrau
Director of Communications	Director of News Service	Asst. Director, University Relations
Northfield Mt. Hermon School	Stanford University	University of Manitoba
(413) 498-3000	(415) 723-2300	(204) 474-9518

THE ABRUPT DEPARTURE OF A CHIEF EXECUTIVE OFFICER

May 1992   A CASE Issues Paper for Advancement Professionals   No. 9

College and university presidents and independent school heads are leaving their positions at a faster rate than ever before. In 1991, in one month alone, four presidents unexpectedly announced their resignations from higher education institutions in Vermont. In fact, the average tenure of a college president at a public institution is now only about 3.5 years.

While each situation differs, all resignations have certain principles in common. For one thing, advancement professionals can be best prepared by putting good ongoing communications approaches in place before any such crisis arises. In addition, the departure of a president or school head usually goes through three phases: (1) the build-up before the fact, (2) the announcement of the situation or its resolution, and (3) the follow-up.

Ron Nief, director of public affairs at Middlebury College, gained firsthand experience handling such an instance when his president suddenly resigned in September of 1991. He also consulted with senior advancement experts from around the country, including those at larger public institutions. He recommends the following to other advancement officers who must handle a similar crisis at their own institutions.

BEFORE THE CRISIS

1   **Determine your philosophical framework.** Especially in cases where the chief executive officer and the board are at odds, your own personal allegiance may be called into question. Unfortunately, people on one side or another may try to avail themselves of your talents to present their particular position--a situation you should carefully and skillfully avoid. It's best to establish right off that your allegiance is to the institution, its character, and its good name. All your subsequent decisions and activities should fit within the context of this overarching philosophical framework.

2   **Establish good long term relations with your trustees.** If you haven't already formed strong ties with the members of your institution's board, start today. At times of turmoil, such as the departure of a chief excutive officer, you will want to be able to work with them as naturally and routinely as possible. Of course, you can't develop such a relationship overnight. Attend trustee meetings whenever possible and make yourself available and helpful when board members are on campus.

3   **Organize, or at least help identify, appropriate members for a crisis team.** This group should include trusted people in various areas of the campus. It is critical to organize key administrators in charge of communicating with various constituencies—directors of development, alumni affairs, student affairs, and the like—in advance so they can work effectively together. You don't want to wait until a crisis occurs—and things are inherently pretty chaotic—before you call upon them. Work with them to develop a crisis plan as an integral part of your long-term communications efforts.

4   **Anticipate the possibility.** Unlike other crises (such as a fire, car crash, or sexual attack) that are truly unanticipated, there are usually signs that there is a problem afoot with the chief executive officer a few days, if not months, ahead. Each situation, however, will vary as to how much warning you'll actually receive. Clearly, a case of the chief executive departing in connection with some crime, during an investigation of his or her behavior, due to a vote of no confidence by the faculty, or as a result of accusations gives plenty of signals well in advance. The process of accusers and defenders debating on campus—of accusations, denial, evidence, more denials, and so on—provides plenty of time to examine the possibilities.

In other cases, such as when the chief executive abruptly decides to resign due to his or her own frustrations on the job, you may have a lot less time to plan. *In fact, in extreme cases, you may have only minutes.* Therefore, the best approach is to at least consider a sudden departure as one of the options for the chief executive in a controversial situation.

THE CRISIS BEGINS

1 **Evaluate the reasons for the departure.** After you first sense an imminent resignation or dismissal, you need to evaluate the reason or reasons behind it. Is it because the fit between the chief executive officer and the institution is not right? Or has he or she engaged in inappropriate behavior or malfeasance? The underlying reason for the potential departure is the most important variable in the approach you, as an advancement professional, should follow.

Where accusations are involved, determine exactly what the charges are and how the chief executive might respond. Evaluate his or her personality: Is the person gracious in defeat, combative, manipulative? Try to predict the CEO's reactions, both in the short and long term. Identify the accusers and consider the position the board will probably take. (In most cases, only one person can dismiss the chief executive, and that is the chair of the board.)

2 **Work to dispel rumors.** As information starts to leak out, news—both factual and erroneous—will fly. In such times of crisis, information can travel in a rapid yet disorganized and contradictory fashion. Make sure you know all the facts. As a matter of policy, institutional relations professionals and other advancement officers should always have access to any information pertaining to the departure. However, in the worst cases, you may have to play reporter yourself; don't expect information to come to you. Identify the best sources of information on campus and call them to find out what they are hearing. Use them to spread the right story unofficially. At the same time, make sure people know they can call you at home or in the office to clarify the facts. You may also want to enlist a trusted colleague to take on the role of rumor warden.

3 **Keep opinion leaders, including media representatives, informed.** Dealing with the speculation and brushfires may prove to be the most difficult period of the crisis. If the departure is related to a public scandal over which the board is deliberating, you will certainly be receiving calls from a range of interested constituents. Even if it is of a more private nature, you may still have to field queries based on the aforementioned rumors. In fact, journalists and other external audiences may receive the information as fast or even faster than you. Whatever you do, they will still be calling faculty, board members, and others trying to obtain comments—often anonymously.

Be careful to assure key media figures, top editors in the local community, and opinion leaders in various constituencies that you are on top of things, are thinking of them, and will be back to them as soon as you have something definite to report. For a certain period of time, you can fall back on the "we're still gathering of information" or "we know of no formal charges" or "we haven't seen the document yet" responses to inquiries. But that will work for 24 hours or one newspaper edition at best. Don't leave people hanging. Be as honest as you can without compromising your institution. Make every effort to resolve the issue and get the chief executive officer into a public forum as soon as possible.

4 **Prepare for potential fallout.** If there is a period of investigation or negotiation, or if the chief executive is forced out under a cloud of suspicion, there is a high probability you will have to deal with other issues. These usually originate from disgruntled current or former employees who have been waiting for the chance to vent their anger at the chief executive, others closely associated with the chief executive, and the institution in general. Usually the rumors contain just enough truth to keep the story alive, so you have to deal with them seriously.

5 **Monitor the situation carefully.** You hope that this phase of the crisis will not last too long. Especially if protracted negotiations are involved, the story may play out among the media and attorneys for various parties. Public statements and accusations can change daily, both in positive and negative ways. Daily accusations and denials tend to give the accusers the headlines; the media, unaware of anything more than the rumors, will send reporters generally unfamiliar with higher education—or with your institution, for that matter—to campus seeking quotable opinions of undergraduates and other people wanting to offer their views. You may want to start compiling a notebook of key facts, statements, interviews, news coverage, and the like to keep the record straight during this tumultuous period. These are the times when you earn your pay.

THE ANNOUNCEMENT

1 **Prepare a formal statement.** As soon as information is available, organize it into a statement that's as objective as possible and avoid all speculation or innuendo. This statement, the fundamental document all parties should agree to abide by, forms the basis for all other communications. You will be working closely with the trustees to address their concerns while also being fair and open.

The statement should explain very clearly the chief executive officer's future with the institution. Will he or she hold tenure? If you are at a public institution, you will probably have to communicate the financial terms of the agreement as well. You may also have to justify paying a separation package in these times of campus cost cutting and retrenchment. (Before you get to this stage, in fact, you may want to advise your trustees that substantial golden parachutes often have negative effects on an institution's reputation.)

Also, if there are specific reasons for the chief executive stepping down, the chair of the board must address them, and if appropriate, announce some definite plans for dealing with them. If your trustees don't do it now, somebody else will demand it and force the trustees to do it later. However, you should always request a copy of the chief executive's resignation letter and be aware of any agreement not to disclose exact reasons. The increasing risk of litigation makes it difficult for some boards to announce the specific reasons behind a departure. Such cases are more challenging for the advancement professional: You need to be as honest as possible but, at the same time, more careful.

2 **Keep in mind the dignity of both the individual and the institution.** The most important aspects of this phase are fairness and respect. If appropriate, have the board chair praise the chief executive for his or her contributions and accomplishments. In cases of malfeasance, the chair should express concern and sympathy for the individual and his or her family.

Keep the statement simple and direct. Detail tends to sound defensive. Hiding suggests a feeling of guilt. Blaming others is undignified. Remember that over the long term, it is the institution that can suffer the most. Your board and administrators' response to the situation must embody the sensitivity, character, and dignity expected of the academy. If your institution appears to be cold and heartless, it may reflect an internal problem that is much larger than the chief executive's departure.

3 **Alert each key institutional leader personally.** Advise top administrators and work with them to schedule meetings with the leadership of the faculty, staff, and student government immediately. (The chief executive officer will have already informed close friends and colleagues, so the rumor mill will already be in overdrive.) You will need their support to help communicate to the rest of the campus and to important external audiences.

While this is going on, other members of the crisis team should assemble lists of key people—including the governor or local leaders, key donors, trustees and other governing boards, alumni leadership, parents committee leaders, and the like—and contact or meet with them personally. However, no matter how thorough you try to be, you may accidentally neglect someone in the process. In fact, you may want to have a letter of apology ready for any individuals you unintentionally overlook.

4 **Communicate the news to the general campus community.** As soon as the crisis team completes these calls and meetings, you should deliver the written statement to student and faculty mailboxes or post it on key bulletin boards throughout the campus. You might also want to schedule an address by the chair of the trustees to the campus community several hours later or the following day—and include a release announcing this address with the statement. Or, it may be most effective to send a letter from the chair of the board to every faculty and staff member. Also, as soon as possible, begin working with the faculty newspaper and alumni magazine staffs to develop stories to include in their periodicals.

5 **Inform the media.** At the same time you are telling the campus community, you must begin the faxes and phone calls to the media. It's important you orchestrate the timing of your communications to both internal and external audiences carefully. You don't want faculty and staff reading about the situation in the newspaper, but you also don't want reporters to receive only rumors and second-hand information.

The method for distributing the information depends on various factors. In some cases, a release to the media, drafted at the same time as the formal statement, will suffice. In others, you may need to organize a full-blown press conference. If the chief executive officer desires or the situation requires a press conference, it would be most ideal if the chief executive is available to speak. The trustees should be in the wings. Otherwise, the public relations director should become the conduit for communicating information about the situation to external audiences—or, at least, should orchestrate the efforts.

Keep in mind the special needs of the broadcast media. For instance, you may want to develop special audio releases for local radio stations. Pay close attention to the student newspaper as well. Also, if the chief executive officer is not able or willing to speak to the media, he or she should truly be unavailable. Otherwise, the chief executive may find reporters camping out at his or her home in search of quotes and comments.

6 **Enlist your board members to serve as public relations ambassadors.** This is also a time when the trustees earn their stripes. Encourage trustees to join you and other administrators in communicating about the situation throughout the community your institution serves—at the local, state, and national levels. Make sure they receive a copy of the final statement and understand the key issues. Provide them with appropriate background and brief them on questions they should be prepared to answer. Help schedule them to speak at campus events, alumni reunions and gatherings, and community meetings like local Rotary or chamber of commerce functions.

THE FOLLOW-UP

1 **Announce the interim or new leadership as soon as possible.** Getting on with things is always the best way to start rebuilding confidence. The announcement of the new or the interim leader is critical. If speculation about the new leader is given too much time to spread, it will become speculation on the direction, role, and leadership of the institution. Especially after a long period of negative publicity and difficult negotiations, most people on and off campus are ready to jump on a positive bandwagon and move forward.

2 **Introduce the new leadership to key constituencies.** Organize a major announcement from the new chief executive officer to the campus community. Such an announcement—preceded by a statement of confidence from the board chair—should include lots of supportive people: the faculty, the board, the staff, and the students. It is theater. The announcement should be the message of hope that brings the campus together and points everyone in the same direction. As this message goes out, attitudes will start to change. Be sure to have lots of copies of the announcement and background on the new chief executive available immediately. Also begin the process of substituting the new or interim chief executive's signature on all recruitment, alumni, donor, and other literature.

3 **Issue a statement on the institution's immediate future.** The new leader must be a visible symbol of confidence for alumni, students, donors, and the broader community. With your help, he or she must present the direction the institution will follow from this moment forward. Most immediately, he or she must spend the next 48 hours meeting with campus groups; appearing in the dining halls; receiving people from the local community; and communicating with representatives of the broader college, university, or school community. You may want to encourage news coverage of some of these events.

4 **Follow up with key constituencies.** You will spend the next week on the phone. Be as responsive as possible. Everyone may have a theory as to what actually happened. If the outgoing chief executive has had successes during his or her tenure—as many have—it makes the situation even tougher. Choosing up sides can continue for some time after the separation. Stay with the statement. It is the only element of consistency in the whole unpleasant scenario. Concentrate on the future and avoid debating the past.

5 **Expect surprises.** Even after the dust appears to be finally settling, the departing chief executive may recant, change his or her attitude from agreeable to argumentative, or offer a different reason for his or her departure. Be prepared to take the offensive; don't just sit back and let the former chief executive grab the headlines. Keep open the lines of communication to both internal and external audiences. A specific tip: Videotape all public statements involved with the resignation or dismissal. That way, you can always substantiate your institution's position and point out any discrepancies between the chief executive officer's previous and current comments.

6 **Look to the future.** This time of transition can be a period of opportunity. Although the resignation or dismissal of a chief executive officer may be a difficult and tumultuous time for your institution, you can use the occasion to develop innovative ideas and approaches. Show leadership by initiating contact with the new administration and by developing an exciting, revitalized plan for the future.

The senior professionals listed below contributed to this paper and can share their expertise on dealing with the sudden departure of a chief executive officer. Also, as a matter of policy, you should regularly consult with your institution's legal counsel.

Jim Bennett
Assistant Vice President
Office of University Relations
University of Tennessee
Knoxville, TN 37996
(615) 974-2225

Linda Gibbs
Director of Administrative Services
National Association of Independent Schools
75 Federal Street
Boston, MA 02110
(617) 451-2444

Sandra Golden
Associate Vice President,
Public Affairs and Information
Cuyahoga Community College
Cleveland, OH 44155
(216) 987-4804

Sharon Jones
Director of College Relations
Mills College
Oakland, CA 94613
(510) 430-2100

Paul Kincaid
Director of University Relations
Southwest Missouri State University
Springfield, MO 65804
(417) 836-5139

Christine Koukola
Assistant Vice Chancellor for University Relations
University of Missouri, Columbia
Columbia, MO 65804
(314) 882-4523

Joel Lonergan
Director of University Relations
University of Alabama at Huntsville
Huntsville, AL 35899
(205) 895-6414

Nicola Marro
Director of Public Relations
University of Vermont
Burlington, VT 05401
(802) 656-3131

Michael Mulnix
Executive Director of University Relations
University of Nebraska, Lincoln
Lincoln, NE 68588
(402) 472-2116

Gail Raiman
Vice President for Public Affairs
National Association of Independent
Colleges and Universities
122 C Street, NW, Suite 750
Washington, DC 20001
(202) 347-7512

David Taylor
Director of Communications
University of Maryland, Baltimore
Baltimore, MD 21201
(410) 328-7336

William Walker
Director of University Relations
College of William and Mary
Williamsburg, VA 23815
(804) 221-2624

HIV/AIDS ON CAMPUS

October 1992   A CASE Issues Paper for Advancement Professionals   No. 11

AIDS continues to challenge our society. Like other major institutions, colleges, universities, and independent schools must grapple with a multitude of issues surrounding HIV and AIDS.

According to a survey conducted by the National Association of People With AIDS, more than one-third of Americans diagnosed with AIDS believe they became infected when they were 18-21 years old. However, besides traditional-aged students, HIV/AIDS is affecting people of all ages and occupations, including faculty, administrators, health care workers, and others on campuses. Experts at the University of Alabama at Birmingham predict that by 1993, AIDS will become the No. 1 cause of years of productive life lost among people between the ages of 21 and 44.

At the same time, thanks to medical and scientific advances, people with HIV have greater life expectancies and are continuing to live relatively normal lifestyles more frequently than in the past. As a result, it will become increasingly common for colleges, universities, and independent schools to have greater numbers of people with HIV living and working in the campus community.

The federal Americans with Disabilities Act, the Rehabilitation Act of 1973, as well as certain state and municipal laws and regulations, mandates that there be nondiscrimination in the treatment of persons with HIV/AIDS regardless of their role within an institution. What's more, because of increased HIV/AIDS awareness, today it's much less common for a campus situation to cause the kind of panic or attract the widespread media attention it did in previous years. The communications challenges for advancement officers now focus much less on dealing with HIV/AIDS as a crisis and more on ongoing education to help accommodate the needs of persons with HIV/AIDS—while building knowledge, sensitivity, and understanding among others in the campus community.

Institutional advancement officers are taking the lead in helping their colleges, universities, and schools acknowledge and understand the realities of HIV/AIDS and in educating a wide range of on- and off-campus constituencies about the disease. They are helping communicate the most effective ways for these constituencies to protect themselves against HIV and reassure these groups of the high standards of education and awareness at their institutions. In addition, if a situation ever becomes a public relations crisis—as sometimes is the case when a health care worker who has treated many patients tests HIV positive—advancement professionals are often among the first called to help deal with such an incident and the potential misconceptions that could accompany it.

Michael Lawrence dealt with this type of challenge in 1991 when he served as interim director of the Office of News and Information at the University of Texas Health Science Center at San Antonio and a dental student tested positive for HIV. In addition, he has consulted with other institutional advancement experts around the country who have also had hands-on experience dealing with HIV/AIDS-related incidents. He has compiled the following general suggestions to help advancement professionals cope with HIV/AIDS education and incidents on their own campuses.

It should be stressed, however, that HIV/AIDS is an exceptionally complex issue and each situation varies, especially as the issue continues to develop over time. For instance, while a few cases—such as those involving health care workers—may under some circumstances suggest a public announcement, most do not. While the following are guidelines, you, your administration, and your trustees should always work with medical professionals, legal counsel, and other experts on your campus to determine the best approach for your specific situation.

GENERAL GUIDELINES

1 **Educate your trustees, president, school head, and other administrators on the critical importance of HIV/AIDS awareness and education.** Help them understand that HIV/AIDS is not going to go away and incidents will occur on your campus—no matter how insulated it may currently appear. Explain that an effective continuing communications program can require significant amounts of time and effort, but that the investment is definitely worth it. (To help make your point, you may need to highlight cases that reflect the costs of doing otherwise.) Consider organizing a retreat or special staff function, and invite a public health expert to talk about the speed with which the epidemic is spreading and the increasing importance of being prepared to deal with it—both from an ongoing education and a crisis management standpoint.

2 **Recommend that your trustees and administration establish a high-level HIV/AIDS task force.** If they haven't already done so, your president, school head, and other senior officials should bring together a group of trusted people from various areas of the campus and charge them with the responsibility of understanding and dealing with the medical, legal, ethical, moral, and psychological aspects of the disease. Besides student affairs administrators, medical experts, and health officials on your campus, the group could include experts from the institutional relations, legal affairs, personnel, and counseling offices, as well as representatives from faculty, students, and other administrative areas. (This group would, of course, vary depending on the nature and size of your institution.) You may also want to include, if possible, appropriate trustees, donors, alumni leaders, or other respected members of the community on this team. If involved and supportive, these opinion leaders can provide valuable perspective.

Work with the task force to develop a crisis plan as an integral part of your long-term communications effort. You could also designate a special crisis mini-team from among the task force that can come together to help trustees and administrators make decisions quickly. The task force should also oversee development of an official HIV/AIDS policy to help direct your institution in dealing with HIV/AIDS issues and incidents in the future.

3 **Help trustees and senior administrators establish an official HIV/AIDS policy and distribute it widely.** If you don't have a policy, start developing one. If you already have one, review it periodically to include new information, changes in statutes, or innovative approaches and strategies in dealing with HIV/AIDS on your campus. Make sure the policy addresses issues including your own state laws on the subject—which can vary significantly from other state and federal laws and change frequently. Also make sure it deals with confidentiality; legal liability; condemnation of discriminatory behavior; access to care and insurance; access to campus facilities, including housing; admissions, hiring, promotions, and dismissal; HIV antibody testing and counseling; and day-to-day modification, if needed, of the duties of the person with HIV/AIDS and those of his or her co-workers and classmates. Once completed, you should disseminate the policy to all members of the campus community. [The National Association of College and University Attorneys offers a 500-page legal compendium on HIV/AIDS on campus that includes sample policies from 12 institutions. To order a copy, send $35 to NACUA, Suite 620, One Dupont Circle, Washington, DC 20036.] (See Nos. 4 and 9 for more on policies.)

4 **Keep the policy flexible.** Experts recommend that rather than adopting blanket policies concerning students, faculty, administrators, or others with HIV/AIDS or AIDS-related conditions, an institution should establish general guidelines and then analyze and respond to each case as required by its own particular circumstances. According to the American Council on Education (ACE), which has spelled out guidelines in the form of a general statement of institutional response to HIV/AIDS: "The best statement for now is one that is based on principles of flexibility, simplicity, and concern for individual as well as community welfare. Campuses that have already issued such policy statements primarily have chosen to consider each case of AIDS on a case by case basis, attending to the principles stated above."

To request a copy of the ACE document, *AIDS on Campus*, send a self-addressed, large (9"x12") envelope showing 98 cents postage to the Office of Women in Higher Education, ACE, One Dupont Circle, Suite 800, Washington, DC 20036. The document is free, but postage must accompany requests. For additional information, contact Donna Shavlik, director of the Office of Women in Higher Education, at (202) 939-9300. In addition, the Association of Governing Boards of Universities and Colleges also offers "AIDS and HIV: Policy Guidelines for Boards." [Call Matt Stevens at (800) 356-6317 to order a copy of the 45-page report.]

5 **Offer HIV/AIDS awareness and education programs for all students, staff, and faculty.** Even if an HIV/AIDS situation has not yet arisen at your institution, education should always be a top priority. With student affairs personnel, include educational programs as part of freshman orientation or HIV/AIDS awareness days. Provide educational sessions during lunch or in-service training for employees, administrators, and faculty. Write about HIV/AIDS-related issues and education in your employee, faculty, student, and even alumni publications.

Because information dissemination alone does not necessarily lead to behavioral change, it's important to offer as many opportunities as possible to discuss and process information in a group. Also make sure training includes informing faculty, employees, and students about sensitivities in working, living, and/or studying with persons with HIV/AIDS. A part of the educational effort should point out that discrimination or failure to treat someone appropriately could result in disciplinary action.

6 **Promote the availability of these HIV/AIDS education programs widely and tailor them to specific campus audiences.** Work with student affairs and other experts on campus to publicize educational programs through videotapes, brochures, pamphlets, posters, and the like, as well as through advertisements and publicity in campus media. Make sure it's clear that these programs are widely available to all—graduate and professional students as well as undergraduates, faculty members, and staff at all levels including senior administrators.

Again working with student affairs experts, make sure programs also pay attention to the needs of specific student groups--such as women; gay, lesbian, and bisexual students; U.S. students studying abroad; and international students. For example, Florida International University offers its students and makes available in bulk to other campuses a four-color brochure titled "What Do You Know About AIDS? Information for International Students in the U.S." [For more information contact Florida International University's director of publications, Terry Witherell, at (305) 348-2236.] Also, if your institution has medical facilities, it should provide educational programs about HIV/AIDS and the reduction of risk to health care providers.

7 **Establish a central health care office or identify a key individual who will serve as an HIV/AIDS counselor or resource person.** This individual's primary role should be to serve as a first point of contact for students, faculty, administrators, and others about HIV/AIDS and refer them to other experts and community services.

The resource person should be able to inform those with HIV/AIDS-related concerns about such aspects as (1) clinics where HIV antibody testing and counseling are available, (2) services available for people testing HIV positive, (3) names of physicians known to be sympathetic and experienced in dealing with persons with HIV/AIDS, (4) arrangements within the institution that can be made to accommodate the needs of a person with HIV/AIDS while maintaining confidentiality, and (5) disability benefits available to full-time, permanent employees who have HIV-related illnesses.

8 **Enlist student volunteers to help educate other students, and publicize their efforts.** Students often respond more to HIV/AIDS education when it comes from peers. Many institutions are increasingly relying on student volunteers to teach and counsel other students in classrooms, residence halls, fraternities and sororities, and other sites where they congregate. Help student affairs, health service, and counselling personnel establish a peer education network and then communicate about these volunteers to the campus community. Your administrative team will need to provide these student volunteers with training, as well as brochures, pamphlets, and other materials to distribute. If any questions arise that the students aren't prepared to answer, make sure they know the appropriate experts to contact. Also, while you must be especially sensitive to their feelings and concerns, some students with HIV may even be willing to help inform others and serve as spokespersons.

9 **Keep current.** Use qualified medical personnel with the latest information for your education programs, since procedures and knowledge on this topic are changing rapidly. The Centers for Disease Control also offers a toll-free hotline [(800) 342-AIDS] that provides callers with the most up-to-date information. Also, an excellent source of information specific to colleges and universities is the American College Health Association, which offers detailed recommendations for developing HIV/AIDS policies and establishing effective prevention programs. It offers, for example, free workshops on developing peer education programs, as well as a manual to help each institution improve its peer education program. It has also developed informative, easy-to-read brochures—on topics such as safe sex, HIV infection, the HIV antibody test, and women and AIDS, among others—to distribute on your campus. In addition, ACHA and six other higher education associations have compiled a campus self-assessment inventory to help colleges and universities develop, promote, and monitor HIV/AIDS prevention and support programs. [For information, contact the American College Health Association at (410) 859-1500.]

10 **Work with your local public health department or other agencies.** Your area health districts publish materials and provide statistics you can distribute on your campus. Experts at local health departments are often willing to serve as spokespersons for any public announcements you decide to make. They can offer both background information and an objectivity to put any incident on your campus in a larger perspective.

11 **Establish guidelines for informing the media about specific incidents, and always keep in mind the individual's legal right to privacy.** Now is the time to establish clear guidelines for communicating with the media about any possible future HIV/AIDS incidents on your campus. While, again, you must be flexible, make sure your policy includes such guidelines and appropriately balances the right of the person with HIV/AIDS to privacy with the community's right to know. Privacy laws are strict; under the federal Americans with Disabilities Act, an employer must keep all medical information absolutely confidential except where there is a "need to know." This need—when an identifiable risk to others exists—is defined narrowly. Because most job descriptions for faculty or administrators and student academic/extracurricular activities do not involve either the exchange of body fluids or any contact with body fluids, usually there would be no need to inform anyone of an individual's HIV/AIDS status—with some exceptions, such as health care workers. Work closely with personnel and legal experts on your institution's HIV/AIDS task force to develop your guidelines. You can also contact the American College Health Association [please see No. 9], which has prepared general guidelines on AIDS confidentiality.

12 **Work to help educate the media about HIV/AIDS in general.** When possible, provide background for the media, and encourage journalists to cover the problem from a broad and in-depth perspective before any crisis occurs. If you have medical experts on HIV/AIDS or its associated public policy issues, and it's appropriate, invite media on campus for a briefing on the latest information on the disease and describe the precautions, educational programs, and other measures your institution is taking to deal with it. Working together with the media in the longer term will help put any incident that may occur in a more accurate and balanced perspective.

13 **Designate external spokespersons.** Decide in advance who will speak to outside audiences if a crisis occurs and provide those individuals with media training. In many cases, besides a media relations professional, you should identify a medical or public health expert as well. (If you don't have a medical unit on your campus, contact your local public health organization. Please see No. 10.) Make sure these spokespersons are well acquainted with how to communicate highly sensitive information.

IF A CRISIS ARISES

As mentioned previously, it is rare for an HIV/AIDS incident to require dissemination of information to the public. However, those institutions with medical facilities where health care professionals are treating patients might find themselves confronted with the need to advise others of an HIV/AIDS case on campus. These cases can present especially difficult communications challenges for institutional advancement professionals. You will need to protect the identity and privacy of the affected individual, but at the same time you might need to advise those who might also need to know for their own health and protection. Again, before taking any action, you should always thoroughly consult with legal counsel based on the specifics of your own situation. The following are only meant as general guidelines.

1 **Convene the crisis team and determine your communications objectives and strategy.** In most cases, your most fundamental objective will be to reach those individuals most directly affected and help them through this extremely difficult situation. This is a time for compassion and support. You must ask yourself key questions, such as: What are the most immediate needs of the individual with HIV? How much information does this individual want to release? Who else may be directly at risk?

2 **Inform the person with HIV about any proposed public or in-house announcements regarding the situation.** In many instances, a public announcement will not be necessary. However, when you must make an announcement, be particularly mindful of confidentiality laws and the individual's right to privacy. Also, if the individual retains his or her own legal counsel, you should inform this counsel about any proposed public announcements.

3 **Don't presume to know what anyone in-house or in the community knows about HIV/AIDS or how they will react to it.** Regardless of any previous educational efforts, proceed as if all individuals need maximum explanation about the disease itself and the institution's plans for handling the situation.

4 **If there are patients involved, work with other institutional administrators to inform them about the situation and see that they receive an immediate test for HIV antibodies, if appropriate.** This may be especially important if the individual performs any procedures in his or her capacity with your institution that could be considered high-risk, such as surgery. Be prepared to offer significant support and reassurance, and to offer free, anonymous testing to anyone contacted. Administrators should send registered letters and make phone calls *before* making any public announcements.

(NOTE: Ironically, however, officials at the University of Texas Health Science Center at San Antonio found the most helpful way to avoid leaks and rumors was to bring the media into their confidence early. The university development board president invited leading media representatives to her home and explained the situation—and the need to protect the individuals involved and prevent potential panic. The audience was supportive and agreed to wait until the university contacted patients before demanding further information and breaking any stories. Of course, this approach may not always be possible and involves some risk.)

5 **If the situation warrants a public announcement, prepare a statement and background information.** The statement will form the basis for all your communications efforts. The statement should include: your general policy on HIV/AIDS, the facts of the situation, the steps your institution is taking to deal with it, and specific information offering help to any other individuals directly affected by it. You could also compile information giving a national perspective on HIV/AIDS, a list of telephone numbers of health organizations concerned with HIV/AIDS, and, if possible, letters from professional organizations and state and federal health officials supporting your institution's handling of the situation.

You should always protect the person with HIV/AIDS and make no reference to age, sex, or any other aspect that might reveal his or her identity. Make sure your legal counsel reviews in advance all documents for public release. Remember, under current laws, your institution could be held liable if the identity of the individual is revealed without his or her consent.

6 **Enlist knowledgeable and credible faculty and other experts to help field questions.** Identify a central telephone number that anyone in-house or in the community can call for information and reassurance. Ask faculty from your medical and dental schools or psychology department to help in field calls and queries. Or, if you don't have such individuals on your own campus, try to find outside experts to help out. It's best to route all calls through the institutional relations office, but make sure these staff members know to refer callers to the experts. Also don't forget to enlist experts who speak Spanish or other commonly spoken languages in your community.

7 **Alert the media.** If you decide to advise the general public, you could hold a press conference or briefing or simply send out a release and the background materials. Sometimes a press conference is preferable because it enables administrators to answer questions as effectively and efficiently as possible, as well as hear each other's responses and reinforce them. The president or school head and—depending on your institution—the dean of students or academic affairs, the deans of the medical or dental school, infection control experts, and outside experts from local or city health organizations should attend. Allow plenty of time for questions and answer honestly, keeping in mind confidentiality issues. If appropriate, use the opportunity to educate the audience about the state-of-the-art infection control measures—including masks, gloves and chemicals—your institution's medical facilities use.

You should also determine in advance any sections of your medical or dental facilities—or other areas of the campus—where you can escort camera crews to shoot.

8 **Continue to distribute information through other campus communications vehicles.** For instance, prepare a campus news bulletin with the same information contained in the background statement for institutional staff. Post it on all general bulletin boards and send it interoffice mail to all departments. Also work with other communications outlets—your student newspaper, faculty newsletter, and alumni periodical—to get information to as many in the campus community as possible. For more information on specific communications and advancement aspects dealing with HIV/AIDS on campus, see "A Case of AIDS" and "The Best Defense" in the July 1988 CURRENTS.

9 **Evaluate and follow up.** In the days and weeks that follow, remain open to the media; expect journalists as well as others to follow up with further questions. Keep in touch with the infected individual and his or her legal counsel to make sure you continue to respect his or her privacy and release only appropriate information.

Finally, review your policy as well as any specific incidents and determine whether you might have done anything differently. Then adjust your policies and procedures accordingly so you will be well prepared for the future.

The senior professionals listed on the following page contributed to this paper and can share their expertise on dealing with HIV/AIDS cases on campus. This information is not intended to be legal or medical advice for your specific institution. You should always consult your institution's own legal and medical experts about HIV/AIDS policies, programs, and incidents on campus.

Karen Adams
Director, Marketing and Public Relations
Dundalk Community College
Dundalk, MD 21222-4692
(410) 285-9690

Susan Bonnett
Assistant Vice President for University Relations
University of Miami
Coral Gables, FL 33124
(305) 284-5500

John F. Burness
Senior Vice President for Public Affairs
Duke University
Durham, NC 27706
(919) 681-3788

Connie Crowther
Director, University Relations
Florida International University
Miami, FL 33199
(305) 348-2233

Toni Eisner
Assistant Vice President for
Equal Opportunity Programs
Florida International University
Miami, FL 33199
(305) 348-2785

Carol Fox
Director of News Services
University of California, San Francisco
San Francisco, CA 94143
(415) 476-2557

Richard P. Keeling
Director, Department of Student Health
University of Virginia
Charlottesville, VA 22908
(804) 924-2670

Michael Lawrence
Assistant Director, Public Affairs
University of Texas Health Science Center
at San Antonio
San Antonio, TX 78284
(512) 567-2570

Jack McCune
Head of the Upper School
Saint Albans School
Washington, DC 20016
(202) 537-6435

Alice Trinkl
Manager, News Services
San Francisco General Hospital Campus
University of California, San Francisco
San Francisco, CA 94110
(415) 476-3804

Ken Wildes
Director, University Relations
Northwestern University
Evanston, IL 60201
(708) 491-5000

Ken Wittingham
Director, Public Relations
Concordia University
Montreal, Quebec H3G 1M8
(514) 848-2424

ACQUAINTANCE RAPE ON CAMPUS

December 1992   A CASE Issues Paper for Advancement Professionals   No. 12

While most experts agree that acquaintance rape has occurred from time to time on campus for many years, only recently has extensive public attention been paid to it. In fact, many observers still object to even the term "date rape" or "acquaintance rape," believing that distinguishing it from other types of rape suggests that the act is somehow less offensive. In the early 1990s, however, the news media made acquaintance rape a national issue. As the issue has become more public and better understood, more acquaintance rape victims have come forward to seek redress.

Although the problem of date rape is certainly not exclusive to colleges and universities, its impact on campuses has been formidable. Date rape has tested severely institutional policies and procedures governing student behavior—and the communications surrounding these policies and procedures. Colleges and universities are charged with the education and development of a group of people, many of whom have reached the age of majority and therefore are subject to the laws that govern the behavior of adults. At the same time, the institutions are responsible for maintaining communities where young people can live, work, learn, and develop socially in an environment that is insulated from society. To accomplish this, most institutions have developed rules and regulations—in addition to rules mandated by state and federal law—to govern further the behavior of these young adults.

A woman victimized by date rape off campus may have no effective recourse against her assailant other than through the criminal justice system. If the assault takes place on campus, however, and involves members of the college or university community, the woman has the option of pursuing administrative action short of— and often in addition to—a criminal or civil lawsuit. Whether our institutions should or should not be in the position of adjudicating rape cases presents a serious and legitimate question, but that is not the subject of this paper. The issue addressed here is how we use our skills and resources to deal with this important question of student behavior in ways that promote the best interests of our institutions and the students they serve.

Advancement professionals can play a key role in dealing with the issue by helping organize and publicize ongoing education and information programs about acquaintance rape and other kinds of sex offenses, forcible and non-forcible, both on campus and in the general community. Not infrequently, we are also called upon to deal with specific incidents that occur on our campuses.

An incident that occurred in the fall of 1990 at the College of William and Mary became a nationally known case that sparked much public debate in early 1991. A freshman woman said she had been raped by her date, and subsequently reported the incident to the administration for adjudication. Unsatisfied with the outcome of the hearing, she took the unusual step of going public—asking the local news media to use her name and photograph and launching extensive news coverage. **William Walker**, director of university relations at William and Mary, handled this incident and based on his own experience offers the following advice to other advancement experts. He also draws suggestions from other senior advancement professionals and student affairs experts who met to discuss the topic at a recent special CASE forum at Bryn Mawr College. While the optimal approach to this subject is likely to depend on applicable state and federal legal requirements, prevailing college or university policy, and other institution-specific requirements, the following suggestions should be useful to many institutions.

ONGOING COMMUNICATIONS

1 **Work with other top administrators to develop sound official policies and codes of conduct.** If your institution doesn't have such policies and procedures, it should develop them now—and, indeed, is compelled to do so by recently enacted federal law. Senior administrators should review the policies and procedures periodically. Work with others to establish a task force representing various key constituencies—including student affairs, legal, and communications experts as well as faculty members and students—to get in-depth advice from each. Consider including representatives from campus women's groups and community experts from local women's centers and rape crisis centers. For a national perspective, one source of information is the Center for Women Policy Studies, 2000 P Street NW, Suite 508, Washington, DC 20036 (202/872-1770).

Make sure your institution's policy carefully specifies procedures for handling complaints and disciplinary actions. Codes of conduct should identify not only kinds of misconduct but also possible sanctions. Also, make sure that your institution's policies include orientation and training of a wide range of individuals—campus health professionals, counselors, student affairs experts, security officers, and resident assistants—to help prepare them to receive and respond to student complaints. Legal counsel should be consulted on policy formulation in this sensitive area.

It's important that your president or other appropriate senior official reinforces your institution's commitment to the policy, provides leadership, and sets the tone for how your institution handles complaints of acquaintance rape and other sexual assaults on campus. He or she should play a key role in student orientation sessions and other forums, by making clear that acquaintance rape and other sexual assaults will not be tolerated on your campus, that fair-minded procedures for institutional review of complaints are in place, and that students are encouraged to use institutional and community resources to help resolve issues and problems. Consideration should also be given to having students participate as members of a standing committee that regularly investigates the campus environment and reports to and advises the president and other top administrators.

2 **Define your terms clearly.** As your institution's policies and procedures are developed, their terms should be defined with care. It is important that all the institution's representatives use the same definitions. What exactly is rape? Sexual assault? Sexual harassment? Students in particular often use such terms as rape or sexual assault to signify a wide variety of activities and incidents. The confusion is exacerbated because society itself is not clear about what constitutes sexual misconduct. For instance, if rape is sex without consent, how should consent be defined and communicated, and when and by whom? One way to begin addressing these issues is to know your state's laws. Each state's laws contain their own definitions—for example, limiting assault to cases of actual physical harm. State laws and court rulings in the area of sexual misconduct vary and sometimes are not entirely clear. In addition, federal laws, such as the Student-Right-To-Know and Campus Security Act, and new federal requirements that FBI uniform crime reporting definitions be used, must be taken into account. Consult your institution's legal counsel on these points.

3 **Determine the proper balance between the individual's right to privacy and the public's right to know.** Sexual misconduct is among the most difficult issues college and university advancement professionals must address. One reason for this is the tension between the individual's right to privacy under the Buckley Amendment—and sometimes under state law as well—and the public's right to know about criminal activity on campus, a right reinforced by recent federal laws. Each situation may demand a different approach, depending on the institutional context, the nature of the particular case, and the applicable legal requirements. However, it's important to work to achieve the most appropriate balance and to begin agreeing on some guidelines as early as possible, before an incident arises.

4 **Develop an overall communications plan for the issue.** Create a strategy for reaching important groups to educate them about your institution's policy and procedures and to provide them with information, when appropriate, about specific instances. Establish ongoing multiple communications channels among internal constituencies—administration to faculty, administration to student, student to faculty, student to student, and so on.

5 **Strive with other administrators to establish a sense of trust within the institution.** If students believe the campus administration will treat them compassionately and fairly, they will work with designated institutional officials to resolve their problems. Without this sense of trust, many students are prepared to expect the worst from administrators. They may not report assaults or, conversely, may bypass institutional officials and take their case directly to the media. Make sure that sound procedures are in place, and that students can count on your administration for understanding and support.

6 **Focus on developing strong ties with student affairs administrators.** You should also strive to develop trusting relationships with other administrators, especially student affairs experts. Advancement officials must understand the action of student affairs professionals thoroughly to serve as knowledgeable and effective advisers to them on communications issues that affect their work. Help other responsible institutional officials understand that you are on their side and support their efforts. By working together with student affairs professionals to identify and address major social issues such as acquaintance rape, you can help shape your campus cultural and social life for the better. In addition, good relations with student affairs experts will help you learn more about current students—how they view acquaintance rape, how their attitudes differ from previous generations of students, and so on. The more you know, the more effectively you'll be able to respond to any incidents that may arise.

7 **Review your relationships with other administrative units on campus.** Initiate and encourage ongoing communications with campus security officers, affirmative action professionals, legal counsel, and others on campus who are also involved in issues of date rape and sexual assault. As advancement officers, it's important to stay in the loop and informed. If an incident does arise, you will need to be able to communicate clearly and immediately with each other in a controversial and often fast-breaking situation, so it's best to start working together as early as possible.

8 **Work with student affairs staff to educate the campus community.** In accordance with sensible judgment and taking into account pertinent federal and state legal requirements, inform students, faculty, and others about the existence and purpose of sexual assault prevention, educational programs, and services to victims as well as procedures for dealing with sexual assaults. With student affairs personnel, develop programs on campus to discuss the issue of date rape and sexual assault. Consider holding such programs during freshman orientation, residence hall functions, fraternity and sorority gatherings, and faculty meetings. As part of these discussions, you and other administrators should help students, faculty, and administrators examine how they are socialized and the particular views they hold toward date rape and sexual assault. How do they personally define date rape? Do they tend to blame the victim or the accused? Also invite campus and local police to attend and brief the participants. Reinforce these sessions through speeches by the president or other appropriate administrators, and articles in the campus newspaper, the student handbook, and other publications.

A key objective of these education programs should be to teach students and others in the campus community about personal safety, including the need to take responsibility for their own safety—to control alcohol consumption, lock residence hall doors, travel with others after dark, and avoid reckless behavior. Help them realize that the campus is not a protected haven and they are not invincible.

Another key objective should be to help educate campus groups about fairness and the need to see that there are two sides to every incident. Accused students may not necessarily be found guilty in campus administrative proceedings; however, in the minds of many of their fellow students and others, they are guilty when charged, and are often made to feel that way. Help students and others understand that significant damage can occur if they polarize the issue by taking unyielding sides.

9 **Organize peer counseling programs.** Because students often learn best from each other, you and other administrators might consider establishing a cadre of students willing to help lead discussion sessions and develop other methods of educating their peers. Identify and work with individual students who might be willing to write op-eds and other thoughtful articles on the subject. Also, since most students enter colleges and universities with their attitudes already formed, consider working with student affairs experts to enlist such students to help in a partnership program with local high schools. In addition, you and student affairs professionals might consider encouraging not only students but faculty, administrators, and others to volunteer as special companions to victims of acquaintance rape or sexual assault on your campus.

10 **Begin an ongoing dialogue with the media.** As mentioned before, the term "rape" is variously under-stood to cover a spectrum of assaults and incidents, from sexual relations on dates, to stranger-in-the-bushes-attacks, to general harassment. Work with the media to define the terms more precisely and explore with them the many complexities surrounding date rape and sexual assault both on your campus and off. Send the media background materials on any programs you've developed. Where possible, ground the issue in broad societal trends, rather than focus only on your institution's specific activities.

11 **Identify a spokesperson in advance.** You will want to determine before an incident occurs who will serve as spokesperson both to internal and external audiences. Often, this may be the head of student affairs. It is essential that the designated individual be someone who can effectively speak publicly about controver-sial and sensitive information, respond thoughtfully to questions from the media, get his or her points across, and provide appropriate information, while scrupulously observing privacy laws and other legal require-ments. You and your colleagues should train the appropriate person for the job, and make sure he or she coordinates all appropriate steps through your institution's media relations experts.

IF AN INCIDENT OCCURS

Each incident of date rape varies and requires a specific approach. Many such matters should properly remain confidential and will not require any public announcement or disclosure. At the other extreme, such as in the case of William and Mary, a student may choose to make the incident public and you will have to deal with it. In between, you may confront gray areas that will require sound and informed judgment to determine the appropriate response. The senior advancement officers who assembled at Bryn Mawr offer the following general guidelines.

1 **Deal with the incident promptly.** Your institution should take disciplinary action, where warranted, as soon as practicable. Speed in handling such matters is often extremely difficult, because, among other rea-sons, typically only the two conflicting parties are witnesses, entailing a "he-said, she-said" situation that is very challenging to resolve. If the persons involved believe that the institution's policies and procedures are indeed fair and supportive of both parties' rights, trust will be earned and a constructive, educational dia-logue on the topic will be fostered in the campus community. Focus on the positive actions your institution is taking and will take regarding date rape and sexual assault. (See "ongoing community actions.")

2 **Evaluate how much information you will release.** Under the federal Student Right-To-Know and Campus Security Act, colleges and universities are now required to monitor and report statistics on forcible and non-forcible sex offenses, including acquaintance rape. Reporting under the Act takes two forms. First, institutions must compile annual summaries listing the number of such instances "reported" to "campus security authorities" or "local police agencies." Exactly when "reporting" occurs or who is considered to be a "campus security authority" is still under discussion within the government, but the requirement will likely extend to complaints filed with campus deans and residence directors, as well as reports filed with local and campus police. The Act requires many levels of administration to be responsible for reporting campus crime, and this factor must be addressed in developing procedures for reporting such incidents.

Colleges and universities are also required under the Student Right-To-Know and Campus Security Act to notify the campus community of crimes that are considered to be a threat to students, faculty, and staff. The Act requires that warnings be made in a manner that is timely and that will aid in the prevention of similar occurrences. The law provides no specific legal requirements as to the precise nature of the information to be disclosed. This leaves your institution some flexibility to determine as a matter of sound policy and practice the information to be released without infringing on privacy interests. A prompt public notice that describes the nature and location of the crime that occurred, and the type of precautions that students, faculty, and staff should take to try to prevent similar occurrences, is one option.

Although institutions are required to report certain crimes, they are simultaneously required under the Buckley Amendment to keep certain student information private. Ordinarily, without the consent of a student or the student's parents, any personally identifiable information contained in the student's educa-tional records may not lawfully be released. There is a limited exception to the privacy requirement for reports maintained by local enforcement authorities, if the reports are kept only for law enforcement purposes and not for other educational reasons. Your institution should be aware that this exception may leave a victim vulnerable to exposure if the public seeks to obtain information about the crime from campus police records through freedom-of-information laws.

In keeping these legal requirements in mind, note that even when it enacted the Student Right-To-Know and Campus Security Act—a measure designed to promote disclosure of information about crimes—Congress was concerned about protecting victims' privacy. Efficient, sensitive, and lawful institutional response to a reported acquaintance rape incident should emphasize safety, but take care to avoid use of information that could identify either the alleged victim or the accused. Make sure that you always consult your institution's legal counsel and the victim before disseminating any information to the public.

William and Mary circulates an anonymous reporting sheet that every office involved uses to report and share incidents. Thus, the institution coordinates any information to be released and can be consistent when it makes facts public. Once a date rape case is resolved, the institution gives students, the media, and others access to as much appropriate information as possible through a summary report of all incidents that occurred within a given time period.

3 **Frame the issue.** Try to raise the level of the debate as high as possible—ideally to a national level—to establish context. Don't focus only on the incident at your institution. Before agreeing to do interviews, ask yourself: Will this exposure add anything to the legitimate national debate in which we are engaged, and if so how?

4 **Avoid putting yourself in an adversarial position with a student.** Even if a student takes a stance opposing the institution and the way it handles a particular incident, make sure you always support the student's right to express such views. Don't, for instance, allow yourself to be positioned as the student's adversary when discussing the incident with the media. If that happens, you may win the battle of the interview, but you will lose the war of public trust and support.

5 **Determine different constituent reactions and respond to each.** If the incident becomes public, you will likely need to communicate directly and clearly with students, faculty, alumni, parents, the media, and selected other constituencies. Develop a communications protocol to ensure that other campus administrators are aware of who will be communicating with key constituencies. As soon as possible after a major incident occurs and rumors begin circulating on campus, you may want to set up counseling sessions for key campus groups to help them cope with various aspects of the case. Consider also other effective vehicles for reaching people. Establish a rumor hotline for students or a fax network for faculty and administrators; develop alumni magazine articles and special internal newsletters.

6 **Analyze and separate the issues.** Often, date rapes involve other issues as well, such as student drinking and alcoholism or racial incidents. Incidents of date rape are often related to misuse of alcohol. If that is the case at your institution, you should probably enhance alcohol and drug abuse education programs. If the incident has racial overtones, you will probably have to focus on diffusing the situation with minority groups on campus. Often, only the president or another very senior and experienced administrator can bring together divergent constituencies.

7 **Err on the side of overcommunicating.** Don't be unduly concerned that by communicating about an incident (subject to the pertinent legal limitations) and the risks of similar incidents occurring again, you may stir up unnecessary fear and panic. Efforts to apprise the campus community of the dangers of date rape and sexual assault—both in terms of specific incidents as well as ongoing education—can often outweigh the risks. At the very least, you will reassure the campus community that your institution takes the issues seriously and instill that important sense of trust. At the very best, you will help bring the community together to reduce substantially the threat of date rape and sexual assault and build a better, safer environment for all.

This information is not intended to be legal advice for your specific institution. You should always consult your institution's own legal experts. The senior professionals listed below attended a special CASE forum on acquaintance rape on campus and contributed to this document. They are willing to share their expertise in more detail with other campus professionals confronted with acquaintance rape and sexual assault on their own campuses.

Mary Louise Allen
Director of the Women's Center
Haverford College
Haverford, PA   19041-1392
(215) 896-1183

Gordon Brown
Director of Communications
Hobart and William Smith Colleges
Geneva, NY   14456-3397
(315) 781-3540

Amy Dmitzak
Director of Public Relations
Millersville University
Millersville, PA   17551-0302
(717) 872-3586

Linda Grace-Kobas
Director, University News Service
Cornell University
Ithaca, NY   14850
(607) 255-4206

Matthews Hamabata
Dean
Haverford College
Haverford, PA   19041-1392
(215) 896-1232

Joe Hargis
News Bureau Director
Carleton College
Northfield, MN   55057
(507) 663-4183

Roland King
Director of Public Information
University of Maryland
College Park, MD   20742
(301) 405-4621

Robert Lyons
Director, News Bureau
La Salle University
Philadelphia, PA   19141
(215) 951-1080

Joel Blumenthal
Associate Vice President for University Relations
University at Albany, State University of New York
Albany, NY   12222
(518) 442-3070

Paul Brown
Director of Public Relations
University of Scranton
Scranton, PA   18510-4615
(717) 941-7661

Judith Phair
Vice President for Public Relations
Goucher College
Towson, MD   21204
(410) 337-6116

Sharon Poff
Director of Public Relations/Publications
Bucknell University
Lewisburg, PA   17837
(717) 524-3260

Samuel Sadler
Vice President for Student Affairs
College of William and Mary
Williamsburg, VA   23185
(804) 221-4000

Pam Sheridan
Director, College Relations
Haverford College
Haverford, PA   19041-1392
(215) 896-1333

Debra Thomas
Director of Public Information
Bryn Mawr College
Bryn Mawr, PA   19010
(215) 526-5137

Karen Tidmarsh
Dean of the Undergraduate College
Bryn Mawr College
Bryn Mawr, PA   19010
(215) 526-5000

HANDLING ISSUES OF SEXUAL MISCONDUCT AT INDEPENDENT SCHOOLS

June 1993   A CASE Issues Paper for Advancement Professionals   No. 14

Sexual misconduct at independent schools can include sexual innuendoes, sexual harassment, sexual assault, and date rape, among other actions. Such misconduct can occur at any time and any place—with both adults and students in any combination. These incidents occur in day schools and boarding schools, coed schools and single-sex schools. Although it may appear that coed schools or those becoming coed must confront issues of sexual misconduct most directly, single-sex schools are certainly not immune to problems. They must contend with issues arising between their students and those at brother or sister schools, as well as between students and teachers and between individuals of the same sex. No school can afford to take an "it will never happen here" attitude.

Managing the questions and problems of sexual misconduct while students are immersed in the normal stages of child and adolescent development is especially complicated. As a recent (May 24, 1993) cover story in *Time* magazine notes, "Bombarded by mixed messages and values, students are more sexually active than ever, and more confused." A *Time*/CNN poll offers hard statistics that support this assertion. Its results show more than a third of 15-year-old boys report having had sexual intercourse, as do 27 percent of teen-age girls—up from 19 percent in 1982.

At the same time, it found that no consensus had been reached among parents as to when and if their children should have sex before marriage and that a majority of parents still reinforce a double standard and expect and support different sexual conduct from their sons than they do from their daughters. More than ever, schools must act *in loco parentis*, playing roles many parents can't or won't play. This can be particularly the case for independent boarding schools, where students live together 24 hours a day; however, all schools are experiencing it to some degree. "Schools are attempting to fill in where parents have failed," the *Time* article says. "But it has been hard for educators over these past few years to know what to teach when society itself cannot agree on a direction."

The changing composition of school populations further complicates the situation. Today, students come from a wide variety of ethnic, cultural, and social backgrounds and often hold radically different views about what is—and what isn't—appropriate sexual conduct.

Advancement officers can play a key role in helping their campuses deal with issues of sexual misconduct—by helping advise on policies and procedures, by working closely with their school head and other administrators to help develop programs to educate both students and adults at the school, and by handling the communications and other aspects of an incident if one occurs. A group of senior advancement professionals and others from independent schools came together at a special forum at CASE Washington to discuss the issue and develop guidelines for other advancement professionals to consider—as well as share with deans of students, counselors, and other administrators at their school. Their recommendations follow.

ONGOING COMMUNICATIONS

1 **Encourage your trustees, school head, and other top administrators to make the issue a priority.** Given all the daily demands on school administrators, faculty, counselors, and staff, it's easy to neglect concerns about sexual misconduct until an incident occurs and a crisis erupts. Help trustees, your school head, and other top administrators understand the importance and pervasiveness of issues concerning sexual misconduct and that incidents will occur—no matter how insulated your school may currently appear. Explain that an effective education and communications program can require significant amounts of time and effort but that the investment is definitely worth it. (To help make your point, you may need to highlight cases, including perhaps even lawsuits, that reflect the costs of doing otherwise.) Stress that the best approach always is to tackle the issue *before* a problem arises.

2 **Work with other top administrators to develop sound official policies and codes of conduct.** If your institution doesn't have a basic policy governing issues of sexual misconduct, it should develop one now. Work with others to establish a schoolwide task force representing various key constituencies—including trustees, student life professionals, counselors, students, faculty, public relations and other administrators, legal counsel, and external audiences such as parents—to get in-depth advice from each. The policy should include both a statement of why it's important to your school to prevent incidents of sexual misconduct, as well as procedures to follow if, in fact, specific incidents of sexual misconduct do occur. It should also include an educational component. (See No. 10 and No. 11 below.) Also, if your school establishes a grievance committee, you need to make sure your top administrators clearly define who will serve on it, how they will be selected, and how their findings will be reported back to the school community.

3 **Be thorough.** The policy should be as comprehensive as possible and articulate all potential types of misconduct. This can be especially difficult because society itself is not clear about what constitutes sexual misconduct in every instance. Students in particular can use terms such as harassment, assault, and rape to signify a wide range of activities and incidents. Consider sexual harassment alone: It is defined by law in the United States and judicial precedents in Canada, yet many areas of ambiguity remain. The U.S. courts are still interpreting federal law, for example, on how to more precisely define what is a hostile, offensive, and intimidating environment.

However, it's important to try to develop as much consensus as possible among faculty, counselors, staff, students, and others as to what clearly constitutes inappropriate behavior. Cite examples in the policy of the various types of activities that would be viewed as misconduct and articulate all the potential combinations of misconduct the policy covers: student to student, faculty to student, student to faculty, etc. You will also have to determine whether the school will have appropriate jurisdiction—i.e., incidents that may occur between students or to a student outside of school at a nonschool function. Don't reinvent the wheel; collect statements and procedures from similar institutions to see how they've tackled the issue. Without fail, make sure knowledgeable legal counsel reviews the policy. (For more information, contact the National Association of Independent Schools, which has a packet on sexual harassment including sample policies, case studies, and other resources at (202) 833-4757; after August 1993, (202) 973-9700.)

4 **Know your state laws.** As you develop your policy, one way to address issues of ambiguity is to make sure you and other adults in the school, including trustees, administrators, staff, faculty, and spouses, are aware of the major laws in your state affecting various aspects of sexual misconduct. State laws and court rulings in the area of sexual misconduct vary and are sometimes not entirely clear. Work with knowledgeable legal counsel to stay abreast of confidentiality laws, statutory rape laws, and other legal requirements, especially as they relate to your *in loco parentis* status (e.g., child abuse reporting laws). It may also be important to hold educational sessions during which expert counsel briefs school adults as well as students in some detail on the various legal aspects they should consider. (See No. 10 below.)

5 **As much as possible, adapt your policy and general approach to your school's individual culture.** At boarding schools, for example, close relationships—often much more familiar than at other institutions and settings—develop between students and their faculty, administrators, and staff. This can make dealing with sexual misconduct even more complex. Adults in those institutions are often called upon to perform parenting roles as well as their regular functions. This makes it particularly hard to spell out appropriate behavior in rigid, rule-bound codes. Putting a comforting arm around a young student whose beloved family pet has just been killed should not be a questionable act. Your school should allow some flexibility in the policy and educate all constituencies about the appropriate distinctions they will need to make.

6 **Encourage your school head to take the lead.** It's important that your school head reinforces your institution's commitment to the policy, provides leadership, and sets the tone for how your school handles complaints of sexual misconduct. If possible, he or she should consider convening school leadership regularly—at least once a year—to discuss the issue candidly, including progress being made and any areas of continuing concern. He or she should also play a key role in student orientation sessions and other forums by making clear that sexual misconduct will not be tolerated, that fair-minded procedures for review of complaints are in place, and that students, faculty, administrators, and staff are encouraged to use school resources to help resolve issues and problems.

7 **Communicate about the sexual misconduct policy widely.** A top priority should be to communicate the policy as widely as possible so all key constituencies are aware of it and its contents. Include it in new student orientation packets, send it in letters to trustees and parents, post it throughout the school, feature it in articles in your alumni periodical. Make sure everyone is aware of how the policy was developed, the processes for reporting transgressions and for handling cases once they're reported, the possible disciplinary actions, and whether notification of any proper government authority is required. Educating key audiences in advance will make communication much easier if a specific incident of sexual misconduct occurs.

8 **Recommend appointing a special adviser charged with handling sexual misconduct issues.** As part of the policy, work with other top administrators to ensure that at least one highly credible person serves as a primary grievance resource and coordinates the educational component. In some cases, your school may want to appoint more than one person to receive complaints and offer guidance. This is because students, faculty, staff, and other groups may not be comfortable dealing with the same person or office. Make sure you consider the needs of both the victim and the accused.

9 **Strive with other administrators to establish a sense of trust within the school.** If students, faculty, and other members of the school community believe school administrators will treat them compassionately and fairly, they will work with designated institutional officials to resolve their problems. Without this sense of trust, many are prepared to expect the worst from top administrators. Reinforce continually that the school administration takes the issue seriously, that the school has established a policy and procedures, and that complaints will not be ignored or handled unfairly.

10 **Educate faculty, counselors, staff, administrators, and other adults closely associated with the school.** Whenever possible, help student affairs professionals reinforce among the adults involved closely with the school that they must be accountable for their actions and that inappropriate behavior will not be tolerated. Also, although it's important for these adults to remain comfortable with students, school officials may need to remind them that students can misinterpret innocent actions. Help organize educational sessions that raise the faculty and administrator consciousness about their own behavior, the legal issues and liabilities surrounding sexual misconduct, the school policy and its implications, and the appropriate steps they should take if a student comes to them with a complaint.

11 **Educate students.** Similarly, you need to help educate students as much as possible. Keeping in mind the turnover among the student body from year to year, work with student counselors, deans of student life, dorm representatives, and others to educate and re-educate students and to seek fresh, creative approaches. Organize special residential mini-courses and develop educational pamphlets and brochures on the topic. If your school has just gone coed, it might be especially timely to hold educational sessions on various aspects of sexual misconduct.

Besides educating students about the policy and what to do in cases of actual misconduct, concentrate on teaching students of both sexes how to avoid and manage uncomfortable sexual situations. School officials should also use the opportunity to remind students of security precautions to avoid sexual assaults by strangers on campus as well as the surrounding neighborhood. It's also a time to reinforce to students the importance of principles of due process—that no one, even if accused, is guilty until proven so. And, in all programs, for adults as well as students, make sure the education process focuses equally on both sexes.

12 **Help establish peer counseling or other student-to-student education.** Students often learn best from each other and may also be more comfortable opening up about such sensitive issues as sexual misconduct to peers than they are to adults. You and other administrators might consider establishing a cadre of students willing to help lead discussion groups and develop other methods of educating their peers. They can also serve as contacts for students who want to report incidents but don't feel comfortable going first to an adult. Your administrative team will need to provide these student volunteers with training, as well as any printed materials they might distribute. Also, make sure they know what not to say or do, and whom to go to if any questions or situations arise that they aren't prepared to—and should not—deal with. You may also consider some form of peer counseling for faculty and administrators.

13 **Always take into account the increasing diversity of the student body.** Increasingly, schools are homes to a widely diverse population, comprised of individuals from many countries and cultures. Based on their different backgrounds, these individuals can each hold distinct views toward what does or doesn't constitute sexual misconduct. An offhand gesture that may be accepted without second thought by one may be seen as highly inappropriate and offensive by another. A policy will help bring all groups together with some generally accepted guidelines and standards. However, in the educational process, it's also important to remember cultural, social, and other nuances to help students, faculty, and administrators from different backgrounds understand each other's perspectives.

14 **Educate trustees, parents, alumni, donors, and other concerned constituencies.** Parents are often the most concerned constituency when it comes to sexual misconduct, and they can also be the most vocal with outside audiences, such as the media, when an incident occurs. Make them aware of the policy, the education programs, and the other ongoing efforts you've established to deal positively with sexual misconduct issues. Discuss these efforts at trustee and parent meetings, write about them in alumni and key donor letters, and always keep good lines of communication open—before any incident may occur.

15 **Form partnerships with other local schools.** At single-sex schools, issues of sexual misconduct most often occur between students at their brother or sister school. Work with these schools to develop written policies and procedures together. Even if you don't develop identical policies, it's good to share ideas and approaches and support one another. Beyond the obvious partnerships between brother and sister schools, your school may also find it advantageous to work as a group with schools in the area—coed or single-sex, day or boarding. Working to tackle the issue as a team may not only improve your results, but it will present a consistent, united voice to key constituencies—students, parents, alumni, media, and others.

16 **Educate the media.** Whenever appropriate, raise awareness among the media of the positive efforts your school is making to deal with this major societal issue. Frame the issue in broad terms and establish context. Again, it may be most effective if you work as a group with other local schools to hold backgrounding sessions or send joint informational materials to the media describing various schools' policies and programs.

17 **Develop a crisis communications plan and educate key constituencies about it.** Whether or not your school has a public relations department, you need to develop a crisis communications plan in advance. It should outline who's responsible for each activity if a crisis occurs. Make sure you define the proper relationships between the school head; those who must communicate with internal audiences such as students, faculty, and staff; and those who must talk to the media, parents, and other external audiences. In particular, there should always be close coordination between student counselors and public relations professionals. After you've developed these ground rules, share them with board members, faculty, students, and others so they are aware of the plan in advance and understand the importance, for example, of having one external spokesperson.

18 **Establish an external spokesperson in advance.** It's always good to identify one person in charge of responding to outside queries from the media, parents, and others. This individual could be the school head, the director of public relations, the chief advancement officer, or—at smaller schools—even the head of the English department. The key requirement is that he or she be a good communicator and know how to handle highly sensitive issues and information.

WHEN AN INCIDENT OCCURS

1 **Deal with the incident promptly.** Your school should follow investigative procedures—including involving legal counsel—and take disciplinary action, where warranted, as soon as practicable. This can be quite difficult because, among other reasons, only the two conflicting parties may be witnesses. You may have to resolve a "he-said, she-said" situation—which is extremely challenging. However, if the persons involved believe that the school's policies and procedures are indeed fair and supportive of both their rights, you will earn their trust and reach a constructive resolution.

2 **Develop a statement.** Schools should not release the names, or in any way identify, those individuals involved in any cases of sexual misconduct. However, because schools are often small close-knit communities, information can leak out. If that happens, school authorities may be required to offer some explanation. Work with other top administrators to develop a clear, concise statement that outlines the complaint, the process, and the educational programs you have in place. Even if you don't actually send this document to anyone, it can serve as a talking paper for all those who will have to communicate to various constituencies about the incident. It can become the basis for all other communications so that each audience will receive the same clear, consistent messages.

Be sure that not only those who deal with students but those who will have to communicate to outside audiences, such as public relations professionals, are involved in managing the crisis after it occurs and developing the statement. And, again, always be sure to involve knowledgeable legal counsel to avoid making damaging admissions or defamatory statements.

3 **Convene and brief key individuals identified in crisis communications plan.** Follow your crisis communications plan. Use the statement you've developed, as a basis for your discussion and to brief all those in charge of working with various internal and external constituencies about the incident. This might include counselors, dorm representatives, and others who will be hearing rumors and getting questions from students. Work with them to develop appropriate responses.

4 **Communicate with students and other internal groups.** The communications team should provide students with prompt and appropriate information while maintaining confidentiality. To create faith in the system, it's important that students and others realize that violations of the policy will not be ignored, but dealt with fairly. At the same time, all spokespersons should strive to communicate compassion for both the victim and the accused—and the understanding that the school is not operating in an irresponsible, capricious, or dictatorial way.

5 **Communicate with parents, the media, and other external audiences.** Your ongoing communications efforts (see previous section) are of most importance in dealing with parents and other outside audiences. Because you will not be able to legally disclose much information at the time of the incident, you will have to rely in many ways on their faith that you already have a fair internal system in place to handle the incident—and a clear understanding of your legal obligations regarding required reports, if any, to government authorities.

In most, if not all, cases, you will not want to provide any details about the specific incident. However, you may receive unsolicited questions about it and should be prepared to respond both truthfully and legally, based on advice of counsel. Make sure in your conversations with outside audiences such as parents that you distinguish between any rumors they may have heard and the actual facts. Explain to the media that student matters are confidential, and stress that a system is indeed in place to deal with any incidents. If an angry parent begins spreading inappropriate or erroneous information to the media, you might be able to enlist the president of the parents association or a trustee to intervene.

6 **Analyze and separate issues.** Often, sexual misconduct involves other issues, such as alcohol or substance abuse. If that is the case at your school, you should probably consider establishing or enhancing substance abuse education programs. Or, instead of immediate disciplinary action, you may recommend that the accused undergo individual counseling for alcohol and drug abuse if appropriate.

THE FOLLOW-UP

1 **Review your programs.** Work with other administrators to evaluate how your school handled the incident, with an eye toward improving your policy and procedures. If problems arose, determine what aspects you need to update and revise.

2 **Keep educating.** One school has developed an "issue book" in which students can raise any questions they'd like about sexual misconduct, and any other issue, in writing. The school head responds in writing to student concerns and distributes her answers throughout the school. Although this particular idea may not be appropriate or feasible for every school, you should strive to create similar opportunities that encourage ongoing discussion of the topic. Whenever possible, use what could be a divisive incident to foster a constructive, educational dialogue that makes your school community even stronger than before.

The senior professionals listed below contributed to this paper and can share their experience on dealing with sexual misconduct at independent schools. This information is not intended to be legal advice for your specific institution. You should always consult your institution's own legal experts.

Jessica Ackroyd
Director of Publications
Episcopal High School
1200 N. Quaker Lane
Alexandria, VA 22302
(703) 379-7686

Laura Amick
Diretor of Public Affairs
The Bryn Mawr School
109 W. Melrose Ave.
Baltimore, MD 21210
(410) 323-8800

Winnie Anderson
Guidance Counselor
The Holton-Arms School
7303 River Rd.
Bethesda, MD 20817
(301) 365-5300

Margaret W. Goldsborough
Director of Public Information
National Association of Independent Schools
(202) 833-4757
After August 1993
1620 L St. NW
Washington, DC 20036-5605
(202) 973-9700

Christopher A. Massi
Director of Institutional Advancement
Washington International School
3100 Macomb St. NW
Washington, DC 20008
(202) 364-1833

Jennifer J. Salopek
Director of Marketing and Communications
The Madeira School
8328 Georgetown Pike
McLean, VA 22102-1200
(703) 556-8200

Tracy Savage
Director of Development and Public Relations
National Cathedral School
Mount Saint Alban
Washington, DC 20016
(202) 537-6347

Mary Spencer
Director of Women's Life
Virginia Episcopal School
PO Box 408/VES Rd.
Lynchburg, VA 24505
(804) 384-6221

Christine Turek
Director of Public Relations
The Holton-Arms School
7303 River Rd.
Bethesda, MD 20817
(301) 365-6033

Crisis Resources

CHAPTER • 32

Campus Counsel on Crisis Management

Shelley Sanders Kehl

Most of us define a crisis as a natural or human event that dominates a campus and a community. Many colleagues may think first of obvious tragedies, such as an earthquake, murder, or hurricane. Others may suggest that a Justice Department subpoena, a congressional investigation, or the indictment of the college president (or football coach) also meet the definition of crisis.

Whether campus administrators take a narrow or expansive view, senior level administrators, perhaps including campus counsel—often in the capacity of a "risk manager" —must play a key role in crisis management. College and university administrators should look to their legal counsel for help in drafting the crisis management plan and guidance from applicable cases and statutory law.

In the view of this college counsel, a basic crisis management plan should include, at minimum, the following elements.

• *The crisis management team.* This group will be responsible for responding to the crisis and coordinating the institution's actions.

• *A communication chain that serves immediately to contact members of the crisis management team.* This communication system must be operational regardless of the time at which an emergency occurs.

• *Operations protocols for the first few hours of an emergency when the situation is most fluid and team members may be in the process of assembling.* These protocols must set priorities among actions for the most senior administrator available at the scene, specifying what should be done, what can wait, and what should not be done.

• *A resource manual listing the external agencies to contact in the event of a crisis.* In addition to such obvious contacts as police, fire, and medical support services, a crisis resource manual should cover, for example, disaster relief, hazardous materials response offices, U.S. State Department officials (for foreign study programs), and major utilities. Once compiled, the crisis team should update the manual regularly to reflect both changes in

Shelley Sanders Kehl is an attorney in private practice with McGuire, Kehl & Nealon in New York City. She specializes in counseling educational institutions and systems.

government departments and the needs of the college or university.

• *Dissemination of information about the crisis plan so the campus community knows where to turn when an emergency occurs.* A plan kept in a file drawer is of no use; the existence of the plan, the make-up of the team, and the basic protocols for response must be known and available in written form.

The crisis management plan

1. *The crisis management team should include senior administrators from across campus.* Generally, representatives from public relations, security, student services (especially counseling), health services, the physical plant, campus operations, risk management, housing, and legal counsel will make up the core team members. Team assignments should be position-specific (not individual-specific) and should also include designations of alternate team leaders.

Take time to identify administrators who are based on or near campus at non-business times or who can function during the early stages of a crisis. One or more of these individuals should either be part of the team or at least be especially familiar with the crisis management plan. Be sure to develop and distribute on campus a written summary of the plan that identifies team members and their functions.

2. *Develop a communications system for alerting team members and other appropriate campus officials in the event of a crisis.* The communications chain should operate even when ordinary communication systems are disrupted. So in addition to a telephone contact plan, specify alternate arrangements. Provide team members with wallet-sized cards listing the names and home telephone numbers of other team members.

3. *Draft first response protocols for predictable types of emergency situations.* Make clear assignments regarding who contacts police, fire, and other emergency services; who coordinates their activities; and the like. Reviewing protocols in advance will help develop a general consensus on acceptable actions. This consensus will increase the likelihood that the initial response will address the crisis on all appropriate levels—human as well as institutional.

4. *As soon as practicable, the team's designated PR person should be available to coordinate all media relations.* This will help the institution limit the spread of rumors and will also encourage the media to look to the public relations office for continuing information.

The media spokesperson should take the initiative by providing press releases and public statements that distinguish fact from speculation. Of course, the spokesperson should also understand the issues of confidentiality and privacy and, if appropriate, should coordinate with the police and prosecutors both the nature and timing of released information. Legal counsel should consult on press releases.

5. *Early in the crisis, the institution should initiate a thorough investigation of the situation, preferably under the direction of counsel.* Detailed factual investigation—including the identification of witnesses, gathering of evidence, and taking of statements—will preserve information and make it possible to assess liability.

6. *Coordination and cooperation is essential—especially when the police or other government agencies will become involved in the crisis.* As part of effective crisis management, an institution should establish and maintain cordial relations with police, the district attorney, the fire department, and emergency medical services. Team leaders should review the crisis management plan with representatives of these local agencies. When solid relationships already exist, cooperation will be made easier during times of crisis.

When a crisis has occurred, the crisis team leaders should work closely with the specific government agencies involved to help shape the institution's response. These off-campus officials should become, in effect, an extension of the crisis management team.

7. *Once the initial phase of an emergency has abated, the crisis team must focus on assessment and response. The institution will need to take certain steps immediately.* These actions may range from closing a damaged facility to increasing security patrols to evacuating students studying abroad. But remember, potential liability is a factor in these early actions. The crisis team must consider both the impact of possible action—and inaction. As part of this analysis, it may be appropriate to seek advice from legal counsel.

Longer-term actions are the next focus of consideration. If the crisis has revealed the need for a particular service or action—and the institution determines that it can and will take that step—the institution should announce the decision to the campus community. Doing so may serve to reassure students and staff that the institution has taken the situation seriously and is responding appropriately. However, legal counsel should caution senior management against being stampeded into taking action that cannot or should not be implemented. The crisis team should carefully review all possible actions so responses do not constitute gratuitous admissions or otherwise act as red flags to potential litigants.

Reassuring the broader campus constituency is a crucial aspect of crisis communications. Although most campus administrators are reluctant to draw attention to negative events, parents and alumni will become aware of a crisis that garners media attention. It may be appropriate to communicate directly with these groups, in addition to board members and trustees, to address their concerns and assure them that the institution is managing the situation.

The institution should also offer a range of services to the victims of an emergency and to the general campus community. Counseling services, telephone hotlines, and open meetings all help provide support to those constituents affected by the crisis.

8. *A crisis management plan requires examination after the emergency has passed.* While the experience is still fresh, the team and other key campus officials should meet to review the effectiveness of the plan. But remember, the purpose of this review is not to find fault or to fix blame but to modify the crisis plan in light of actual experience. The institution must also determine if there are any actions it can take that would prevent a similar crisis in the future or minimize the impact of one.

A note on case law

An early history of judicial reluctance to hold colleges and universities responsible for injuries and criminal actions has been eroding. Clear or consistent court trends are not emerging. The judicial decisions turn on fine distinctions arising from the facts of specific cases, making broad generalizations problematic. The general wisdom to be derived from cases in which institutions have been held liable is that when an institution is on notice of a likelihood of danger as a result of prior information and therefore a risk is foreseeable, there is a duty to warn and protect members of the campus community. Courts have been slow to impose special duties on colleges, but have been willing to hold them to the same degree of responsibility that would be imposed, for example, on a landlord.

An example of standard judicial analysis can be found in a well-known New York case, *Eiseman v. State of New York*, which involves a student—admitted through a program for disadvantaged individuals—who murdered another student. The killer was a paroled felon, and a lower court ruled that the college was liable to the family of the murdered student. However, New York State's highest court ultimately reversed the decision. The issue in the case was whether the college had a heightened duty to protect students from potential harm when the college had a program to admit economically and educationally disadvantaged students. The court determined that the law imposed no heightened duty of inquiry where colleges had special admissions programs or admitted paroled felons. The court further determined that, once admitted, the college undertook no additional duty to monitor or restrict the ex-felons' activities in order to protect others.

Familiarity with case law is, of course, helpful in shaping responses to a crisis, but it does not substitute for a considered crisis management plan.

CHAPTER 33

Emergency Communications Manual Excerpts

Wilfrid Laurier University

Wilfrid Laurier University
Emergency Communications Manual

Table of Contents

April 1993

Designated Sites for Communication Uses

During an emergency, the sites listed below are reserved exclusively for uses related to communications; their use will be controlled by the Institutional Relations Emergency Unit. This designation has been authorized by the president.

Library Basement: L124, L125, L126, L127
 two pay telephones in hall
 washrooms
 adjacent to computer services lab in
  Rm. 123
 TV/VCR in closet outside L126

Athletic Complex: 201, 202 A, B, and C
 pay telephones in lobby
 washrooms
 flexible room size
 TV/VCR in closet next to 202A
 telephone jacks

Frank Peters Building: P1004, P1005, P1017
 telephone jacks
 washrooms
 lounge space
 TV/VCR in back of P1017 and P1035
 personal computer and laser printer in
  Rm. P1035

202 Regina: 102, 103, 137, and 139
 pay telephone off lounge
 lounge space
 photocopier and fax machine in Rm. 115
 TV/VCR in Rm. 102

232 King Street: B14, B15, and B16
**** near alternate site for Emergency
  Response Team
 numerous telephone extensions nearby
 washrooms
 private printshop nearby

Seagram Stadium: Ticket Office, Rm. 4, 13, 14
 telephone in Ticket Office and Rm. 14
 washrooms
 easy access to gym and field

Paul Martin Centre
 internal telephone
 flexible room size
 washrooms
 TV/VCR

Faculty and Staff Lounges
 internal telephones
 kitchen facilities

Security Office
 near Emergency Response Team
 photocopier, computer and printer

April 1993

Wilfrid Laurier University
Emergency Communications Manual

3.3

Contacts for News Media

OUTLET	ADDRESS	TELEPHONE	FAX	CONTACT(S)
Kitchener-Waterloo Record	225 Fairway Road S., Kitchener N2G 4E5	894-2231	894-3912	Bill Bean, Assignment Manager
Waterloo Chronicle	201-75 King St. S., Waterloo N2J 1P2	886-3021	886-9383	Melodee Martinuk, Editor
				Pete Cudhea, sports & business; Debra Crandell, entertainment
CHYM/CKGL Radio	305 King St. West Kitchener N2G 4E4	743-0611 / 570-2454 (Control Booth)	743-9025	Fred Lehmann, Assignment Editor
				Joyce Gaudet, Cynthia Colby, Cathia Maxwell
CKCO-TV	864 King St. West Kitchener N2G 4E9	741-4401 / 578-1313	743-0730	Dave Carswell, Jeff Soltysiak
				Daiene Vernile, Province Wide; Gary McLaren, Sunday AM; Brian Bourke, radio; Willa McLean, Morning Magazine
AM96	46 Main Street Cambridge N1R 1V4	621-7510	621-0165	Laird Elcombe, Jeff Hicks, Brad Skinner, Roger Vokey
Cambridge Reporter	26 Ainslie St. S., Cambridge N1R 3K1	621-3810	621-8239	John McGhie, City Editor
				Christina Jonas, Managing Editor; Gordon Paul, Business Editor
Cambridge Times	1425 Brishop St., Cambridge N1R 6J9	623-7793	623-7337	Brian Reid
CKLA/CJOY Radio Magic	75 Speedvale Ave. E., P.O. Box 217, Guelph N1E 6M3	1-824-7000 / 1-823-1416	824-4118	Paul Osborne, News Director
				Norm Jary, Craig Campbell, Neill Clemens
Daily Mercury	8-14 MacDonnell Guelph N1H 6P7	1-822-4310 / 1-822-4313 after hours	1-767-1681	Al Ferris, City Editor; Bob Zeller, business
The Royal Tribune	40 Cork St. E., Guelph N1H 2W8	1-763-3333	1-763-4814	Chris Clark
DC103	287 Broadway Ave., Orangeville L9W 1L2	1-800-265-9663 / 1-942-0950	1-942-2550	Joe Snider, News Director
Ingrid Clark	41 Verney St. Guelph N1H 1N5	1-837-3973		

April 1993

Guidelines for Emergency Communications Decisions

It is the university's policy to be forthright and timely in its communications with the university community, the media, and the public at large.

It is the university's policy that decisions regarding communications will be guided by due concern for the right to privacy, personal security, legal liability, *and* the public's legitimate right to be informed.

It is the university's policy that all media and public inquiries will be referred without comment to the Institutional Relations Emergency Unit. Only the official spokesperson and alternate will articulate the university's position upon the authorization of, and as directed by the President or the Emergency Response Co-ordinator.

- Recognize and address the information needs and/or demands of those who will converge on the campus: members of the media, concerned families and friends of employees and students, area residents, local politicians, and idle spectators.

- Place priority on guarding the long-term credibility and reputation of the university. This may mean swallowing hard in the present.

- Take control of the issue by initiating communications to present the facts of the emergency and articulate the university's position.

- Be timely in the release of information to the media and the public; otherwise, rumors will multiply and the media will develop other sources. Provide regular updates.

- Consider the interests of different constituencies; the communications may vary by group, but they must be consistent.

- Try to communicate with internal audiences first, then external audiences. Or communicate with them simultaneously.

- Be forthright. Lies, untruths, and cover-ups will be found out and cause damage.

- Try to accommodate the logistical needs of the media. In an emergency, the media can assist the institution and an investment in goodwill can pay dividends.

- Refer legal questions to the "Legal Guidelines for Emergency Communications" in the *Emergency Communications Manual* or to the university solicitor.

- Correct major errors, challenge rumors, and dispel misperceptions about the emergency.

April 1993

Guidelines for Official Spokesperson and Alternate

The spokesperson will be responsible for articulating the university's position only upon the authorization of, and as directed by the President or the Emergency Response Co-ordinator.

Never offer your personal opinions: you are representing the university's position.

Stay in contact with the Institutional Relations Emergency Unit. Keep the unit informed of your location and a telephone number or other means of reaching you.

Be well-groomed. Keep a fresh change of clothes and other personal items (razor, toiletries, make-up) at the university. Don't wear brights, plaids, or checks.

Under this policy, *The Cord* and *Laurier News* are considered external media and are to be treated as such.

In a news conference or interview:

- identify the university's key messages and put them in point form
- rehearse your statement; go through a mock news conference or interview
- keep statements brief, simple, and to the point
- stay within pre-determined boundaries for the communication
- don't be afraid of "dead air" when you've finished what you want to say
- take time to breath and think before answering questions
- don't be tempted to relax during an interview
- be politely assertive in communicating, not passive
- remain calm and courteous in face of hostile questions; don't argue
- avoid academic, institutional, and technical jargon
- avoid speculation; don't answer hypothetical questions
- don't accept or lay blame
- challenge loaded questions
- correct major errors, and challenge rumors but don't respond as if they were legitimate
- avoid false assumptions and inflammatory statements
- avoid loaded words but don't hesitate to express compassion
- avoid the words "no comment"
- explain why you can't or won't answer a question:
  (policy; legal matter before courts; confidential personnel matter; facts not available)
- say nothing *off the record*
- answer questions considering the public interest

April 1993

APPENDIX II

Emergency Communications Plan
A Complement to the Emergency Response Plan

I. Rationale

Communication is a key factor in the University's response to an emergency. Good communications policy and practice can assist in the actual management of the crisis; provide direction to faculty, staff, and students; and disseminate information to interested constituencies and the public at large while maintaining the institution's credibility and mitigating damage to its reputation.

II. General

It is the policy of the University to be forthright and timely in its communications with the University community, the media, and the public at large during an emergency. Decisions regarding communications will be guided by due concern for the right to privacy, personal security, legal liability *and* the public's legitimate right to be informed.

III. Emergency Communications Plan

During a declared emergency, communications — both internal and external — will be under the direction of the President or the Emergency Response Co-ordinator as prescribed by the Emergency Response Plan.

This Emergency Communications Plan will also apply in the event of an emergency at an off-campus activity (including evening classes, convocation, and other events for which Laurier has some responsibility or a significant number of its community involved).

In this policy, the President will mean the President or Designate as prescribed by the Emergency Response Plan.

IV. Release of Information

All written or oral statements (including news conferences, news releases, open memorandum or letters, interviews, and switchboard messages) to campus groups, the media, and the public will require the authorization of the President or the Emergency Response Co-ordinator.

CHAPTER 34

Emergency Action Plan Table of Contents

State University of New York Institute of Technology at Utica/Rome

State University of New York
Institute of Technology at Utica/Rome

Emergency Action Plan

EMERGENCY PHONE NUMBERS

PUBLIC SAFETY	792-7105
COLLEGE RELATIONS	792-7113
FACILITIES	792-7456
HEALTH CENTER	792-7172
PERSONNEL	792-7191
RESIDENCE LIFE	792-7810
V. P. ADMINISTRATION	792-7300

If all phone lines are down the following cellular phone numbers are available:

PUBLIC SAFETY	796-3033
	796-3063
FACILITIES	796-7779
RESIDENCE LIFE	796-5999

EMERGENCY ACTION PLAN

TABLE OF CONTENTS

3/1/92

CHAPTER • 35

Office of Student Services Emergency Duty Guidelines

University of Florida

Office for Student Services-Emergency Duty Guidelines

Nature of Emergency	Person(s) to call (Immediately)	Person(s) to call (next day)	Follow-up Paperwork
Serious Injury	Vice President for Student Affairs Dean for Student Services Residence Hall Staff (if applicable) Patient Relations Officer (Shands)	Student Family (if applicable)	Emergency Checklist Emergency Log Sheet Faculty Notice
Accidental Death	Vice President for Student Affairs Dean for Student Services Residence Hall Staff (if applicable)	Family (if applicable) Roommates Campus Minister (if appropriate)	Emergency Checklist Emergency Log Sheet Faculty Notice Registrar Notice
Hospitalization	Residence Hall Staff (if applicable) Patient Relations Officer (Shands)	Vice President for Student Affairs Student Family (if applicable)	Emergency Checklist Emergency Log Sheet Faculty Notice
Sexual Assault	Vice President for Student Affairs Dean for Student Services Residence Hall Staff (if applicable) UPD Investigations	Dean for Student Services Associate Dean for Student Services UPD Investigations Vice President for Student Affairs	Emergency Checklist Emergency Log Sheet Faculty Notice
Mental Health Crisis	Dean for Student Services Residence Hall Staff (if applicable) Crisis Center (off-campus) UPD (if appropriate)	Vice President for Student Affairs Family (if applicable) Residence Hall Staff (if applicable) Dean for Student Services Associate Dean for Student Services	Emergency Checklist Emergency Log Sheet Faculty Notice (if hospitalized)
Suicide	Vice President for Student Affairs Dean for Student Services Residence Hall Staff (if applicable) Crisis Center	Family (if applicable) UPD (if applicable) Vice President for Student Affairs Dean for Student Services Crisis Center (off-campus)	Emergency Checklist Emergency Log Sheet Faculty Notice Registrar Notice (if completed)
Drug/Alcohol Overdose	Vice President for Student Affairs Dean for Student Services Residence Hall Staff (if applicable)	Vice President for Student Affairs Dean for Student Services Family (if applicable)	Emergency Checklist Emergency Log Sheet Faculty Notice (if hospitalized) Registrar Notice (if completed)

CHAPTER 36

Crisis Communications: Generic Action Plan and Backgrounders

Rensselaer Polytechnic Institute

RENSSELAER CRISIS COMMUNICATIONS PLAN
Office of News and Communications

PHILOSOPHY OF CRISIS COMMUNICATIONS

✓ Crises can be opportunities as well as problems. They can prompt us to improve our programs. And, if we respond aggressively and forthrightly, they provide a chance to improve our credibility with the news media and with our key publics.

✓ News and Communications is an advocate for Rensselaer in the news media and for the news media inside Rensselaer. As in all media relations, N&C is honest, efficient, and candid with media during a crisis. At the same time, we speak for, and protect legitimate interests of Rensselaer's students, faculty, and staff.

CRISIS COMMUNICATIONS: GENERIC ACTION PLAN

1. Write a brief summary of the crisis, our reactions, and our efforts to avoid such crises. This can be tailored to serve as a media backgrounder, an internal memo, or a fact sheet that other offices can share with their constituents.

    Assigned to: _____ Deadline: _____
    Comments: _____
    _____
    _____
    _____

2. Prepare statements for the media, and then identify and prepare spokesperson(s). We'll use existing backgrounders and the crisis summary (step 1) to prepare responses to expected media inquiries and the persons who will deliver them.

    Assigned to: _____ Deadline: _____
    Comments: _____
    _____
    _____
    _____

3. Draft a PR plan to tell our side of the story to publics that could be concerned about the crisis. Key publics could be students, employees, the Capital District, alumni, parents, members of a certain profession or minority group, etc.

    Assigned to: _____ Deadline: _____
    Comments: _____
    _____
    _____
    _____

2

CRISIS COMMUNICATIONS PLAN
Office of News and Communications
Rensselaer Polytechnic Institute
Page 2

4. <u>Share our communications plans with the Crisis Committee.</u> Eddie Knowles and/or Tom Yurkewecz, as co-chairs of Rensselaer's Crisis Committee, will be briefed on our communications plans.

Assigned to: _____ Deadline: _____
Comments: _____
_____
_____
_____

5. <u>Inform campus offices that may get calls about the crisis.</u> We'll give information on the crisis, along with advice on what to say about it, to offices that can be expected to get questions from their constituents -- such as development, admissions, alumni relations, constituent programs, and government relations.

Assigned to: _____ Deadline: _____
Comments: _____
_____
_____
_____

6. <u>Inform News and Communications staff about the crisis.</u> We'll tell staff what they need to know, what they should say to non-media callers, who is handling media calls, and what their assignments are.

Assigned to: _____ Deadline: _____
Comments: _____
_____
_____
_____

7. <u>Gather information from relevant campus offices.</u> Campus offices affected by crises may have literature that's relevant to the crisis. We'll get copies of relevant materials, including brochures, organization charts, crisis plans, and so on.

Assigned to: _____ Deadline: _____
Comments: _____
_____
_____
_____

3

BACKGROUNDER:

ATHLETICS

<u>Primary Contact:</u>
Bob Ducatte
Director of Athletics
Work: Home:

GENERAL INFORMATION

To promote a healthy lifestyle, Rensselaer encourages students to take part in sports. Athletics are conducted under the same general rules and regulations as other phases of education at Rensselaer. The intercollegiate athletic program conforms to policies of the National Collegiate Athletic Conference and the Eastern College Athletic Association.

There are about 4,400 undergraduates at the Institute. Approximately 70 percent of them participate in intramural sports. About 10 percent are members of an intercollegiate team. There are 22 varsity teams at Rensselaer -- ten are women's teams. Rensselaer intercollegiate athletes compete at the NCAA Division III level except for men's ice hockey, in which Rensselaer competes in Division I.

INTRAMURALS

Rensselaer's very extensive intramural program involves thousands of students, as well as some faculty and staff. There are literally hundreds of teams fielded each year for indoor and outdoor sports. Any group of students or faculty and staff members is welcome to pull together a team and register to compete. Games are scheduled and records are kept by the intramural director, a paid Rensselaer staff member. The contests are refereed by the players.

ACADEMIC EXPECTATIONS OF STUDENT-ATHLETES

Academics are stressed as the first priority of all Rensselaer students. The registrar provides grade point averages of varsity athletes to the athletic department each year. If a student-athlete is having academic difficulty, his or her coach works with Rensselaer's Office of Academic Advising to try to improve the situation. Occasionally, an athlete will sit out a year in his or her sport so he or she can focus on studying.

4

BACKGROUNDER: ATHLETICS
Page 2

Sanctions against student-athletes: Student-athletes who are involved in an incident requiring adjudication or discipline are referred to Rensselaer's Dean of Students' Office just as any other students are. They have no special privileges and face no special punishments. A coach has the discretion to decide if a member of his or her team who has been convicted of some infraction off the field or court may remain on the team.

OTHER REQUIREMENTS FOR INTERCOLLEGIATE ATHLETES

Coaches in each intercollegiate sport are responsible for giving each of the athletes on their team a copy of the "Rensselaer Intercollegiate Athletic Handbook" and for reviewing it with the team. Rensselaer was one of the first Division III schools to adopt such a policy and the handbook has been used as a model by several other schools.

The 25-page handbook sets out Rensselaer's basic philosophy of intercollegiate competition (which appears in the first paragraph of this backgrounder) as well as medical, alcohol, and drug policies for athletes. Also included are NCAA principles, NCAA Division III rules and regulations, and a statement regarding student aid. Excerpts from the handbook appear below.

INJURIES

All intercollegiate athletes must pass a medical history program administered by the athletic training staff before they are allowed to report for team practice or play in any game. Entering freshmen may substitute their health service physical exam by submitting their entrance physical prior to admittance. Some teams are subject to campus physical exams administered by the college health service.

It is Rensselaer policy that all injuries, no matter how trivial, must be reported to the trainer or to the coach if the trainer is not available. Athletes treated for an injury are instructed to follow the doctor's or trainer's directions exactly. High-risk intercollegiate contests, such as football and hockey, have a team physician in attendance.

ALCOHOL AND DRUG POLICIES

Alcohol: Rensselaer students are bound by New York State law and Rensselaer regulations regarding alcohol consumption. In addition, each Rensselaer coach sets his or her own rules pertaining to the use of alcohol and has the authority to suspend or drop from the team any athlete who violates the rules set by the coach. Alcohol is considered a drug and athletes are encouraged not to use it.

5

BACKGROUNDER: ATHLETICS
Page 3

Cases of continued abuse or chronic use are handled by a committee made up of the athletic director, the medical director, and the coach. A rehabilitation program is initiated. Athletes are urged to confide in their coach, athletic director, dean, or medical director about problems of chronic use.

Drugs: The use of banned substances and performance-enhancing drugs is prohibited for student-athletes who are members of Rensselaer intercollegiate teams. Use of banned substances may result in suspension from participation (practice and games) on a team. Reinstatement may be made upon agreement by the coach, athletic director, and medical director that the athlete is not a user or is rehabilitated.

To implement this policy the athletic department has established a substance abuse program consisting of information and educational activities, counseling services, and a testing procedure. The testing procedure is administered by the student health service to determine whether student-athletes have used banned substances.

RECRUITING

There are no athletic scholarships available to students participating in Division III sports, and Division III regulations prohibit communication between coaches and the financial aid office on behalf of their athletes. Division III coaches do recruit athletes, but since they are not able to offer them financial aid, recruiting abuses are rare.

The hockey team, which competes in Division I, follows the much more stringent guidelines for recruiting that are established by the NCAA. Rensselaer has never had any sanctions leveled against it by the NCAA or been investigated for any violations of recruiting rules.

BOOSTERS

Donations to the university's athletic booster club are treated in the same way as other university income. All income and expenses are monitored and subject to audit. Rensselaer controls the activities of the booster club.

Rensselaer's Let's Go Red! booster club was established in 1980 by the athletic department. In recent years, it has generated about $50,000 annually for Rensselaer's athletic programs.

-30-

6

BACKGROUNDER:

GREEK LIFE AND GOVERNANCE

Eddie Knowles
Dean of Students
Work: Home:

GENERAL INFORMATION

There are 30 fraternities and five sororities affiliated with and recognized by Rensselaer Polytechnic Institute. About 40 percent of Rensselaer's undergraduates (about 1,600 students) belongs to a fraternity or a sorority.

Fraternities have existed at Rensselaer since the mid-1800s. The first sorority on campus was founded in 1976. Institutionally, the Greek system is seen as a very positive part of student life. Greeks at Rensselaer are expected to provide social and leadership opportunities and to encourage scholastic endeavors and community service among their members.

THE INSTITUTE/GREEK RELATIONSHIP

Each fraternity and sorority is an independent institution. Most are governed by a national organization and an alumni/ae board. Fraternities and sororities are accountable to their nationals, to their alumni/ae board, to various levels of student government, and to the Institute.

Rensselaer provides fraternities and sororities with recognition: a formal process by which the school agrees that a social fraternity/sorority may function on its campus, enroll undergraduate members through established rush procedures, use campus facilities and services, and identify its chapter with the university. The Dean of Students Office is the primary focus of university interaction with Greek-letter organizations.

To be recognized, fraternities and sororities must adhere to the federal, state, and local ordinances and laws as well as rules established by the Institute, their national chapters, and the Inter Fraternity Council (IFC) and Panhellenic Council (PHC), the student groups responsible for governing Rensselaer Greek-letter organizations.

7

BACKGROUNDER: GREEK LIFE AND GOVERNANCE
Page 2

The most serious penalty Rensselaer can inflict is the withdrawal of recognition. This last happened in the fall of 1987 when the Institute's Review Board suspended recognition of the Rensselaer chapter of the Chi Phi fraternity for two years after several women charged they had been harassed at a fraternity party. In addition, the fraternity's national governing board evicted the chapter from its house.

A statement of relationship between Rensselaer and its Greek organizations was written after a task-force effort that last several years and include students, administrators, and citizens of Troy. It was formally adopted in April, 1991, after two-thirds of all Greek organizations signed it. To retain recognition, organizations must adhere to the rules and obligations set forth in the relationship statement.

POLICIES ON ALCOHOL AND HAZING

✓ Hazing and pre-initiation rites are unequivocally opposed by Rensselaer and the student groups governing Rensselaer's Greek organizations. Hazing is any action taken or situation created to produce mental or physical discomfort, embarrassment, harassment or ridicule. Greek organizations which haze members are in serious danger of having their recognition withdrawn.

✓ The use of alcohol on chapter premises during a official event or in any situation sponsored or endorsed by the fraternity must comply with all applicable laws. Rensselaer imposes additional requirements on fraternities and sororities, and many chapters' national offices have policies on hazing, alcohol, and other drugs.

The IFC requires that Greek parties be closed. Fraternities must register parties at least two days in advance and submit guest lists to the IFC for all parties where alcohol will be present. Up to 25 non-registered guests are allowed at the party, but a supplemental guest list containing their names must be submitted to the IFC by 2 p.m. the day after the party. No advertising of parties at which alcohol will be present is allowed.

The IFC has also prohibited the use of alcohol during "rush," when new students are recruited for fraternity membership since 1989.

Last fall, the IFC sponsored a series of seminars called "Party Positive." The seminars emphasize the legal ban on underage drinking and give information about low-risk drinking. Beginning with members of the class of 1995, a student who does not have proof of having attended a Party Positive seminar (a sticker on his or her college ID card) is not permitted to attend fraternity parties where alcohol is served. Having a sticker does not imply that a student can drink, only that he or she can attend the party.

8

BACKGROUNDER: GREEK LIFE AND GOVERNANCE
Page 3

COMMUNITY ISSUES

A Greek Neighborhood Relations Committee was established in 1989 to monitor the relationship between Rensselaer's Greeks and their neighbors. The committee is comprised of representatives from the IFC and Panhellenic, each chapter, the community, faculty, and the Dean of Students Office. the committee encourages communication between Greeks and their neighbors. For instance, members of each chapter are encouraged to ask their neighbors to call the fraternity first when they have a problem.

Greeks are expected to maintain their properties to community standards and to contribute positively to the life of the neighborhood.

SEXUAL MISCONDUCT

Rensselaer's rape education efforts are aggressive, continuous, and extensive for all students. In addition to the rape education programs that are offered during student orientation and the numerous programs offered year-round by the Department of Public Safety and the Dean of Students Office, there are several special programs specially directed at members of fraternities and sororities.

PHYSICAL FACILITIES

Fraternities and sororities must be physically safe and meet all required building and safety codes. Emergency loans of up to $10,000 may be obtained from Rensselaer to make repairs considered crucial to maintaining health and safety standards.

ENCOURAGING EXCELLENCE

In recognition that it is at least as important to encourage good behavior as it is to punish bad behavior, the Institute annually gives awards to those chapters meeting established criteria including academic excellence, social responsibility, campus involvement, chapter management, and alumni/ae involvement. Winning chapters receive a plaque and a gift not to exceed $300 in value. They are also recognized in campus publications.

In addition, each year the PHC sponsors a "Panhel Tea," an awards ceremony at which Panhel member sororities recognize achievements of both individual women and whole chapters.

9

BACKGROUNDER:

PUBLIC SAFETY AT RENSSELAER

Bernie Drobnicki
Director of Public Safety
Work: Home:

GENERAL INFORMATION

The Department of Public Safety patrols the campus 24 hours a day every day. It also investigates crimes and offers crime prevention and education seminars. This is a highly trained private security force. Officers do not have police or peace officer status (see page 8), but current training exceeds the levels required for peace officers. All new officers undergo 100 hours of intensive classroom instruction and three months of on-the-job training. All new officers are on probation for one year.

PATROLS

Public Safety officers patrol the campus in cars, on foot, on bicycles, and, on special occasions, on horseback. Their patrol areas include the main academic campus in Troy, dormitories, research facilities in Watervliet and Schenectady, and the Rensselaer Technology Park in North Greenbush. Part-time officers provide enhanced coverage for special events such as concerts at the Field House.

INVESTIGATIONS

William Canavally, an experienced former police officer, private investigator, and trained bodyguard, is investigator for the Department of Public Safety.

How investigations begin: Investigations begin with complaints filed with the Department of Public Safety. A uniformed officer takes a report. Canavally, who is on call around the clock, will conduct a more detailed investigation if one is deemed necessary by the patrol supervisor or administration. He routinely investigates a variety of crimes, including assaults, burglaries, harassment, indecent exposure, etc. As in any police agency, investigations are prioritized based on the seriousness of the crime.

10

BACKGROUNDER: PUBLIC SAFETY AT RENSSELAER
Page 2

Involvement of external police: When and whether to involve Troy police or other external law enforcement officials is a judgment call made by Canavally and department administration. Troy police are generally called any time a gun is involved, if the reported crime is fairly serious, or the victim requests it after the responding officer tells him or her of this option. (Crime victims have the right to report crimes to both Public Safety and the Troy Police Department, and Public Safety and other offices on campus always tell victims that.)

Canavally's background and special training: Canavally has worked for more than 30 years in various police and private security jobs around the country. He has completed advanced training in personal protection -- i.e., bodyguarding -- at the nationally recognized Nine Lives Training School in Washington, D.C. He served as personal bodyguard to Olga Korbut, the former Soviet gymnastics star, when she toured the United States in the 1970s. Canavally also has completed hostage negotiation training. He is a licensed private investigator.

CRIME PREVENTION AND COMMUNITY SERVICE

The Office of Public Safety's public information officer (Bill Denn) frequently gives presentations to students, faculty, and staff on personal safety. He presents a "basic lesson plan" for personal safety during student orientation, at well-advertised campus lectures throughout the year, and to student groups or whole dormitories. He makes more than 30 such presentations each year.

This presentation always includes information on crime prevention, rape prevention, and assault prevention. He talks about scenarios in which such crimes are likeliest to occur, and he passes out leaflets on rape prevention. He emphasizes that a person is never more vulnerable to violent crime than when walking alone in the dark, and he urges people to use the escort service and the buddy system.

Publications: As part of his community service, Bill Denn produces a variety of newsletters, pamphlets, and brochures:

✓ Each incoming freshman receives a brochure about the Ride in Safety Escort (RISE) in his or her orientation packets. (Information on this service is also mass-mailed each year to all campus mailboxes (student, faculty, staff).

✓ A brochure describing safety and crime prevention is being published by Public Safety in compliance with a new federal law on campus safety. This brochure should be completed by summer of 1992. It is to be distributed to all students, faculty, staff, and, on request, to all prospective students and staff.

11

BACKGROUNDER: PUBLIC SAFETY AT RENSSELAER
Page 3

✓ A brochure describing safety and crime prevention is being published by Public Safety in compliance with a new federal law on campus safety. This brochure should be completed by summer of 1992. It is to be distributed to all students, faculty, staff, and, on request, to all prospective students and staff.

✓ A monthly newsletter on campus safety includes detailed reports on crimes reported on campus as well as information on preventing crimes. Each issue of the monthly safety newsletter is mass-mailed to each campus mailbox, left in bulk at public distribution drops, and posted on bulletin boards. Special editions of this newsletter are created whenever there is a special need, such as an unusual crime.

RAPE AND SEXUAL ASSAULT

Rensselaer's programming to educate students about rape and sexual assault is aggressive, continuous and extensive.

Student orientation: Rape education starts at student orientation, where students see three separate programs. Incoming students see a vignette and a presentation by the Department of Public Safety that includes role-playing of a rape scene and engages participants in discussion; a second program by the Department of Public Safety for new students and their parents addresses rape prevention; women students and their parents also see a special presentation by the Dean of Students Office (DOSO).

Programs throughout the year: Both DOSO and Public Safety offer programs on rape prevention to dozens of groups all year long. The groups include sororities and fraternities, RAs and dormitory floors, and freshman seminar classes.

Training in rape prevention: Training in rape prevention is made available to freshmen, to all residence life staff, in residence halls, through women's student organizations, at fraternities, and elsewhere. Videos, booklets, brochures, and other resources are available at the office of women's student services. RAs receive special training on rape from DOSO.

Peer Sexuality Program: DOSO sponsors a Peer Sexuality Program in which students are trained to offer their own programs on sexuality-related issues, including rape.

Public Safety Newsletter: The Department of Public Safety's monthly newsletter regularly provides detailed tips on crime prevention, often focusing on sexual assaults. An entire issue of this newsletter is devoted to preventing sexual assault in September of each year, in compliance with New York State law.

12

BACKGROUNDER: PUBLIC SAFETY AT RENSSELAER
Page 4

THE RIDE IN SAFETY ESCORT SERVICE (RISE)

This offers free, safe escorts anywhere on campus and in the immediately surrounding area along a pre-determined and widely advertised route. Students trained and managed by Public Safety drive the two RISE buses between 6:30 p.m. and 1:30 a.m. Sunday through Thursday, and an hour longer on Fridays and Saturdays. The buses run a pre-ordained route identified by students as a high-traffic route. During other hours, students may call the Department of Public Safety to be escorted by officers on duty. Basically, escorts are offered 24 hours a day, seven days a week. Operational hours have been extended which, has resulted in an increase in riders from 2,065 in '88-'89 to 4,417 in '90-'91.

CAMPUS LIGHTING

Rensselaer has invested heavily in improved lighting on campus since 1990:

- ✔ approximately $50,000 per year spent to improve lighting on campus walkways

- ✔ 75 new locations utilizing high pressure sodium light source

- ✔ 38 upgrades of campus walkway lighting from mercury vapor (incandescent) to high pressure sodium lights

- ✔ upgrading of Sherry Road street and sidewalk lighting utilizing a high pressure sodium light source, completed as a joint venture with the City of Troy

BUILDING SECURITY

Rensselaer maintains a 24-hour locked door policy on outside doors of all residence facilities. Dorm rooms and campus building locks were recently upgraded. In 1992, Rensselaer completed installation of modern dead-bolt locks in every campus dormitory and apartment complex. All residence hall laundry rooms have locks.

EMERGENCY CALL BOXES

Emergency call boxes are provided at 20 locations on campus, mostly in residential areas. Six are emergency radios linked directly with the Office of Public Safety. The additional call boxes are regular campus phones clearly marked for emergency use but able to make other on-campus calls. Located throughout the campus, they can be used to call Public Safety, residence halls, dorm rooms, and offices on campus. Each of these phones has an emergency button for one-touch dialing of Public Safety.

13

BACKGROUNDER: PUBLIC SAFETY AT RENSSELAER
Page 5

In the summer of 1992, nine other high-tech, high-visibility call boxes will be erected, mostly in academic areas. The cost of these new call boxes is approximately $50,000.

HOW RENSSELAER KEEPS AND REPORTS CRIME STATISTICS

Since 1976 -- long before campus crime became the concern it is today and long before new laws required aggressive reporting of statistics -- Rensselaer has taken a very public stance on campus crime and how it is reported. Rensselaer submits a uniform crime report for every crime committed on campus. These reports go to the FBI and the state Department of Criminal Justice Services (DCJS). These statistics are reported not only to the campus community, but also in state and federal crime reports and publications. Rensselaer is one of only three private colleges in the state that report these statistics to DCJS for its Uniform Crime Report.

WHAT HAPPENS WHEN A CRIME IS REPORTED

When a crime is reported to Public Safety, students are encouraged to report the crime to the Troy Police Department. Other campus offices, such as DOSO and Residential Life, may report incidents to Public Safety, which then follows up with the victim to determine if the victim wants to make a criminal complaint.

In accordance with state and federal law, the <u>victim</u> decides whether and how to press charges. Victims may file a criminal complaint, bring civil action, request action in Rensselaer's own judicial system, or any combination of the above. Rensselaer cannot require victims to press charges or file reports. Victims are advised of their rights to file a complaint either internally or externally when they first report the incident. The Dean of Students Office helps victims get medical care and counseling.

RENSSELAER'S JUDICIAL SYSTEM

The Dean of Students Office administers, with heavy involvement of elected students, a judicial system that is considered a national model. This system has jurisdiction over violations of Rensselaer's Grounds for Disciplinary Action (GDA). These violations can 30 seconds occur on campus or off. (See pp. 10-20 of the Rensselaer Handbook.) This judicial system is independent of external criminal civil courts, and Rensselaer emphasizes this to anyone who reports a crime to Rensselaer.

PRESIDENT'S TASK FORCE ON PUBLIC SAFETY

After a Rensselaer student reported that she was abducted and raped near campus in December 1990, President Roland Schmitt appointed the President's Task Force on Public Safety.

14

BACKGROUNDER: PUBLIC SAFETY AT RENSSELAER
Page 6

That task force, which included students, faculty, and staff, identified three areas for improvement: the escort service, campus lighting, and call boxes. The task force's major recommendations in all three areas will have been implemented by the summer of 1992. The Campus Safety Non-Academic Discipline Committee, which has been in existence in various forms since 1980, will continue to monitor compliance with the recommendations of the 1990 president's task force.

GUNS ON CAMPUS

Public Safety suspects that the number of guns on campus is increasing -- a reflection of the reality of society in general and the increasing prevalence of guns in high schools in particular.

Under New York State law, students are prohibited from having guns on campus. However, this law pertains only to campus property, and therefore exempts off-campus housing and fraternities.

Rensselaer policy requires students to store guns and other deadly weapons with public safety. (See page 23 of the Rensselaer Handbook.) During hunting seasons, Public Safety stores about 20 guns. At other times, the number goes down to 10. Most guns are for hunting or target practice. Public Safety and DOSO may send guns home at their discretion (e.g., assault weapons).

All Public Safety Officers receive bullet-resistant vests and must wear them on duty.

FIRE SAFETY/HAZARDOUS MATERIALS

Rensselaer's Department of Public Safety responds to reports of fire and hazardous materials on campus and takes charge until the Troy Fire Department arrives. Public safety then remains at the scene to provide information on facilities, on hazardous materials stored in facilities, and so on.

CONTINGENCY PLANS

The Department of Public Safety, like other offices on campus, maintains contingency plans for hazardous waste spills, bomb threats, power failures, and other potential problems. Copies of those documents are attached.

AMBULANCE SERVICE

Lieutenant Wes Marshall administers Rensselaer's state-certified on-campus ambulance service. This service is run by students and funded by the Rensselaer Union.

BACKGROUNDER: PUBLIC SAFETY AT RENSSELAER
Page 7

TRAINING

Rensselaer is involved in the Capital District Campus Law Enforcement Consortium, a recently formed regional consortium comprising schools that are members of the International Association of Campus Law Enforcement Administrators. In conjunction with this group, the Department of Public Safety has initiated a 40-hour intensive campus law-enforcement program for entry-level officers. This program will be increased to 80 hours in June of 1992. This increase will mean that officers who complete this course receive more training than that required for peace officers. Public Safety is asking the state Department of Criminal Justice Services to certify this course. Public Safety also provides administrative support for Rensselaer County's Emergency Medical Response Program.

Public Safety officers receive an intensive 80 hours of entry-level classroom instruction, followed by three months of on-the-job training and an additional 20 hours of classroom programming. Senior personnel receive approximately 80 hours of training each year in critical disciplines of law, arrest procedures, use of physical force, emergency management and response, sexual assault response, cultural diversity, and patrol technique.

POLICE OFFICERS/PEACE OFFICERS/PRIVATE SECURITY OFFICERS

Private colleges in New York State are not permitted by law to have police or peace officers. The Department of Public Safety wants to have police officer or peace officer status, as do most private institutions in the state. The differences among them:

Police Officer: Police officers have statutory power to make arrests and execute warrants anywhere in the state whether or not they are on duty. They have access to intensive, 16-week, full-time training programs. They also have special authority to carry weapons. They can make arrests based on reasonable cause or suspicion.

Peace Officer: Peace officers also have special authority to carry weapons. They also have the same statutory powers as police officers, but only when they are on duty at their place of employment. The state criminal procedure law identifies officers in approximately 60 different agencies as peace officers. Peace officers also can make arrests based on reasonable cause or suspicion.

Private Security Officer: These are simply private citizens. They make only citizens' arrests and have no special authority to carry weapons. Training can be nonexistent ("rent-a-cops"), or intensive and professional, such as Rensselaer's training. There is no state-certified training for these officers.

16

BACKGROUNDER: PUBLIC SAFETY AT RENSSELAER
Page 8

These officers cannot make arrests based solely on reasonable cause or suspicion. They must see a crime occur in their presence in order to make an arrest. Private security officers' arrest powers also are limited to misdemeanors and felonies. In cases of lower-grade violations of law (violations of the state drinking-age law and other parts of state liquor law; disorderly conduct; trespass), private security officers cannot make arrests.

Private institutions want upgraded status for their safety personnel mainly because police and peace officers generally have access to longer, better, more detailed training. Police officers receive 16 weeks of full-time training; peace officers at the State University of New York get 14 weeks of campus law enforcement training. By requiring that officers who take this training be sworn in as peace officers or police officers on the first day of training, state law effectively forbids colleges and universities from taking these training programs.

Legislation to permit private institutions to retain peace or police officers on campus has been introduced, with encouragement from Canisius College, for the last five years. It generally is approved by the Senate but fails to get out of the Assembly Codes Committee. Bernie Drobnicki chairs a group of private-institution security officials that has lobbied for such legislation for several years.

DROBNICKI'S PROFESSIONAL ACTIVITIES

Drobnicki is a director (representing New York and Pennsylvania) of the International Association of Campus Law Enforcement Administration (IACLEA).

-30-

CHAPTER • 37

Bibliography

ASE and the cooperating associations that helped make this book possible offer a variety of books, articles, and other materials on crisis management and campus communications. The following list includes additional resources you may wish to consult to complement the information presented in *When Crisis Strikes on Campus*.

For your convenience, Chapter 38 provides a list of these cooperating associations—complete with their addresses, phone numbers, and fax numbers—to help you find out more about ordering these resources. To order any of the CASE publications listed below, call toll-free (800) 554-8536, or check your RESOURCES catalog for more details.

Council for Advancement and Support of Education

Bennett, Joseph L. "The Best Defense: How Five Campuses Are Using Education to Battle AIDS." CASE CURRENTS, July/August 1988, 48-50.

Carter, Lindy Keane. "A Case of AIDS: When AIDS Hits a Campus, A PR Director Has to Answer Everyone." CASE CURRENTS, July/August 1988, 42-46.

Ellis, Richard, Irene Haske, and Emily R. Turk. "The Day Reagan Was Shot: How a University Hospital PR Staff Handled the Crisis." CASE CURRENTS, December 1981, 20-23.

Enger, John K. "Strategy During a Strike." CASE CURRENTS, November 1977, 20-21.

Haglund, Elizabeth. "Plan for Lightning Before It Strikes." CASE CURRENTS, February 1979, 10–12.

Hay, Tina M. "Survival of the Fittest: For Campus Communicators, the Battle over Animal Research Means a Struggle for Control. Here's How to Stand Your Ground." CASE CURRENTS, October 1991, 20-25.

Jensen, Nordy, comp. *Communicating About Intercollegiate Athletics*. 1994.

Johnson, William J. "Crime Report: Don't Think of the Campus Security Act as Just More Red Tape." CASE CURRENTS, January 1992, 30-34.

Lauer, Larry D. "Putting a Lid on a Crisis: Issues Management Can Control a Crisis Before It Boils Over and You Get Burned." CASE CURRENTS, April 1983, 38-40.

Moore, Paula. "Coping with Crisis." CASE CURRENTS, December 1975, 15-17.

Reichman, Michela. "UCSF Turned the Tide from Crisis to Credibility." CASE CURRENTS, June 1979, 26-28.

Renner, Tom. "Fire! What One College Did When Fire Struck—Twice." CASE CURRENTS, September 1980, 50-53.

Sheffield, Wesley. "Two Strikes: A PR Crisis." CASE CURRENTS, February 1979, 13.

Vickrey, Jr., James F. "Academic Unionism: The Florida Experience." CASE CURRENTS, September 1977, 35-39.

American Council on Education

Plante, P.R. *The Art of Decision Making: Issues and Cases in Higher Education*, 1987.

Siegel, Dorothy. *Campuses Respond to Violent Tragedy*, 1994.

Smith, M.C., ed. *Coping with Crime on Campus*, 1988.

Association of Governing Boards of Universities and Colleges

Burling, Philip. "I Think Someone Is Following Me." In *Crime on Campus,* 1993.

Goodale, Thomas G. "I Thought I Could Handle It." In *Alcohol and Drug Abuse,* 1992.

Keeling, Richard P. "I Didn't Think It Could Happen to Me." In *AIDS and HIV,* 1990, 1992.

Sandler, Bernice R. "No Means No." In *Sexual Harassment and Date Rape,* 1993.

Association of Higher Education Facilities Officers

Asbestos in the Workplace: Managing Small-Scale Abatement, 1991.

Cotler, Stephen R. *Removing the Barriers: Accessibility Guidelines and Specifications*, 1991.

Dillow, Rex O., ed. *Facilities Management: A Manual for Plant Administration*, 2d ed., 1989.

Emergency Preparedness, 1992.

Hazardous Materials and Solid Waste Management, 1992.

Rush, Sean C., and Sandra L. Johnson. *The Decaying American Campus: A Ticking Time Bomb,* 1989.

College and University Personnel Association

Deane, Nancy H., ed. *Sexual Harassment—Issues and Answers: A Guide for Education, Business and Industry,* 1986.

"Sexual Harassment—Issues and Answers," 1991 (videotape).

National Association of College and University Attorneys

Ansell, Edward O., ed. *Intellectual Property in Academe: A Legal Compendium,* 1991.

Barber, Charles A. *What to Do When OSHA Comes Calling,* 1991.

Burling, Philip. *Crime on Campus: Analyzing and Managing the Increasing Risk of Institutional Liability,* 1991.

Burling, Philip, and Kathryn Mathews. *Responding to Whistleblowers: An Analysis of Whistleblower Protection Acts and Their Consequences,* 1992.

Cole, E.K., ed. *Sexual Harassment on Campus: A Legal Compendium,* 1990.

Houpt, Corinne A., ed. *Academic Program Closures: A Legal Compendium,* 1991.

Hustoles, Thomas P., and Walter B. Connolly Jr., ed. *Regulating Racial Harassment on Campus,* 1990.

Strohm, Leslie Chambers, ed. *AIDS on Campus: A Legal Compendium,* 1991.

National Association of College and University Business Officers

Balbresky, Paul. "When Catastrophe Strikes." *NACUBO Business Officer,* December 1992, 27-29.

Halfmann, Robert, and Ted Balser. "AIDS in the College Housing Workplace." *NACUBO Business Officer,* March 1990, 46-47.

McIntyre, Jim. "Natural Disasters Force Institutions to Examine Their Plans." *NACUBO Business Officer,* December 1989, 26-28.

Rothman, Michael. "Three Campus Crises." *NACUBO Business Officer,* December 1992, 30-34.

National Association of Independent Schools

The Americans with Disabilities Act and Independent Schools, Part I, 1991 (booklet).

The Americans with Disabilities Act and Independent Schools, Part II, 1993 (booklet).

The Next Marketing Handbook for Independent Schools, 1991.

Risk Management for Schools, 1988.

Sample Policies on AIDS and Other Serious Infectious Diseases, 1993 (packet).

The Search Handbook: A Step-by-Step Guide to Selecting the Right Leader for Your School, 1992.

The Sexual Harassment Packet, 1992.

National Association of Student Personnel Administrators

"Complying with the Campus Security Act—1990," May 1991 (white paper).

"Complying with the New Federal Laws: Sex Offenses on Campus." ACE and NASPA, March 1993 (white paper).

"Confronting Sexual Harassment on Campus," November 12, 1992 (teleconference).

Jacobs, B., and J.E. Towns. "What Residence Hall Staff Need to Know About Dealing with Death." *NASPA Journal*, Fall 1984, 32-36.

Miser, K.M., ed. *Student Affairs and Campus Dissent: Reflections of the Past and Challenges for the Future.* NASPA Monograph Series no. 8, 1988.

Scott, J.E., and others. "The Trauma Response Team: Preparing Staff to Respond to Student Death." *NASPA Journal*, Spring 1992, 230-37.

"Statement Concerning Campus Disciplinary Procedures and the Criminal Law in Sexual Assault Cases," March 1993.

Walton, Spring. "Date Rape: New Liability for Colleges and Universities." *NASPA Journal*, Spring 1994, 195.

West, E.L., C. Reynolds, and J. Jackson. "Addressing Sexual Harassment: A Strategy for Changing the Climate in Higher Education." *NASPA Journal*, Winter 1994, 130-36.

Other Resources

Agron, Joe. "Safety Net." *American School and University*, February 1994, 38.

American National Red Cross. *Tornadoes: Nature's Most Violent Storms: A Preparedness Guide Including Safety Information for Schools*. Washington, DC: 1992. ERIC Document Number ED361146.

Archer, J. "Campus in Crisis: Coping with Fear and Panic Related to Serial Murder." *Journal of Counseling and Development,* September-October 1992, 96-100.

Berlonghi, Alexander. "Managing the Risks of School District Special Events." *School Business Affairs*, June 1991, 12-16.

Bovet, Susan. "Educators Need to Communicate Better On and Off Campus." *Public Relations Journal,* September 1992, 14.

Burns, Carter. "What to Do When the Crisis Is Over." *American School Board Journal*, March 1990, 31-32.

"Cal State-Northridge Rocked by Earthquake." *Black Issues in Higher Education,* February 10, 1994, 22.

"Campus Journalism: Cry 'Censorship' and the Media Will Come." *Editor and Publisher,* November 27, 1993, 12.

Caylor, Mary Jane. "Trial by Fire (and Tornado) Taught Us to Plan for Crimes." *Executive Educator*, February 1991, 22-24.

Christenberry, Nola J., and John L. Burns. "School District Policies for Response to Death-Related Crises: Fact or Fiction?" Paper presented at the Annual Meeting of the Mid-South Educational Research Association (Lexington, KY, November 1991). ERIC Document Number ED341169.

Christenberry, Nola J., and Mitchell Holifield. "A Death in the School Family." *American School Board Journal*, May 1992, 39.

Colorado State Department of Education. *Be Aware—Be Prepared. Guidelines for Crises Response: Planning for School/Communities*. Denver, CO: 1990. ERIC Document Number ED330919.

"Deaf Women at Gallaudet University Claim that Rape on Their Campus Is Chillingly Common—and Kept Under Wraps." *People Weekly,* June 20, 1994, 36.

Derrington, Mary Lynne. "Calming Controversy." *Executive Educator*, February 1993, 32-34.

DeWitt, Robert C. *Effective Crisis Management at the Smaller Campus*. Beaver, PA: Pennsylvania State University—Beaver Campus, 1989. ERIC Document Number ED313999.

Dodge, Susan. "With Campus Crimes Capturing Public Attention, Colleges Re-Evaluate Security Measures and Stiffen Some Penalties." *Chronicle of Higher Education*, February 6, 1991, 29-30.

Dunne-Maxim, Karen. "Keeping Afloat in Suicide's Wake." *School Administrator*, May-June 1991, 20-25.

Finley, Colleen. "Rape on Campus: The Prevalence of Sexual Assault While Enrolled in College." *Journal of College Student Development*, March 1993, 113.

Fox, James. *How to Work with the Media.* Newbury Park, CA: Sage Publications, 1993.

Golden, Sandra. "The Media and Your Message: Getting the Coverage You Want." *Community, Technical, and Junior College Journal*, October 1992, 48.

Gottschalk, Jack A., ed. *Crisis Response: Inside Stories on Managing Image Under Siege.* Detroit, MI: Visible Ink Press, 1993

Heller, Robert W., and others. "Disaster, Controversy—Are You Prepared for the Worst?" *Executive Educator*, March 1991, 20-23.

Keeling, Richard P. "Campuses Confront AIDS: Tapping the Vitality of Caring and Community." *Educational Record*, Winter 1993, 30-36.

Kessler, R. "Preventing Violence and Crime on Campus." *Journal of Security Administration*, June 1993, 53-65.

Levy, J. "Death, Grief, and Solidarity: The Polytechnique Case." *Omega: Journal of Death and Dying,* 1993, 67-74.

Lyman, Linda. "Tough Calls in Tough Times." *American School Board Journal*, February 1992, 35-37.

"Make Your Campus a Safer Place for Students with Gai-Tronics Emergency Telephones." *American School and University*, January 1994, 107.

McQuinn, John, and Robert C. O'Reilly. "Adolescent Suicides and High Schools: Recommendations for Administrators." *NASSP Bulletin*, February 1989, 92-97.

Moriarty, Anthony, and others. "A Clear Plan for School Crisis Management." *NASSP Bulletin*, April 1993, 17-22.

Munro, Penny, and David Wellington . "When Crisis Strikes: Strategies for Managing Student Grief." *Schools in the Middle*, Spring 1993, 18-22.

Perry, Lester. "A Catastrophe Can Happen." *Journal of Educational Public Relations*, 1993, 23.

_____."The School Disaster Recovery Team: A Concept Whose Time Has Come." *School Business Affairs*, December 1989, 14-16.

"Preparing Schools for Terrorist Attacks." *School Safety*, Winter 1991,18-19.

Rajacich, Dale, and others. "An Institutional Response to Date Rape." *Canadian Journal of Higher Education*, 1992, 41-59.

Seltzer, Joel A. "Crisis at a Bronx Junior High: Responding to School-Related Violence." Paper presented at the Annual Convention of the American Psychological Association (Washington, DC, August 1992). ERIC Document Number ED357304.

Shannon and McCall Consulting Ltd. *AIDS: Preparing Your School and Community*. Ontario, Canada: April 1991. Funded by the Centre for AIDS Health Protection Branch, Health and Welfare, Canada. ERIC Document Number ED333585.

Sheckler, Paul. "When a Student Is HIV Positive." *Educational Leadership*, December-January 1992-93, 55-56.

Siegel, Dorothy. "Crisis Management: The Campus Responds." *Educational Record*, Summer 1991, 14-16.

Simon, Adam. "Student Perspectives on Facilitating Rape Prevention Programs." *New Directions for Student Services,* Spring 1994, 43.

Smiar, Nicholas P. "Cool Heads: Crisis Management for Administrators." *Child Welfare*, March-April 1992, 147-156.

Smith, M.C. "Vexatious Victims of Campus Crime: Student Lawsuits as Impetus for Risk Management." *Journal of Security Administration*, 1992, 5-17.

Stacy, Cheri, and others. "It's Not All Moonlight and Roses: Dating Violence at the University of Maine 1982-1992." *College Student Journal,* March 1994, 2.

Twineham, Lawrence. "A Media Cloud Can Have a Silver Lining: Opportunities for Positive Coverage." *Journal of Educational Public Relations,* 1993, 4.

"Violence: Gun-Toting Campus Security Officers Are Becoming Fixtures at Many Black Colleges as Administrators Grapple with Maintaining Academic Success in an Atmosphere of Fear." *Black Issues in Higher Education,* February 24, 1994, 22.

Zimmerman, Sam. "Violence in the Schools: We Need Solutions to Increase the Peace." *Journal of Educational Public Relations,* 1993, 34.

CHAPTER • 38

Cooperating Associations

On behalf of the more than 6,000 CASE campus communications professionals, we thank the following associations for sharing our belief in the significance of effective and cooperative crisis communications.

American Association of Collegiate Registrars and Admissions Officers
One Dupont Circle, Suite 330
Washington, DC 20036
Phone: (202) 293-9161
Fax: (202) 872-8857

American Association of Community Colleges
One Dupont Circle, Suite 410
Washington, DC 20036
Phone: (202) 728-0200
Fax: (202) 833-2467

American Council on Education
One Dupont Circle, Suite 800
Washington, DC 20036
Phone: (202) 939-9300
Fax: (202) 833-4760

Association of American Universities
One Dupont Circle, Suite 730
Washington, DC 20036
Phone: (202) 466-5030
Fax: (202) 775-9242

Association of Catholic Colleges and Universities
One Dupont Circle, Suite 650
Washington, DC 20036
Phone: (202) 457-0650
Fax: (202) 728-0977

Association of Governing Boards of Universities and Colleges
One Dupont Circle, Suite 400
Washington, DC 20036
Phone: (202) 296-8400
Fax: (202) 223-7053

Association of Higher Education Facilities Officers
1446 Duke Street
Alexandria, VA 22314-3492
Phone: (703) 684-1446
Fax: (703) 549-2772

College and University Personnel Association
1233 20th Street, NW, Suite 301
Washington, DC 20036
Phone: (202) 429-0311
Fax: (202) 429-0149

Council of Independent Colleges
One Dupont Circle, Suite 320
Washington, DC 20036
Phone: (202) 466-7230
Fax: (202) 466-7238

**International Association
of Campus Law Enforcement
Administrators**
638 Prospect Avenue
Hartford, CT 06105
Phone: (203) 586-7517
Fax: (203) 586-7550

**National Association of College
and University Attorneys**
One Dupont Circle, Suite 620
Washington, DC 20036
Phone: (202) 833-8390
Fax: (202) 296-8379

**National Association of College
and University Business Officers**
One Dupont Circle, Suite 500
Washington, DC 20036-1178
Phone: (202) 861-2500
Fax: (202) 861-2583

**National Association of Independent
Colleges and Universities**
122 C Street, NW, Suite 750
Washington, DC 20001
Phone: (202) 347-7512
Fax: (202) 628-2513

**National Association
of Independent Schools**
1620 L St., NW
Washington, DC 20036-5605
Phone: (202) 973-9700
Fax: (202) 973-9790

**National Association
of State Universities
and Land Grant Colleges**
One Dupont Circle, Suite 710
Washington, DC 20036
Phone: (202) 778-0818
Fax: (202) 296-6456

**National Association
of Student Personnel Administrators**
Universal North Building, Suite 418
1875 Connecticut Avenue, NW
Washington, DC 20009
Phone: (202) 265-7500
Fax: (202) 797-1157